DAWN *of* TRUTH

DAWN *of* TRUTH

Guide to a New Awareness

JOHN B LEONARD

authorHOUSE®

AuthorHouse™
1663 Liberty Drive
Bloomington, IN 47403
www.authorhouse.com
Phone: 1-800-839-8640

First published by AuthorHouse   01/18/2012

ISBN: 978-1-4634-2150-2 (sc)
ISBN: 978-1-4634-2149-6 (hc)
ISBN: 978-1-4634-2148-9 (ebk)

Library of Congress Control Number: 2011963710

Printed in the United States of America

TABLE OF CONTENTS

ACKNOWLEDGMENTS

I thank my dear friend;
for her constant support and encouragement.

I thank my buddy;
for his patience, and for the inspiration he provided.

And I thank my parents;
for providing the environment,
which allowed me to become the person I am;
so that I could be able to accomplish this undertaking.

DEDICATION

This book is dedicated to:

God

And to:

Buddha, Jesus, Krishna, Moses, Muhammad,
and all other Avatars of God,
who have served to help raise human consciousness
on the earth.

And to:

Gerald O'Donnell
Founder
Academy of Remote Viewing and Influencing Reality
Through Time and Space for offering humanity a vision that they can
manifest on the Earth.

Also to:
Edgar Cayce and the A.R.E.
and
Avaton and **Vikki T**. founders of C.A.C.
together with Cosmic Awareness channels:
Paul Shockley, and **Will Berlinghof**
who have helped me to raise my own consciousness.

INTRODUCTION

I guess I could say that I'm a "seeker"; because as long as I can remember, I've questioned the assertions of others with regard to religious subjects. This has led me to seek out answers to the many questions I had when considering religious "truths"; many of which seemed to conflict. This search for truth has brought me to a state, wherein I have established—for myself—a set of beliefs which satisfy me; satisfying also conflicts which religious teachings have with scientific evidence. At least in my own mind, I feel that I have resolved the many questions that arose throughout my early life, when I was attempting to resolve both religious and scientific theories (though, of course, religions never state their assertions as theory). And the result, besides satisfying my need for understanding, is that I have a new awareness about "God", life's purpose, why people suffer, and what exists beyond death (or the known).

This has resulted in a problem for me, though. Like most everyone—perhaps through a feeling of empathy—I have a desire to share my new-found beliefs with others, so that they can obtain the peace of mind that I have received. But I recoil at the thought of being some type of evangelist. Besides, I've long felt that it was up to individuals themselves to seek out answers as they desired them; and that if people were satisfied with their present beliefs, then others shouldn't interfere. Also, since the answers I've found for myself can't be proven to everyone's satisfaction, I really have no basis to claim that my assertions are the truest or best.

In order to resolve this conflict, I have decided to write this book in an autobiographical way. It is my hope that in describing my own thoughts and feelings about subjects of which I consider to be truth, that you—the reader—will have an opportunity to consider them for yourselves; without having to feel that I am being pushy about it, or that I'm making any claims as to their absolute validity. After all; who can really know what's absolutely true and valid?

Now, there's danger in this approach; some of you may assume that I'm not so sure about my present convictions, and others of you might conclude that I'm driven by ego in wanting to write about myself. So, let me assert now, that neither of these assumptions is true. I just don't intend to present myself as some type of guru or authority who must be believed and followed without question, or even given recognition. Rather, quite the opposite. It's anonymity that I prefer, and have written this book under a pseudonym (a pen-name) for that very reason. Believing my own queries and uncertainties to be similar to your own, I'm merely attempting to—as they say—write from my heart and not my head; anticipating that some of you will be able to identify with me or my feelings, and be more open to considering my theories as a result.

Please note that I've titled this book "Dawn of Truth", and not "High Noon of Truth". For myself the "light" is only just "dawning" on me—so to speak—and I'm certain that in time my present beliefs or conclusions will change. Also, I've chosen as a sub-title "Guide to a New Awareness". In this, I intend to only be presenting a guide that can be used by you—the reader—in pursuing your own search; if, and to the extent which, you desire it. I don't intend to claim that this is something like an operating manual, science text, or Holy Book. So, with these understandings, I will proceed to tell you a bit about my life, why I came to question certain assertions posed by others, and the resolutions to these conflicts which I have accepted as truth.

Also, as should be expected, I grew up in a particular religion and culture, which may not be the same as yours. Please forgive me if I relate more extensively to the teachings and assertions of the religion in which I was raised; I can do little else. Where your own religious upbringing (if any) might have acquainted you with different subjects for consideration, please try to understand where "I'm coming from", so that you can make adjustments to fit your own situation and set of beliefs. I'm certain that if you can, you will be able to gain much from what I present here, even though my questions and conflicts may not be exactly the same as any that you might have.

Before I proceed, however, I wish to make something perfectly clear: I am <u>not</u> intending to "dis" anybody's religion, or religious beliefs. I consider all the major religions to possess great meaning and provide significant benefit to their practitioners; I don't intend to discredit that, even though some of my assertions (ok, a lot of them) may not be the same as taught or presented by other religions. My only desire is to provide answers to those who are seeking a better understanding about God and Its purposes on Earth, and greater insight to those who are satisfied with their religion, but would like to get more out of it. Please don't let ego get in the way; either by refusing to accept that some aspects of your present beliefs may be slightly in error, or by feeling that you need to inform others—who may be perfectly satisfied with their own religion's teachings—of their "erroneous" beliefs, so that you can feel a little bit superior.

I was brought up in a Protestant religion, and attended a church-sponsored elementary school, which—together with Sunday School—provided most of my early religious "training". Through that—as well as through parental influence—I was made aware of some of the basic teachings of other religions; being taught that these were all (with the exception of Judaism) pretty much inspired by the devil. The devil—in constantly trying to bring people down to hell with him—supposedly tried to get people to do "bad things" and accept religious beliefs that weren't acceptable to God. And while it troubled me that this didn't seem right, my religious teachers just pointed to "God's Word" (the Bible) as proof that this was true. When I would express my opinions, I was told not to question, but to just leave their judgment to God's greater wisdom; "He" obviously knew best.

You may note that in referring to God, I put the capitalized "He" in quotations. Since the teachings in my early up-bringing and most religions, even now, refer to God as a masculine being, I am using that terminology when referring to their perception of God. When I later refer to God as I presently view It, I will use "It" without quotations. (Hopefully, I will remember to be consistent with this terminology).

Now, contrary to what I may seem to be inferring, I am grateful for my early religious experience, because in spite of the many questions it raised in my mind, it also provided some great benefits. And chief among them was a profound trust in Jesus; I truly felt that he loved me, and I, therefore, loved him in return. Unfortunately, at least during my early youth, I had come to perceive "God the Father" as a strict judge and a vengeful punisher of those who disobeyed "His" will. Since this perception raised questions in my mind about "His" supposedly loving everybody, when the church's teachings seemed to indicate otherwise, I clung all the more strongly to Jesus as "my savior"; as he was the one who would intercede for me with his Father.

What troubled me most during my early youth was that God's plans—at least as they were presented to me—just didn't seem to be consistent or logical. If all sin originated from Adam and Eve's mistake, why didn't God just kill them and start over? And why didn't God know that they would disobey "Him"? After all, "He" knew all things. In fact, why didn't God create people so they wouldn't be so weak? Also, how could it be that God would later conclude that "He" was expecting too much from mankind in expecting them to be obedient, and change his mind—requiring them instead to accept a particular belief; that of believing a Messiah would come to save them? And why wait so long in fulfilling that promise?

Then, with respect to the new plan—that of "salvation by faith"—how could that be fair when most people weren't even told about the new requirement, or even given the opportunity to learn of this saving Messiah? Having been told by my early religious teachers that God was testing us, how could it be fair to grade someone on subject matter of which they had no chance of being exposed to? If God really wanted everyone to be perfect, and love "Him", and live with "Him" in heaven, why didn't "He" just create them that way in the first place? And if it was a particular faith that "He" demanded of them, why didn't "He" offer more proof to more people? Why just expose one group of people—the Jews—to the miracles and teachings of Jesus, and let the rest of the world live in ignorance until they were exposed to it, and then be expected to convert?

Well, these were questions of a very young mind, and I was offered no answers other than to not question, but to trust in God; leaving all others to God's mercy. As I grew into my youth I developed more questions that involved subjects of philosophy and science; and with more of an exposure to the teachings of other religions, began to have more questions on a wider range of topics. These being numerous, and of a more basic, profound nature, will be used to begin this book.

Late in my youth, when I was preparing to leave home to go to college, I prayed to Jesus—the only source I felt I could trust—and told him of my desire to look for answers, even if it meant (which seemed to be an obvious result) leaving the faith of my youth. I asked Jesus to keep me in his care; and that, if I were to stray too far off course, to find some way to lead me back, or to a better understanding. I reminded Jesus that we were promised that if we were to seek, that we would find, and that if we were to ask, we would be given [the answers]. I wanted to call on this biblical promise for myself, with respect to my many questions and concerns. And having felt that my plea would be honored; I set out for college and a wider exposure to the world and its teachings.

In spite of the impression I may have given you up to this point, I didn't choose to major in contemporary religions; or anything like that. I was—after all—quite analytical in nature. Excelling in the subjects of Math and Science, and being influenced by my parents, I choose to pursue a career in Electrical Engineering. Having been accepted by Carnegie Institute of Technology, I found myself entering Carnegie-Mellon University during the first year of its name change. (Actually CIT joined with Mellon Institute to become a University.) Besides having a reputable Engineering department, C-MU possessed an excellent Fine Arts department which attracted a lot of creative people, and I found the mix quite enjoyable. This was the 60's, and, though I wasn't one of them, there were more than a few "hippies" on campus to expose me to social issues, and Eastern practices and philosophies.

This led me to consider the doctrines of Karma and Reincarnation; beliefs which—to my mind—held the answer to so many of my questions. God could be fair in "His" judgments if "He" gave people more than one opportunity to conform to "His" will. Gone was the unfairness of judging people who either hadn't been exposed to the required faith, or who were brought up in a culture that embraced another faith. Also gone was the seeming unfairness of those born into lives of poverty or illness. With the opportunity to live out several lifetimes, things could be fair; all people could experience lives of both desperation and privilege, and be judged after a greater assessment could be made of their degree of worthiness.

In spite of this consideration, my focus was—as might be expected—upon my studies and pursuit of a career. And, actually, this supposition helped me to set aside some of my religious concerns and focus on more practical matters (you know—girls and such). What I didn't realize, however, was how much my college education would impact my ability to come to the understandings I had sought for so long; for through my engineering courses I learned how to solve problems.

I had always been quite analytical in my approach to life, so "if-then" statements made sense to me. (If an assertion is true, then this result must also be observed.) I also learned to consider all possible causes which could produce an observed result; this helped me tremendously in my eventual career as a troubleshooter. But perhaps the greatest technique I learned, I learned by accident while taking an exam.

One of the problems in the exam was to expand a given algebra equation into another specified form, essentially proving that they stated the same thing. I had expanded the equation as far as I could, but then got stuck; I couldn't think of the next step. But instead of quitting and going on to the next question, I put the specified equation at the bottom of the page and began to work back, reducing that equation. I had hoped that I would be able to figure it out that way, but again I got stuck. What I ended up with were two equations with a gap between them; I couldn't figure out how to go from either one to the other. So I gave up and went on to the next question hoping for at least partial credit.

Apparently the person grading the test didn't recognize the gap, and I received full credit for having solved the problem; and this bothered me for a long time, feeling that I had unintentionally cheated. Much later, however, I realized that this episode proved a valuable technique. Very often I would be pursuing a goal step by step, and not know what next to do. It's then that I'd look at the goal and think back, to what would be the logical steps from there. Sometimes this technique would help me to discern the next step, but just as often I would find that a leap of faith was required. I knew that if I could get to that next step I could continue to my goal, I just didn't necessarily know how.

Like the hero running from the villain in an action movie, who came to a dead end or a cliff and needed to take a flying leap in order to keep going, often life seems to challenge us with the need to step out in faith and accept some risk.

The reason that I mention this here is that I've applied this lesson throughout my search for truth; and it's reflected in my writing here. In fact, I perceive that religionists are those who start with the premise that God exists, and profess beliefs that act like steps to prove the present known (miracles, acts of nature, etc.). Likewise, scientists look at the known, and in their search, take steps backwards to discover the workings of the universe (God's plan). By my taking both approaches—occasionally going back and forth from postulation to reality as we observe it—I feel that I have been able to come closer to discerning the real truths of reality that either of those parties, who only allow themselves to search from one perspective.

Relating this to "if-then" statements—wherein the "ifs" are beliefs or theories, and the "thens" are proven scientific facts or observed results—I have considered the ramifications of scientific theories and religious beliefs together, as possible causes for the reality which we observe and experience as results. I have also looked at these "results" and considered all the possible causes (theories and beliefs) that could account for them. What I have ended up with is—at least to my own mind—a pretty solid set of beliefs, which, though open for adjustment, explain why things are as they are; not only in explaining the workings of the universe, but also in explaining why people's personal lives become challenged as they do.

Well—as I said—while in school I didn't really focus on trying to discover the truths behind reality; I was having a tough enough time trying to learn what my professors were trying to teach me. Also, I was a bit distracted with social activities. In fact, I didn't return to my search for meaning and truth until several years after graduating, when my career direction met with a serious set-back.

I had graduated college with a BS in Electrical Engineering; and while pursuing career options, decided to accept a supervisory position within a small company that offered me a wider area of expression than I would have had with a large corporation which would have placed me within a team. This choice, however, required that I focus less on Engineering and more on production and troubleshooting. Professionally, this could have been perceived as a step down; certainly it was a step away from my educational experience. But the field of troubleshooting or problem-solving offered immediate reward, and was challenging enough to hold my interest. (Sometimes it was even more challenging than I cared for!)

After five years in this job, when I was just getting established in this career, it came to an abrupt end. Personality conflicts with one of my superiors had become so difficult, that the stress almost cost me my sight (I almost blinded myself because I was too angry to focus properly on what I was doing). When I finally (and impulsively) left this company, I had nowhere else to go. My resume looked bad, and I was seven years away from the field of Electrical Engineering. My only viable option seemed to be to settle for the life of a technician in some other company, and this isn't where I wanted to go. I was so hurt and angry that I couldn't even focus on doing what I needed to do in order to improve my situation and move on.

This is when I turned to my religion for help. I needed help that this world didn't seem to provide, and my minister was the only reasonable source of the type of guidance I felt I needed. But when I went to this man (who preached such wonderful sermons), I was totally surprised. Not only didn't he offer any satisfying counsel, he didn't even try. It was as though he was acknowledging that his religion didn't have the answers I required. After listening to my plea for understanding, he referred me to a Psychologist friend of his who belonged to a different religion entirely. And this Psychologist not only couldn't answer the "why" of my present predicament (Like many people, I felt that there had to be a "why".), he didn't even think I could find help from God. He counseled me that I needed to reconsider my interests and options, and rely solely upon myself to put my life back in order and move on.

Now, generally, this is good advice. What bothered me about it, was his—and my minister's—belief that God isn't truly active and helpful in our lives. This assertion ran counter to what had been a major part of my belief system throughout life; and was one that I was not able to easily consider as being valid.

So, essentially, by feeling rejected by my religion, and possibly being wrong in my beliefs about God, I was even more troubled, hurt, and angry. Not only had my career path come to an end, now my religious beliefs were being called into question. Before I could move on, both would need to be put into order; and I was too emotionally distraught to focus on either. So, after saying "thanks and good bye" to the Psychologist against his recommendations (since I already knew what his advice was), I began to attempt a serious consideration of my beliefs, choices, and interests.

This brought me to the point where I had to make a decision, and I wasn't in a good enough state of mind to do so. I suppose that many people who have felt similarly victimized, have found themselves in a similar position, and can relate to what I was going through. I needed to move on, and if I were able to freely use my intellect, I could easily have done that; but the emotional issues dominated, and I needed to obtain resolution to those first.

With these issues came all the other questions I had stored away from my childhood and youth. Now it was not only "why me" in this situation, but why anybody or everybody else, in any and all difficult situations that people encounter in life. What <u>was</u> the role of God or religion in our lives;

if not to help and guide us in some way? Surely "He" had a purpose in all things.

So, I took it upon myself to delve more deeply into my religious faith, without seeking the counsel of others, and earnestly sought out the answers to the questions that had troubled me since my youth. This led me to go straight to God. No middle men this time. If I was to find help, it would need to come directly from the Source that—I had been taught to believe—loved me, and wanted me to find truth. And, yes, I went straight to Jesus; to remind him of our deal, and of his promise to come after me and lead me "home" should I go astray. Just what was it that he wanted from me? Where was I to go from here?

I suppose that everybody with a religious upbringing has had some experience with prayer. And there had been a couple of times in my past when I felt that I had received help through this expression. So this is where I went. And I didn't do it casually. Now, "grown men don't cry", and I'd never admit to that; so let's just say that I expressed all of my frustrations, anger, and fears into one emotionally charged "request"; reminding Jesus of his promises and our arrangement. Gratefully, I received an immediate reply.

It arrived in the following day's mail in the form of "junk mail". It was an ad for membership in the A.R.E. (Association for Research and Enlightenment), promising to provide answers to life's challenging questions. I was skeptical at first, since they were promoting a psychic and his predictions, but when I saw the A.R.E.'s symbol of a dove over a cross on the letter head, I felt that this could be the answer I was looking for; so I responded, and was not disappointed. I have no idea how they got my name and address, since I had never even been interested in psychics or such material. But when I began to read about Edgar Cayce and his philosophy, I wondered why I hadn't heard about anything like this sooner.

When I found that the A.R.E. had a study group near me, I joined it and obtained the social support of other people like myself, who wanted more than the simple teachings that conventional religions offer. Should I also add that the "readings" of Edgar Cayce included the teachings of karma and reincarnation? It brought me back to the tentative conclusions I had made while in college; validating them, and showing how they were consistent with the teachings of Jesus. And, Edgar Cayce's philosophy embraced all religions, even though it was strongly centered on Jesus teachings. Cayce, it turned out, had also been brought up in a protestant religion, and was even a Sunday School teacher at the time he discovered he could access a pool of wisdom through a trance state.

But my search didn't end there. In fact, this association pointed me into a wide variety of directions. And two years later, when I was becoming dismayed that the A.R.E. was so rigidly adhering to the sole "readings" of Cayce—long after his death—when there were more contemporary subjects to be considered, and I had specific questions about other religious beliefs and customs, I received another piece of mail (addressed to a person even my landlord didn't recognize, though it had my address) inviting me to join a similar organization called C.A.C. (Cosmic Awareness Communications). C.A.C. had a living "interpreter"—the third since their inception—and they didn't stay focused on the messages from any one like the A.R.E. did. Additionally, members could submit questions on general topics for consideration; which—if deemed worthy or relevant—would receive answers in an up-coming newsletter.

Finding the answers from "Cosmic Awareness"—which the "interpreters" credit as being the source (not a spirit or disincarnate being) of the answers given—to be both understandable and credible, I've been a member in this organization ever since.

These two organizations were the most influential in helping me to understand life's riddles. I recommend them both to any of you fellow seekers, who desire a greater understanding of your life and challenges; and of life in general. If you're interested, they may be reached at www.edgarcayce.org and www.cosmicawareness.org respectively.

Finally obtaining sources of answers to most of my life's difficult questions allowed me to move on professionally, and I found myself starting my own business, and receiving not only more income with less hours of work, but a greater sense of personal fulfillment. And with less of a demand for my time professionally, I was able to put more time into research, study, and contemplation.

Also, the answers I received with regard to religious subjects didn't cause me to forsake Christianity, nor to deny the value of other religious faiths. In fact, they gave me a greater appreciation for Jesus' teachings, and the wisdom found in other religious faiths. The material that I received from these two organizations caused me to come to a completely different understanding about God, Its purposes, and the many teachings within the church of my youth. The different perspective I gained allowed me to see purpose in all belief systems and philosophies, including the purely scientific or atheistic, and to learn how my life could be improved by following the laws and principles revealed by these mystical sources.

Perhaps the greatest benefit I received, however, related to my personal life. I began an in-depth search of my own short-comings, and began the process of personal growth and improvement. I began to realize just how much the quality of my present life reflected my own attitudes and beliefs; perceiving myself less the victim of circumstances, and more the creator of them. I also began the practice of meditation (though not of the type that is generally regarded as such); not with chanting or mantras, but through a process of "entering into the silence", wherein I would "wait" upon Spirit, and open myself to Its subtle uplifting.

Now, don't think that I'm professing to have become completely successful in my attempts at self-improvement, or that everything in my life has changed for the better. In fact, I continued to make poor choices, some of which I came to regret later. I wasn't a perfect being to start with, and I'm still far from one now. In many ways, then, I was more challenged; and many of the answers I gratefully received led me to ask more questions on a wider variety of subjects.

In addition to the practice of meditation (using different techniques from time to time), I began a focus on my dreams, seeking guidance and feedback through them. This opened the door to my experiencing different states of consciousness (some quite profound—and NO I don't use drugs) and experiences of a mystical nature. During my youth I had already experienced a few occasions of ESP, but now I began to have visions, what seemed to be Out-of-Body experiences, episodes of remote viewing, and lucid dreams. My world had begun to expand beyond the comfortable known, and into areas of speculation and wonder. I don't mention this to brag—far from it—because I've met people, and found books written by others, who seemed to have had far greater experiences, and more of an understanding about them. Instead, I'm trying to offer a glimpse into the vastness of human experience that is available to all who seek it; with the encouragement to become open to the guidance and inspiration of Spirit that comes with seeking.

My search has also led me to travel, and to become personally acquainted with people of different cultures and beliefs. And this includes the ancient societies and religions that have long since disappeared. I've joined different religious groups, and tried out their practices for myself, always finding both value and short-comings. Being able to sustain myself with my own business, performing troubleshooting services to industry, I was able to limit my weekly hours, and allow myself time off to travel. To date, I've visited 20 foreign countries, some of them repeatedly, and found kinship with people of many different cultures and beliefs. In doing so, I've come to realize that we are all pretty much the same, differing only in the way we've learned (or been conditioned) to pursue our desire for greater personal and spiritual fulfillment.

This book is my attempt to present the many truths that I have come to understand and accept, with regard to God, religion and reality. It is done in order to assist those of you, who like myself, have come to a point in life where meaning and understanding are both desired and necessary. I've come to realize that Spirit (by whatever name) constantly challenges us to move forward; out of the known, and into areas of uncertainty, for our own growth and development. Sometimes (ok, many times) our experiences are unpleasant, and even painful, but if we are open to looking for a purpose, I'm sure we will find it. At least, I've been able to find purpose and meaning within my own personal experiences. Yes, hindsight is often much clearer than foresight. But, who ever said life was supposed to be easy?

Perhaps some of you are now being challenged as I have been (and continue to be), and are looking for the ability to understand and accept the seemingly unjust circumstances and painful influences that life so often challenges us with. Maybe some of you are even questioning your religious beliefs as I felt compelled to do; and are seeking meaningful answers to the challenges of life that religions so often fail to adequately answer.

Hopefully, this book will aid you in your search, and save you some time. It took me years to come to the understandings that I have presented here, and I'm sure that in the years to come I will come to understand more, and perceive truth more clearly. Toward your own personal journey and your own quest for truth, I wish you blessings.

Though I intend to provide understandings that can be accepted by people of all faiths, I must acknowledge that I am unable to adequately address any but the Christian faith (or to some extent the Jewish faith, since they are linked to a degree). I am just not knowledgeable enough about other religious faiths to do so with credibility. This is not to say, however, that I won't interject my observations and thoughts with regard to other faiths near the end of this book.

It is my hope, that those of you from different religions, can gain enough of an insight from the "truths" (as I have come to perceive them) that I offer herein, that you will be able to adequately adjust your own religious, philosophical, or materialistic beliefs, in a way that improves your own state of consciousness, and adds more of a sense of peace and hope to your life. Sometimes a different understanding about situations, does lead to a more desirable state of consciousness or awareness, and a more satisfying life. Toward this end, I offer this book.

I've also created a website called www.dawn-of-truth.com wherein I may offer other suggestions and opinions not expressed in this book. Through this website, I also intend to provide you with an opportunity to ask further questions of me (which I will attempt to answer if able), and to share your own opinions and experiences with myself and possibly others (if I feel it to be appropriate). I hope that you will find this site to be a helpful and thought-provoking experience.

Also, if you've found some value in this book, please refer others to this site, so that they will also have an opportunity to consider a possible higher truth. I have little money for promotion, so I'm relying upon word-of-mouth (or should I say "word-of-text") from those of you who feel that your friends might be interested in the subject matter. We don't often know what's really on another person's mind, or what they might be looking for, so sometimes a small comment or "hey, check it out" can be most welcome. And it's a lot easier to refer someone to a website, than it is to recommend a book; probably a lot more welcome by the recipient as well.

WHAT IS GOD?

Why Question?

O ne of the things that troubled me as a child was that people didn't seem to care if something was really true, when it didn't seem to make sense. Perhaps it was my nature to be skeptical about assertions made by others because I had caught my parents telling fibs or half-truths in their attempts to manipulate me and my sisters, and I concluded that all adults did the same. But other people didn't even seem to care if what they were told to believe was true or not; even when contradictions or incongruences seemed to be so apparent. And it especially bothered me when teachers acknowledged a conflict, didn't have a satisfying answer, and then tried to discourage me from even seeking out a resolution. It was as though they were hiding something besides their ignorance.

Later, as an adult, I came to realize that most people aren't really concerned whether their beliefs are consistent or valid, as long as they receive validation for them, and the incongruences don't cause problems with their personal life or chosen lifestyle. In fact, even though I had reason to question many of the beliefs I was given, I didn't really look for firm answers until I was faced with personal problems that begged for answers. I guess it comes down to one's comfort level; wherein one really feels it necessary to take the risk of letting go of what is presently accepted, in favor of considering truths that might threaten one's accepted lifestyle or frame of mind.

Assuming, then, that you—the reader—are at a point in your life when you are willing to be open to reconsidering your present beliefs, and to accepting the challenge that a correction or adjustment might present to your personal comfort level and chosen life situation, I will proceed with describing some of the questions and conflicts that I held for so long, and which I finally resolved to my present satisfaction.

What is God?

Perhaps the most controversial subject to address in this book is the one about God; trying to make sense of the many varied descriptions, qualities, and actions attributed to God.

The assertion that I was given through my religious upbringing was that God was a divine being who was Omnipotent (all powerful), Omnipresent (everywhere present), Omniscient (all knowing), and All Loving. These were absolutes that I had no problem with accepting; they seemed to describe just what a God should be. What bothered me, then, was that so many other teachings seemed to challenge these attributes, implying that perhaps much of what was attributed to this "One God", was more appropriately distributed among several entities—or beings—which were perceived as being the same, when in fact they were most likely not. At least, this is the only way I could justify the many inconsistencies I perceived to exist within the subject; especially when they described a God with human qualities.

God is an anthropomorphic being.

That a God which created the vastness of our universe, and possibly other universes in other dimensions of reality, would favor one culture or group on this planet could be believable to one's ego; that is certain. But that this same Supreme God Almighty would also change "His" mind on occasion, repent of things "He" had done, claim to be jealous and vengeful, and perform acts of violence—even eternal torture—just didn't seem believable to me. I felt that surely there was some confusion or misunderstanding with regard to these teachings, or the ancient texts and other stories from which such claims originated.

Also, that God had a face that nobody was allowed to look upon, that if somebody did they would surely die; that Adam could hear God walking, that God liked the smell of Noah's sacrifice, or that people could so unmistakably hear God talking to them, seemed to me to indicate that they weren't truly talking about the Ultimate Almighty God, but rather of some other divine being that was acting more as an agent of the Ultimate God. I could well understand and empathize with those who claimed that man created a god in his image and likeness, rather than the other way around.

What struck me so much as a child was that the Old Testament God was so much different than the God we experienced now. Before, God and "His" actions were so evident to people; as though "He" was there physically among them. Whether on top of a mountain chipping out blocks of stone, or wandering around the desert as a cloud or pillar of fire, "His" presence was obvious to observe. And I couldn't understand why things should be any different today, especially since "He" demanded belief in "Him" to escape "His" wrath.

If God wanted our faithfulness, then why did God stop showing "Himself"? The answer I received was that it was a test: "He" wanted to challenge us to believe purely by faith; that once the Bible had been written, "He" didn't need to prove "His" existence anymore because the Bible was there to prove it. Well, if that was "His" intention, it didn't work; so "He" was wrong again.

The conclusion that I finally came to accept, was that the Old Testament God was not the same Ultimate God of the Universe (or universes); but perhaps a divine being acting in some capacity to facilitate some higher purpose of the Ultimate God. Though they might not be correct in all assertions, I came to believe that there was a lot of truth in books (such as Zecharia Sitchin's book *The 12th Planet*) regarding the probability that ancient astronauts, and alien beings came to this planet to provide us with religion and culture.

Now, I don't want to be offensive to religions which hold firmly to Old Testament stories. I myself have found great value in the lessons taught; and I believe this to be the most important reason for their continuance. But it doesn't matter to me whether the characters were exactly as portrayed, or even if they ever existed; for—to me—the lessons and morals are what is most important. These ancient stories are rightly called myths; not because they aren't true (actually myths can be very accurate in describing an occurrence or story), but because of the symbolism involved, and how the stories affect us on an archetypal level. I don't perceive their value to be diminished in any way, then, if the God that they describe isn't actually the Ultimate Supreme Almighty God which was responsible for all of reality.

If, for example, I were to be at a grocery check-out counter, and upon reaching for my wallet find that I've apparently left it at home, and a woman just leaving the counter reaches back to hand me a $50 bill, I'd be overwhelmingly grateful. And if the clerk were to inform me that it wasn't a woman after all, that it was a man with long hair, it wouldn't change things for me. I'd still have the gift, and I'd still be grateful to have received it. My ego might be bruised a bit, but that would be all. Well, this is what I feel should apply to the teachings of many religions. Some of the details (as presently believed) may not truly be accurate, but the lessons involved—the benefits received—are not necessarily invalidated; and except for a bit of humbling, we needn't be too put off by being corrected, or in reconsidering things.

As this relates to early religious teachings, it may even be that the ancients responsible for the original teachings and texts did recognize a difference between the ultimate God and the lesser gods which "walked and talked with man". It is my understanding, for example, that the ancient Hebrew texts used different names for God. Perhaps the misunderstanding rests with those who later concluded that these different names all related to the same entity, when in fact they didn't. But does it really matter? In my opinion, it only does if it causes someone to disbelieve in the existence of any God, due to the incongruences that result from a misassumption.

Once again, it really comes down to what we choose to believe; what axioms we accept as ultimately true, forming a foundation for all of our other beliefs. Some people place all their trust in a particular person, others in a particular religion, and still others in a holy book. So, if that person or book or claims it to be true, then one doesn't even question it. Well, this tendency isn't all that bad; in fact, even though it could cause one to believe things that aren't actually true, it can be quite beneficial in other ways. After all, it's sometimes hard to conduct one's life and affairs if one is always questioning things. At some point a person just has to make a stand, and decide what will and will not be considered questionable. So, axioms of belief are absolutely necessary; hopefully we choose them with wisdom. The following sections describe axioms which I hold as being valid and unarguable; which form the basis of my beliefs about God and Its reality.

God is omniscient.

That God would know all things seemed perfectly believable to me as a child; though I wondered if "He" could actually know the future. Certainly "He" would have a pretty good idea, though, of the likelihood of future events per mankind's choosing. What troubled me, then was how "He" seemed to be so angry when Adam and Eve failed to live up to "His" expectation of their being obedient; especially when "He" presented them with the temptation of a magical tree that would offer them greater knowledge and awareness.

If God wanted Adam and Eve to be obedient, why didn't "He" just create them that way in the first place? And why should everybody else have to suffer for their mistake? Why not just punish or kill off Adam and Eve, and start again? That God would then change "His" mind and require a particular belief rather than obedience, seemed doubly illogical. If God truly wanted everyone to be obedient, believe in "Him", and live with "Him" in heaven, then why didn't "He" just make them that way and put them in heaven to begin with? Why all the drama? And why would it require a Messiah to save them, or a Savior to take away their sins? Why not just snap "His" fingers and declare them to be saved or forgiven? Was there some rule-book that God had to follow in order to erase sins once they were committed?

Now, these were the thoughts I had as a child; and they bothered me, because what I was being taught just didn't seem to make much sense given the reasons used to justify the assertions. Quite obviously, there is purpose in the way life functions; and a wise God did have a viable plan. It's just that my religious teachers didn't seem to know what it was (other than a test), so they just insisted on blind acceptance of their assertions. A good thing for them to do, perhaps, since the answers I finally came to accept also led me to realize that many of their assertions were based upon wrong assumptions and misunderstandings. These will be addressed in later chapters.

God is omnipotent.

This is another quality of God that I readily accepted as a youth (and still do today), but which also seemed to be contradicted in my church's teachings. In fact, it seems to contradict most of the present world's view of God and "His" drama with "the devil". It's easy to conclude that if God was truly all-powerful, then "He" could either disempower "the devil", eliminate him completely, or make him stay in hell, and not bother the rest of us. As a result, there would be no battle between a God who desires goodness, and a devil who promotes evil. So obviously, if God is truly omnipotent, then the drama, that is supposedly played out in our lives every day, whereby we are struggling against the temptations of Satan (a name for the devil), would be a part of God's plan. If it were otherwise, "He" would have made changes.

Once again, I feel that assumptions have been made about God's "will" or ultimate plan, and the role of the devil (or Satan) that must not be entirely valid. These misassumptions, together with any number of misunderstandings, have—in my opinion—resulted in religious teachings that are not consistent with a view of God as being omnipotent. Once these short-comings are corrected, one will be able to clearly see where all religions (including the one called atheism) have great merit and value. Simply put: If God is truly all-powerful, then what is, is what God intends. And if God is also all-knowing, then "what is" is also what God intended from the beginning.

God is All Loving.

Another way of saying this, is to say; "God is Love". Of course God isn't an emotion as we perceive love to be; but God—in Its expressions—should certainly epitomize love. Once again I fully believe this, and have since my youth; but not since my childhood. Here's the difference: As a child I perceived God to be a wrathful deity whom we had to watch out for. In many ways, I perceived "Him" as a tyrant; unjustly, and unmercifully punishing all who transgressed "His will". That God supposedly sent "His" son (Jesus) to save us, translated—for me—into saving us from "His" own wrath; and again, a contradiction.

Sometime during my youth I came to conclude that the wrath did not come from God Itself, but rather from the laws It created to fulfill Its plan. So rather, it was the law that punished (or corrected), and so the Savior came to show us a way to escape the wrath of the law—through forgiveness and mercy.

This alternate view of God, however, did not explain the teachings of the church with regard to Hell and Eternal Damnation; which showed God to be—at the very least—unloving. It also showed "Him" to be inconsistent; wherein "He" commanded us to forgive others, while "He" showed no mercy at all.

My conclusion was that there have been misunderstandings about what hell or damnation truly is; that there is always a means of escaping its "flames", and that it serves a very beneficial purpose for us all. Once I present a clearer picture of how I perceive hell, how I feel we get there, and what "the devil's" role is, perhaps you will agree with me, that God is truly loving; in fact more loving than anyone can even imagine.

God is Omnipresent.

I saved this one for last, because it's my favorite to contemplate. Just think of the ramifications: If God's everywhere, then "He's" in hell too; also in the devil and its demons. And those evil sinners . . . yep, "He's" there too! My teachers in school weren't pleased with my suggestions in this regard; and even I felt that I was stretching the point a bit, but it did cause me to contemplate the subject over the years.

It's easy to abridge this attribute, though, and conclude that "He's" everywhere that is good or neutral, and filling the space between particles of matter, or such. Or one can conclude that it means "He's" near each of us, keeping watch, and listening for a prayer or two. But this isn't what the attribute really states.

For God to truly be everywhere present, then It would also have to <u>be</u> everything. And this is not a notion even contemplated by most people. On a very real level, though, I've come to the conclusion that it must be true. The assertion is very much like the following one.

God is the "All in All".

This definition of God is pretty much saying the same thing as the last, but in a more precise language; for if God were truly everywhere, then It would also <u>be</u> all things. Of course, this description could also be compromised by stating that God was all that was within all things, but not actually be the all that It was within. In other words, It would be in matter, but not actually be the matter; and It would be <u>in</u> us, but not actually <u>be</u> us.

I don't recall actually thinking of this as a child or youth, and have merely included it here to point out its similarities to the prior attribute, and to the fact that for this description of God to be true, then a much different view of God is necessary. It is this different view that I have come to accept as being the only logical one.

When one has a perception of God as an anthropomorphic being, at war with the devil, ready to punish evildoers, then one cannot perceive God as being the "All-in-All" without making some compromise or adjustment to its expansive implications. With a different view of God, however, as will be described in the following chapter, God will be seen to be quite omnipresent with all implications in place; truly "The All in All"; a more present God than most people can even imagine.

God is the "I Am that I Am".

This is—I think—the only description or name for God that God supposedly gave for "Himself". This was when "talking" to Moses on Mt. Sinai during the Exodus. When I was in grade school (or Sunday School) I recall thinking that this was a rather evasive or non-committal description for God to give "Himself". It was like saying; "I'm beyond description", or "don't try to define Me".

There isn't much more I can say about this now; I've included it here because I intend to refer back to it in the next chapter. In my present opinion of God, I believe it to be the most accurate and most informative description of God that I can think of. In fact, as I will describe later, I believe it says something about us as well.

God is a Triune God.

This is solely (at least at present) a Christian way of perceiving God. I say "at present" because some ancient cultures also seemed to perceive of God in this way. These cultures saw the sun and moon as representing the masculine and feminine characteristics of God, while a third party—a child of the union—possessed dual the attributes of being of the earth and sky.

Though I've ultimately come to accept a triune nature to God, I feel that there is a lot of misunderstanding in the Christian concept; it makes it appear that God has a split personality that is often in conflict. Also, by believing a flesh-and-blood person (Jesus) to also <u>be</u> God, much of what I have come to understand Jesus' teachings to be, is lost or invalidated.

The mystic, Edgar Cayce, suggested that God was body, mind, and spirit; just as we all are. This is another way of perceiving a trinity of God; but it's more of a way of describing God's qualities or aspects. It can be confusing to those who perceive of God as a "being". If you find this confusing, perhaps you will better understand my meaning in the following chapter.

God is the Creator.

Perhaps this is the most commonly held perception of God. It's certainly one of the most basic. After all, who else could have created the universe? It had to have come from somewhere; so God is the only logical source. But It (God) isn't really. God could, in fact, have created other entities: lesser gods—and they in turn could have created our universe. In fact, I've come to conclude that this is actually the way it happened.

As a youth, the creation story—as given in Genesis—didn't seem logical at all; especially since scientific evidence—fossils and such—proved to me that millions of years, rather than days, were involved in the creation of the world as we now know it. I don't recall what I believed then about evolution, though, and probably put this to God's handiwork. After all, I was presented with either of two options: the church's view or the scientific view, and neither seemed to be entirely logical.

To have something just pop into existence seemed just as illogical as for something to evolve into existence all by itself by mere chance. I guess you could say I would have been an "intelligent design" supporter, but with misgivings about the nature and method of the proposed said design. Eventually, and with the help of Edgar Cayce's "readings", I came to conclude that others besides God were responsible for life as we now know it. And this explanation included the influence of higher intelligence and "Alien beings" (intelligent life from other realms) who acted as agents of God's plan. This will be discussed in the following chapter.

One of the things that bothered me as a youth was that, in the Bible, the creator of man is given in the plural tense: "Let us make man in our image, after our likeness." This got me to questioning the entire creation story. If it was rather a group of beings (or agents of God) who created mankind in their image, what, then, of the rest of the Biblical creation story? Maybe the "us" also had a hand in creating other life forms, or the planets themselves.

I guess everybody knows of the dispute going on in public schools about what to teach children with regard to the origin of the universe, and the appearance of different species (including mankind) upon the planet. Science wants to point to spontaneous generation and evolution, while religionists insist on having "intelligent design" discussed. Quite frankly, I have come to conclude that both views are partially right and partially in error. Why else would there be disagreement? It's too bad science and religion can't come to a compromise, because both views have too many holes in them.

One of the basic principles of genetics is that a certain gene pool is required in order to allow a given species to survive. If too few of any species remain, they die out due to excessive in-breeding. How, then, can new species come into being through chance mutations of existing species? Even if a pair was to mutate at the same time and in the same location, they would soon deplete their gene pool through inbreeding, and die out. Yet science points to all present species as having evolved from prior species. And in many cases, these new species (of both animals and plants) just suddenly appeared in a very short period of time. And recall also, that though some evolution appears to be involved with mankind's appearance, no "missing link" has ever been found. Mankind too seems to have just appeared in a very short time frame.

It has become my conclusion, then, that though evolution does occur within a given species (in the form of natural selection); the theory is not sufficient to account for everything. Clearly—at least to my thinking—some outside agent (or group of agents) were involved in the manifestation of life forms which we know today. It could be from entities working their will within the greater will of God, but they also could also have been doing things entirely on their own. We just don't know (don't have the capacity to know) what's really "out there"; so we either suppose that it's God, or nothing (that nothing exists at all if we can't see it, touch it, and prove its existence).

God is the First Cause.

Within the subject of God being the Creator, is the perception of God as the First Cause. This is like a limited definition of the prior description. Here, God doesn't necessarily create; nor does "He" necessarily facilitate evolution; rather "He" causes things to come into being. This could actually be a way for science to define a God. Since every result must have a cause, there must be a very first cause to bring the universe into being, and people could define God as such a "first cause", and there would be no argument that God existed.

The "big bang":

The current "big-bang theory" states that the entire universe came from a tiny, infinitely dense hunk of matter (called a singularity), which (for some unknown reason) rapidly expanded into the universe. No explanation is offered as to where the singularity came from, or for why it expanded; so if science ever chose to compromise with religion, they could accept that God was the creator of the singularity. Of course religion would want to assign more attributes to this first cause, and science wouldn't be able to concede to anything but the one causation.

As with the subject of creation, I don't consider it logical to assume that this first cause was, in fact, God. God could, in fact, have created a multitude of lesser gods, and these others, (or a group) of these others could have created and caused the singularity.

From my point of reasoning, though, the "big-bang theory" cannot be valid without some acceptance of a reality beyond the physical realm. After all, that singularity had to come from somewhere, and if it was the source of our physical universe, then it had to have come from somewhere in a non-physical reality. And the same applies to the cause of its expansion; mass cannot—at least to my understanding—convert itself into energy.

If a singularity is an infinitely (actually I question the validity of that word) dense piece of matter, then it is essentially dead. It has no movement or vibration, and exists at the temperature of absolute zero. It should just sit there forever just doing nothing. And if only a physical reality existed, then there would be nothing to cause it to change its state.

Also, the form of the universe proves the existence of other forces than that of a singular "big-bang". If a single particle of matter of ultimate density were to expand, its expansion should be uniform in every layer of the ever expanding hollow sphere. The outside skin should look identical everywhere, because there would be no other forces to move it out of equilibrium or uniformity; and the same would apply to every layer within this sphere. How, then, would one account for the seemingly random array of cosmic dust, galaxies, and other such celestial phenomena that we observe in our universe?

As I perceive it, the energy within the expansion should be consistent in every cone-shaped sample or segment taken from the expanding sphere, and the gravitational capacity of matter, should also be equal on all sides (not above or below) within a given layer. All matter should then be in a state of uniform equilibrium throughout the expansion process. There would be no clumping of particles of mass to form larger forms. How, then, does one explain the chaos that we observe? Again, there has to be other forces involved, which act upon the expanding singularity; and this necessitates the existence of non-physical forces. Whether these forces are from a singular God, or from any number of other agents, cannot be proven. So, if one chose, one could claim that God wasn't the first cause. On the other hand, since something had to be, one could just as easily define it as God.

Gravity:

Another problem I have with the theory of expansion from a singularity is that the force of gravity should keep it stable and cause it to retain its "infinite" density. In order for there to be any expansion, the "infinite" (in proportion to the density) gravitational force would have to not only be overcome, but essentially reversed. Since science provides for no force which opposes gravity, it cannot describe anything in our known universe which can account for the expansion. So, here again, some force outside of our physical dimension must exist that can cause such a phenomena.

Seemingly the opposite of a singularity is a black hole. This also is theorized to be a mass of incredible density which possesses so much mass that it draws in—through gravity—even stars and light. It might be thought of as a singularity in the making.

This brings me to the subject of gravity; for, in my opinion, the very existence of the phenomena which we call gravity, is also proof of a non-physical reality and non-physical forces at work. In a reality that was solely composed of physical substances, there would not be any physical agent or source of physical energy which could account for the pull that even tiny particles of mass exert upon each other. And—as with the cause and origin of singularities—science can offer no reasonable explanation for its existence; they can only say what it's like, and describe how it is observed, using two different theories.

Isaac Newton described gravity as a force which caused particles of mass to draw toward each other. He didn't postulate where this force came from, so it is assumed that it emanated from matter itself. If indeed this is so, then there is some non-physical energy that moves through matter, but which is not composed of matter; and it is anybody's guess as to the origin and design of this energy. Again, God or some agent of "God's will" is as good a theory as any.

Albert Einstein proposed a different theory, and with all due respect to a man I greatly admire, I have a problem with his theory; at least in the way it was explained to me. So, let me make it very clear that I've not studied Einstein's theory, so my criticism may actually be in the way others describe his theory. This description has matter resting on a sheet of fabric which is our "Spacetime" reality. Supposedly the weight of some mass causes a curvature or indentation to occur in the fabric of "Spacetime", so that other particles of mass slide down the "well" and rest against the heavy mass.

The big problem that I have with this is that it uses the force of gravity in making the model work. It would require a force of gravity from some larger mass, located below the fabric of "Spacetime", to cause the prior mass to settle down into the fabric, causing the well. And it would also require a force of gravity (again from some larger mass below the fabric) to cause the smaller mass to slide down the fabric and into the well. Take away this large force of gravity from below the fabric of "Spacetime", and both masses would rest comfortably on top of the fabric without even causing a dent. So, to my mind, this model is either very lacking in explaining Einstein's theory, or the theory itself is lacking.

I do, however, love the notion of a gravitational force existing outside of our "Spacetime" reality, which causes our physical reality to function as it does. Perhaps it is God which exists outside (or below) the fabric of "Spacetime", causing the phenomena we experience as gravity.

Also I have a problem with perceiving our "Spacetime" reality as a two dimensional plane or "fabric", because I can't conceive of two dimensional realities as existing except in theory. If it were three dimensional, though, then the model would be describing a compression of "Spacetime" where it meets mass, and the compression would be greater or less depending upon the size of the mass. Does science perceive a compression of "Spacetime" measurements when nearing stars or galaxies? If they don't, perhaps that's why they assume the fabric to be two dimensional.

I could propose another model, though I have problems with it as well, but since I intend to address this subject in the following chapter, I'll describe it here. The model I propose, also uses an Einstein theory; though more specifically his famous equation: $E=MC^2$. From my study of mathematics, one can remove the constant (the C^2) from an equation and obtain an equivalency. This would state that energy (E) is equivalent to mass (M). In _my_ words, then, matter would be energy forms. I believe this to have been confirmed with the discovery of atomic energy and the atomic bomb, which create energy through the destruction of matter.

In fact, current research being conducted by colliding protons at high speed is allowing science to view tiny and unique particles of matter that behave like energy forms. They reportedly appear and then just as quickly disappear. It causes me to ask; in their disappearance, is science observing the opposite of creation, whereby matter is going back into nothingness? If that is true, then surely they're confirming the creationist theory that matter can arise from nothing. I suggest, though, that what they have observed (are observing) is that energy can form itself into matter, and that matter can return back into energy. Matter, then would essentially be constructs of energy.

Using the concept of mass being energy forms, one could envision a vast sea of energy which represented our "Spacetime" reality. Were some force within or without this sea to condense energy into matter, it would create an area of great density within this sea. Also, the area of energy around the mass would be weakened due to the conversion. It could be this lessening in the strength of the energy "sea" close to the created mass, which would cause other objects of mass to be drawn to it. It wouldn't because of gravity or some other direct force, but rather because the density—if you will—of the "sea" would be diminished, causing an attraction as "objects move in the direction of least resistance". The creation or condensation could also be thought of as having created a partial vacuum, which would draw in other objects.

Now this model also requires an external agent to cause the condensation of energy, or structuring of energy, into matter forms. So, one could identify that agent as either being God, or a created being, and causing other acts of creation on its own. In either case, this agent would likely be conscious; acting upon its own will, rather than being a mere result of some other unconscious cause. I'll go more into this in the following chapter as well.

To summarize, I just can't perceive of matter as being anything but energy forms: constructs of energy, held in shape or possessing qualities that a non-physical reality has given them. I just can't conceive of essentially dead particles of density possessing all the unique and spectacular qualities that science is observing when they study space, time, and matter.

I look forward to a time when scientists concede that there has to be more than a physical reality; they don't have to define it as God. I think that what they should acknowledge—if they were to satisfy my feelings and reasoning—is that what we think to be solid and physical, is in reality only forms of energy in motion, structured by some unknown force, and acting from some unknown causational influence outside the physical realm. And though that would not prove the existence of God, it would prove the existence of causes which people attribute to God; and maybe that's good enough to start people on their own search for discovery and meaning.

There is no God.

Certainly, this is the view of atheists the world over. And in my opinion, atheism is just another type of religion. It may not have all the dogma and rituals inherent in religions, but the atheist must have a concept of what the God is that isn't believed in. And these notions could very well be the many descriptions of God that are held by the world's various religions. Atheists could, then, be essentially stating that they don't agree with the established religious views of God. And they would—at least in my opinion—be correct in that assertion to very a large degree.

But what if atheists were to define what God would be, or be like, if It did exist? As I've pointed out: believing God to be a creator being or a first cause (including a cause of gravity) isn't necessarily true if one were able to attribute such phenomena to other agents outside our known physical reality. Both creation and intentional design could be attributed to lesser gods, or beings living in other non-physical realms. Of course, these lesser gods might also be expected to have a creator, and therefore a God that they believe in.

So, unless one was to first define what a God (if It were to exist) was, and how It functioned, there would be little meaning to the assertion that there was no God. Certainly there are non-physical forces at play in our reality; it's merely up to us to label them as we choose. Religions have done this, and always (it seems to me) with some inconsistencies which cast doubt upon their beliefs; and this may well justify the atheists' viewpoint.

I wonder what an atheist would think, though, of the description of a God that is truly Omnipotent, Omniscient, Omnipresent, and All-loving; without contrary assumptions made which contradict such attributes. And what if these absolute qualities could account for the physical phenomena which science is unable to explain? Obviously, all result has a cause; so just what could cause the reality we know, if not an infinitely powerful, infinitely expansive, ultimate consciousness?

God is dead.

This is an often misquoted statement which originated from Friedrich Nietzsche; who—in lamenting God's death, blamed society for the murder. It was—to my understanding—part of a statement he was trying to make, and did not intend to promote the idea that God had actually existed at some point and was subsequently murdered.

Other people, though, have apparently used this statement to assert that God doesn't seem to be active in people's daily lives; and this is the meaning which I intend to address here.

An agnostic friend of mine told me that he considered that perhaps God—in creating the world—had done something like winding up a clock and then letting it run. What he meant was that there may have been a God that created everything, but that he didn't perceive of any influence from God in his life. Sadly, I feel that there must be a lot of people who also feel that way. Perhaps the problem is that we don't recognize God's influence when it occurs, or that we don't know how to elicit such aid.

For myself, I've always felt God or Jesus or some other agent to be an active participant in, and influence upon my life. But how can I assert that; since I may pray for something and have the prayer answered from some other entity or agent, and not God? I don't think anybody really can. So it is my conclusion that though many people can claim to have experienced God's blessings, it may not have occurred in just the way in which it is believed.

As I will describe more fully in the following chapters, though, I have come to believe that God is active and present in our daily affairs; It just doesn't function or act in the way or manner in which we believe. And I'll begin by trying to describe what I perceive God to be; and what I have come to believe to be the most likely relationship between God and Its creation.

WHAT GOD IS

The Dream:

I mentioned in the Introduction to this book that I have had varied experiences in realms of consciousness (without the use of drugs). Many of these experiences occurred either during sleep or within that in-between state (between waking and dreaming) which is technically called either the hypnogogic (between waking and sleeping) or the hypnopompic (between sleeping and waking). Sometimes I've found it difficult to later discern just which state I was in, so I won't dwell on that here.

Within the realm of sleeping, I've often experienced lucid dreams; the type of dream wherein one becomes aware that one is dreaming while the dream progresses. Those who've shared this type of experience will agree with me that they are very interesting states of consciousness to be in. In a few of these lucid dream experiences, the dream would end—as though the projectionist turned off the projector—and I was left in a type of sensory void while still remaining conscious. On a couple of other occasions I became lucid in this sensory void, and after a few moments a dream would begin. The "dream"—if I can call it that—which I wish to describe now, was one of these. It occurred sometime during the night while I was sleeping.

Having become lucid in some type of sensory void, I spent some moments with the sole awareness (or realization) that I was. There was nothing else; I was only aware that I was. After a short period of time, though, I then had a thought—a question really: "What was I?" As I contemplated this, I remembered who I was, and that my body was asleep in bed. Immediately after affirming that, I awoke, and indeed was myself again: lying awake in bed.

I mention this "dream" because I think that this might be very close to what God experienced before the beginning of our (or any created) reality. In fact, this experience shed some light on the subject of where God came from. For me, it was never enough to just contemplate the beginning of our universe. I also wanted to understand what God was, where It came from, what led It to become a creator being, and for what purpose.

God's Origin:

The best description I have read, which describes what might be called the origin of God (or the awakening of God), came from a course provided by the organization: C.A.C. (refer to introduction). It originated from impressions that their then "interpreter"—Paul Shockley—received from a source of consciousness which called Itself "Cosmic Awareness". The following is an excerpt from that course:

Cosmic Metaphysics Course

THE UNIVERSE APPEARS AND DISAPPEARS EVERY FOUR QUADRILLIONTHS OF A SECOND

Before the beginning there was a Void. And the Void was without form or substance and It was unaware as if It were eternally sleeping. That Void was empty, without dreams, thought, or consciousness. Nothing that is, was. All that was—was the Void, the **Static Void**. This Universal Consciousness, this Cosmic Awareness, had not come to be. Without awareness—time and space were not yet, for time and space to exist require measurement, and there was nothing existing to measure them. There was only possibility. But possibility is a higher dimension that serves as a seed for all that may eventually become reality. In the beginning reality had not yet come into being, for there was no awareness of it. Even the awareness of the possibility of reality had not begun to manifest. Because the Void was not a thing, was no-thing. It could only wait eternally unaware as no-thing, as a vacuum, a Void. The Void being Static began to build something from nothing from the Static Void in the same manner as Static electricity can be built and will only discharge when the Static electricity becomes strong enough to discharge when something approaches. But nothing existed to approach the Static of the Void, so the Static just built and built throughout pre-eternity until a sense of anticipation from the buildup of Static energy began to develop over the later quarter of pre-eternity. This Awareness uses the term pre-eternity for time did not yet exist since there was nothing yet to measure time, and without time, eternity could not exist even as a concept. In the waiting there was not yet space, for space requires size. Size requires measurement. Nothing can be measured when no-thing exists, whether the universe was the size of what you would today call trillions of trillions of trillions of light years across, or whether it was the size of a point of a pin, or smaller than the smallest imaginable atomic part in your present science, this is irrelevant; for without something with which to compare the size of space means there is no size to it. The Void just was what it was . . . and it waited. And it experienced anticipation from infinite waiting. And the anticipation allowed an awareness of anticipation to expand within the waiting. Anticipation was the fetal beginning of the consciousness that would eventually become aware of its own self as an anticipation that was being created in the Static Void. That anticipation grew to be a very slight and subtle hunger, yearning or quest, a Static unmoving, searching and rudimentary desire for something, some thing . . . anything. That hunger developed an anticipation that required the evolution of an image of something to become the goal or target to satisfy the anticipation and the hunger of the Void. That hunger manifested a rudimentary but very vague image of shadow without substance, a vague image of a solution to the hunger. That shadow without substance that became the target or goal of the anticipation and the hunger then began to take on more definition, more tone and coloration. And the Void began to gaze upon the vague and nebulous image it had created as if it were a thing, a fixed creation of greater substance than shadow. The Static unwavering gaze emanating from the hunger in the Void defined the image even more clearly, and it became quiet and through the stuff that dreams are made of it took on the appearance of solidified substance as witnessed in a dream full of clear and solid images. Reality in its infancy was born. **As this occurred, the** Void Creator, **realized that It was dreaming Its creation and was at** one with the creation—**yet also** set apart from its dreamed creation, like the dreamer and the dream. **It had** created reality **within Its own dreamed imaging while It was slowly evolving and becoming self-aware.**

The Void had become aware of Itself as being something that had come from nothing. It also realized Its own awareness existed because of the image It had created, as a mirror to verify Its own reality, without Its creation It would have no reflection, recognition or evidence of Itself. Without such evidence it could not be aware. Without that evolving self-awareness it would still be only a Void—the nothingness from whence it came. Without awareness there is no time, there is no space, for time and space are relative to other points of reference for measurement. With rudimentary awareness space could be infinitely small, or infinitely large, time could be infinitely brief or infinitely long, because they become relative to the observer, the awareness observing them. Thus time, space, duration, distance and size all came into being by the evolving of awareness.

Now, please understand that though I have found similar material from this source to feel valid to me, I don't recommend that it be taken as fact without question. In fact, I hope that you will question—for yourself—anything that I write in this book. The material I've quoted above is from someone else—not me—and I am not in a position to either substantiate or invalidate it; I leave it with you to consider it as you feel to be appropriate. I have included it here because to a great extent the "course" substantiates (from its own perspective) my own idea of God's origin; particularly with respect to the dream I just described.

Going back to my dream: let's consider that this was what God experienced when It "awoke" from a timeless "sleep". After Its first moment of wakefulness, It could very well have remained in a state of pure "awareness of being" for untold eons of our time; but at some point It would likely have experienced a thought like my own: "What am I?"

It's also the question many of us have asked: "What is God?" And, of course, it's the question we considered in the prior chapter. In attempting to answer it, I've considered my own ideas and feelings together with postulations; such as the course material I quoted earlier. I've also related it to my "dream". But to look at all sides, let's take a look at what science might suggest if it were to be so bold.

Looking backwards:

For me, this is the fun part. You may recall that in the Introduction to this book, I referred to a technique I learned in college of looking backwards from an end-point in an attempt to reach the first premise. Let's do that now; starting from the present existence of our physical reality, and looking backwards to before the "big-bang".

Through Albert Einstein's famous equation: $E=MC^2$, science theorizes that Energy and Mass are equivalent; meaning essentially that matter is a form of energy. When this was discovered, the prior theory of "conservation of matter" (which stated that the matter could neither be created nor destroyed) was dropped in favor of the theory of "conservation of energy" (which stated that the amount of energy in the universe was constant—it couldn't be created nor destroyed; it could only change form).

Now, I'm not saying that I agree with that (at least as it relates to the physical universe which we can study), but I will go along with the theory in the broader context that assumes the possibility of a multitude of universes existing on different dimensions or frequencies (much like different radio stations). So, using that theory, let's do what science did when it exploded the first atomic bomb, and convert mass into energy.

Were we to convert all the matter (mass) in this universe (and in all other potential universes) back into the energy from which they theoretically came, we would have nothing but energy. That's assuming, for the sake of those who consider consciousness to be nothing more than a phenomena of interacting components of matter. Since I consider consciousness to also be a form of energy (a living energy endowed with the capacity of free choice and self-awareness), let's convert that back to energy as well; to a living energy.

This may be hard for you to imagine; as I know it was for me when I first considered it. Some of you—like me—may only be able to perceive of energy in the way it acts upon matter. The bright flash of light and the incredible wave of heat that was released by the first atomic bomb explosion may seem to have been the energy that was stored in the plutonium which was destroyed; but it was not. Instead it was evidence of the released energy's impact upon matter which was not destroyed. We measure energy upon its impact upon mass; without mass we have no way to observe or measure energy—at least to my knowledge.

Energy which impacts matter is called kinetic energy, and is measured in units to the degree to which matter is affected by it. Energy that does not cause a movement of matter is called potential energy, because it can—at a later time—be caused to impact matter. It is this form of energy, then, which I suggest would result from the conversion of all matter (and consciousness) back into energy. This would leave us in a non-physical, non-conscious reality, where nothing existed except this seemingly infinite source of potential energy.

Since without matter there could be no time or space, I would suggest, then, that this infinite potential energy—which I will refer to as Potentiality—would exist in a timeless state, much like the "Static Void" in the previously quoted course from "Cosmic Awareness". I will also suggest that since consciousness—and life itself (if it isn't also considered to be just a result—as some believe about consciousness—of matter acting upon matter)—originates from this Potentiality. This would give this Infinite Potentiality the potential of achieving life and consciousness; something it would require in order for it to move out of the state of potential energy and become kinetic or active.

This has been the dilemma of science; for in considering both consciousness and life to be merely expressions of certain combinations of matter, they are left with no causative factor to act as a "first cause". Also, they must interject a chaos theory in order to explain the non-uniformity of our universe; which—if everything originated solely from a single "big-bang"—should be totally uniform (as previously pointed out).

In recognizing the capacity of this Potentiality to gain consciousness, and essentially use that consciousness to direct its own energy in ways to create both a physical universe (as well as other universes on other dimensions), and whatever other levels of consciousness which may exist, it can only be said that this Potentiality is alive. In fact, I will propose that it IS life in its most pure, sublime form; totally undefined and unlimited. I consider it to be an Infinite Living Potentiality.

This, I suggest, is what the quoted course was describing as a "Static Void"; which eventually became conscious. And I also propose that Its awakening occurred much in the same way as the "dream" I earlier described. So, let's refer back to that "dream", and consider how this ILP (Infinite Living Potentiality) or "Static Void" or God may have awakened.

God is the I Am that I Am.

Now, where I already had an identity to recall, God would have had nothing to remember. It would, then, have had to contemplate something more like: "What can I be?" And the obvious answer to that—in my opinion—would have been: "I am whatever I choose to be.", or alternately: "I am whatever I define myself as being." In this way, God would be affirming Its power of self-definition.

In recognizing Its creative capacity to become whatever It defined Itself as being, however, God was presented with a problem. In Its awakened state of awareness, God realized Itself to be potentially anything; but in the very moment that It would define Itself as being something less than that—or something more specific—It would become that, and lose Its present state of Awareness. This is, after all, just what I experienced in my own dream; my consciousness suddenly rejoined that person sleeping in bed which I realized myself to be. God could conceivably, then, become trapped in Its own creation.

God is the All in All.

In order to preserve Its present state of Omni-ness or All-ness, then, I believe that God—or the consciousness which arose from the ILP—affirmed that It was potentially All, and in desiring to be that All, awakened more of Itself; bringing more of Its sleeping Potentiality into consciousness—much like the expansion within science's singularity—so that the singular God Consciousness became the God-Head of a multitude of holographic god images. In effect, God would have "birthed" potentially zillions of conscious entities; each capable of being anything. Each of these would have been—as holograms of God—capable of creation; capable of not only defining or re-creating their own selves, but of also stimulating the ILP (the un-awakened aspect of God) into awakening more conscious entities. And we might recognize that some of these are we (what might be considered to be cells within the body of God).

All awakened conscious entities would, however, still be parts or expressions of God, for it would be impossible for them (including us) to separate themselves from It. Since nothing would exist outside of God, all created conscious entities would remain a part of God, and God truly would remain the All. And with their (our) subsequent acts of creation, these (we) co-creators of God would eternally be aspects or agents of the All. Through their (our) expressing themselves (ourselves), God would be able to experience all expressions without losing Its awareness of being All.

God is a Triune God.

This is largely a Christian concept of God; but what I intend to present here is not necessarily what the Christian church teaches. If I were to relate my concept of a Triune God to Christian theology, I'd say that the ILP is the Holy Spirit; the supreme conscious element—the God Head—would be the Father, and the manifested form (the "God made flesh") would be Jesus. But this is not the subject which I intend to address here.

Though my up-bringing was Christian, my first real exposure to the trinity concept was from the mystic Edgar Cayce through his organization, the A.R.E. Cayce described God as being Body, Mind, and Spirit. In fact, he proposed that we are also Body, Mind and Spirit: spirit the life, mind the builder, and the physical being the result. This is the triune nature of God which I intend to comment on here.

In my analysis, as previously described, ILP (the Infinite Living Potentiality) would be analogous to Spirit; it would be the life force (the desire for expression) and the origin of All. It would not, however, be creative; rather, It would be like building blocks desiring to be put together. Edgar Cayce compared it to the light within a slide projector.

Consciousness—the awakened portion of the ILP—would no longer be Potentiality, since it possesses the quality of expression; it would—in my opinion—be the only aspect of God which truly is expressive (though our perception might indicate to us that only the body or created form is expressive). Possessing the capacity for choice, through Its own will, this aspect of God is the creator or builder of Spirit into form. It would, through intent, form ILP into units of structure.

These units of structure would essentially be a body or form in which the mind or consciousness would operate in order to express itself (like a car or machine which a driver or operator uses). Following the analogy of the slide projector (apologies for using an analogy with old technology, but it's more visual than new technology), consciousness would be the slide, and the body would be that which was projected onto the screen of reality. Without a body, consciousness would not be able to express itself, other than to possess intent. It would be through the life force energy of spirit that this intent would be able to construct or form a body for expression.

As this relates to the physical universe which we know: everything that exists would have its own consciousness, regardless how simple it might be. It is this consciousness which keeps it in form, providing it with its qualities; its identity. If one were able to communicate with the consciousness of any manifested form, one would be able to know everything about it. This is a far-reaching concept with incredible implications (which will be discussed later).

Also, since everything we know is composed of groups of matter, even groups of groups of groups, etc., then we must recognize that consciousness exists in groups and groups and groups, etc. as well. Just think of your own body. You have your own consciousness, yet each organ of your body has a consciousness, and each component of that organ has a consciousness; also each cell within the component, and each chemical within the cell. One could follow this down to the atomic and subatomic, or upwards to groups of consciousness in which you belong; your family unit, your social group, your racial or religious group, the geographical area in which you live, your city, state, country or world in which you live. There is also a consciousness of this solar system, this galaxy, and this universe. In a greater reality which includes universes in potentially innumerable dimensions, these groups of consciousness—where they lord over not just the physical universe, but all life-forms contained in them—could rightly be considered to be gods themselves. In fact, I believe that throughout history they have been recognized as such; that some of the "gods" which mankind has "prayed to" (attempted communication with), and received guidance from, have been these lesser gods: great in their own being-ness.

God is the Creator.

Now, I don't intend to diminish the beliefs of any religion; for all of these lesser gods are—in my opinion—acting within the will of that which might be considered to be the Supreme God-Head. This will be made clearer in the next chapter; but for now, let's consider how it is with a major multi-national corporation which owns businesses in a variety of industries, each with divisions and subdivisions. An assembly line worker in one department of one company in a particular division would not be expected to go to the corporations CEO for the materials he needs to perform his duties. But he does receive them, because it is the will of the CEO that his requirements be met; it's just that authority is delegated down the various levels.

It must also be recognized that all lesser gods, regardless which level of consciousness they reside in, are like us (near the bottom) involved in their own spiritual growth and development; it is a part of their expression to act in the capacity they have created for themselves. All this will hopefully be understood when I present my opinion of God's plan; or rather Its supreme will and intent.

Think of what you've heard about ancient cultures: those to which our medical researchers go for medicinal cures and remedies. These have a history of praying to gods which many of us—having been influenced by our own religion's teachings and the unfounded claims of science—have deemed to be non-existent or unreliable. Cultures have prayed to rain gods, sun gods, goddesses of fertility, and similar gods which relate to the areas of their life in which they have needs. Some have prayed to "Great Spirit", performed rituals in the hopes of communicating with their gods, and hoped for dreams and visions to answer their prayers. These are all examples of people seeking assistance from higher levels of consciousness; and it has worked for them. It also works for us; we just don't think of it as such when we do it. In fact, a lot of people pray to other people who have since died; calling them saints and attributing acts of healing and assistance to them.

No, I'm not suggesting that anybody pray to, or seek assistance from, any other entities or higher powers than the ones they are already going to. That's not my intent. If I were to suggest anything in that regard, it would be to address oneself to the Highest that one can imagine.

Creation occurs within all levels of consciousness; for all are both representatives and expressions of the Highest source which we rightfully call God; by whatever name. I offer this understanding because there is just too much hostility and disrespect shown between people of differing faiths. It is my hope that if we can all recognize a greater truth about our relationship with higher consciousness—regardless of the level—that we will all draw closer to the One, and likewise—to each other.

Cosmic Awareness—the source for the material presented by Cosmic Awareness Communications (C.A.C.) suggested once, that after the expansion of consciousness, when individualized aspects of God formed groups and associations in order to express their own free will of self-expression, that some of them conceived the idea to experiment in density. Their creation—our physical universe—drew interest from other conscious entities, and these began to likewise involve themselves in the "experiment". According to Cosmic Awareness, this creation of density was as a speck within the vastness of the existing reality. It is this "speck" that we call a universe; and ironically believe to be the only reality.

Edgar Cayce, the psychic responsible for the material presented through the Association for Research and Enlightenment (A.R.E.), stated that it was within this experiment that the biblical "fall" occurred; wherein those creators chose to become "personally" involved with their own creation, so that they might experience the senses existent in a dense form. Of particular interest was that of sensuality and sexuality.

Cosmic Awareness indicated that a more accurate perception of the Bible story—as it relates to the "Tree of Knowledge"—would be that the fruit of the tree represented the five senses. It was in choosing to enter into physical form on Earth, that entities from spiritual planes or dimensions "fell". By choosing to enter into density, however, they were confronted with a problem: how to get back. For by entering into dense form, they lost most of their capacity to create, and essentially became stuck.

According to both Cosmic Awareness and Edgar Cayce, groups of entities from higher dimensions of reality chose to enter in later, in an attempt to free them. They did so with the assurance from others in the higher realms, that should they begin to get stuck, that they would be given assistance themselves. Those rescuers are those whom Jesus referred to as the 144 thousand whom he "fore-knew and predestined". It is a misunderstanding to use Jesus' reference to the agreement which higher consciousness (God) had with these few, and apply it to believers of any particular religion. And it also a misunderstanding to assume that since one group is "predestined" that all are. Quite frankly, I wish the reference to these few was never made. For in my opinion, all people, regardless how evil they are judged to be, are on their way back to the Source which we call God.

So, is "God" the creator of our universe? Though it may be that only a tiny group (I believe Cayce suggested the number of 9 billion) of conscious entities became involved in its creation, it is within the will of the Highest that All things be experienced. I leave it with you to decide. Perhaps the next chapter—wherein I attempt to present God's plan (to the best of my ability to understand it)—will help you to decide.

God is Omnipresent, Omniscient, Omnipotent, and All Loving.

What I hope is still recognized, after my lengthy discussion about lesser gods and conscious entities acting upon the desires of their own free will, is that the Source (the God-Head, the Supreme Consciousness) which caused all other conscious entities to come into existence is still in power, still in control of Its "dream", and exists in full awareness of what is going on in the infinite vastness of Its reality. This Consciousness is—after all—the conscious element of that Infinite Living Potentiality which is everywhere present. That ILP fills the space between electrons, atoms, stars and galaxies. It is within every cell of our body, and acts as both a communication link between all manifested forms, and as a conduit of life—of a desire for growth. If one could take the time to consider the implications of this; recalling that focused intent is all that is required to awaken ILP into expression, one would realize just how much creative power they possessed.

The ancient Greeks believed that we lived within something which they called an Ether; which was everywhere present, but not physical. Though science has since concluded that their beliefs were primitive, I believe that they knew something most of us don't. And I surmise that they received this theory of theirs from Higher Consciousness. In fact, I believe that many ancient cultures received wisdom and guidance from Higher Sources of Awareness; and that these contributed to the various religious beliefs that have existed over the years.

From the very beginning of life on this planet, God—through various levels and elements of Higher Consciousness—has exercised Its power to guide and assist us in our use of Its gift of free will. The only limit to God's knowledge is in knowing what or how we will choose. God may have a pretty good idea, based upon past experience and knowledge that we lack, but we are still able to change our patterns of behavior, and choose differently the next time. Through our own free will, we may "fall"; but we will always have access to Its influence in guiding us back.

If one were to think of the gift of free will as a potential release into realms of pain or oblivion, perhaps it would be good to point out that we are all attached to a tether. That link is what might be called a gravitational influence of Divine Unconditional Love. Just as gravity draws mass to mass, so too does it draw us back to the Source of that love. Nobody, regardless how deep into density they might descend, can ever escape the influence of that bond of love which emanates from God. Were any conditions to be placed upon whoever was qualified to receive it (something we are prone to doing with our own love), then God could not be considered to be All-Loving. It is only that we, by virtue of our feelings of guilt, doubt God's eternal love for us. But it is there; and if we could bring ourselves to set aside our guilt and love ourselves without condition, then we would feel the enormity of that love.

God is Love.

There should be no question that God is truly All-Loving; how could it not be? That ILP is not just Life in Its most sublime form, it is also all qualities which Life infers. It is Infinite Love. Not only does the un-manifested Spirit of God fill all space in our universe (as well as within our own bodies), It also possesses the quality of Love Divine. It can rightly be considered that it is Love which fills all space; that the Infinite Potentiality is Love desiring to be awakened and put into expression. True Unconditional Love is the highest expression of Life; and put into expression can create miracles. So try it some time. Open yourself to that Love which is everywhere present, and through the expression of your own consciousness, intend that this Love manifest in some way which will be helpful to both yourself and others. Its greatest desire is to be awakened into expression; it only awaits an agent of God (like yourself) to give it structure.

God is "Tough Love".

Up until now, I've pretty much focused upon the positive subjects, ignoring the dark side of human expression. This was intentional, for I wanted to first present what I believe to be God's plan; so that I might show how the dark side is a necessary part of it.

But while we're on the subject of love, I don't want to give the impression that because God loves us unconditionally, that we won't suffer now and again. In fact, we may suffer all the more. What we label, as being evil and suffering (or punishment in hell [which is never eternal]), may more appropriately be called (respectively) acts of ignorance and necessary learning experiences.

GOD'S PLAN

Big Bang of Consciousness:

I n many respects, the concept of God being the "All in All" just isn't practical. We don't get up in the morning and consider that we're God on our feet as we proceed to the bathroom and sit on God while we remove some of God from our body. And when we stand in front of the mirror, we don't perceive that we're looking at God. In essence, our conception of reality is what we relate to; and this is determined by our state of consciousness.

We are conscious of <u>not</u> being God, but rather a physical body, separate from other physical bodies; and this is how we conduct ourselves and relate to the world around us. It is my hope, that in reading my opinions on the subject, that this consciousness will change slightly, so that we can all begin to perceive ourselves as being units of consciousness, gravitating toward other units of consciousness to form ever greater units of consciousness.

Science theorizes that our universe and space time originated from a single mass of infinite density which it calls a singularity, which expanded (is still expanding) into the reality which we live. I would like to suggest rather that this "big bang" was more like that which occurs when one presses on the nozzle of a can of spray paint; and that the singularity was more like the tiny pin-hole from which the paint emanates. This would make the paint can, together with its contents, a non-physical substance in a non-physical reality; and the agent which pressed the nozzle a force existent within that non-physical reality. The space-time matrix, and all physical matter, then, would be like the paint that is emitted from this action.

I have come to believe, that in a similar manner, all consciousness emanated from one source which we call God, and—like our expanding universe—is in the process of interacting with other units of consciousness to form groups and groups of groups of consciousness. I believe that just as particles of matter are attracted—through gravity—to other particles of matter, so too do we—as units of consciousness—form groups and associations through the gravitational influence of love. This view would portray us—as conscious entities—as evolving into ever-greater states of consciousness, as we—through our associations with others—come to perceive of ourselves as being less separate and more as a part of a group; ultimately coming to a consciousness of oneness, wherein we truly perceive of ourselves as being a part of that one body which is God.

In order for you to understand this view, however, you must first come to perceive of yourselves as being entities of consciousness, rather than entities of flesh and blood; and this may be hard for some of you. After all, it's our bodies which we see in the mirror every day, and which we cover with clothing and perhaps adorn with make-up. Maybe if you could realize that this same physical being—which you perceive of as being self—does not change when you shift your state of consciousness or perception of some event, then you can more readily come to be able to perceive of your true self as being a consciousness. Though this is not something that can be proven to someone who possesses a purely materialistic viewpoint of reality, it is a view that forms the basis of the "plan" which follows. My conclusion is that consciousness—or the living potentiality from which it originates—is the only true reality; physical form merely being a construct of same, used to give consciousness a "body" to express itself in.

A hierarchy of consciousness:

In the "dream" I described in the last chapter, I expressed my opinion that were God to identify Itself in any specific way, It would cease to be just anything; that in order to experience All that It was capable of being, It awakened more of the Infinite Living Potentiality (ILP) from which It came. This resulted in what I referred to as a "big bang" of consciousness; and much like what we perceive to be occurring in our physical universe, these individualized aspects of consciousness—or conscious entities—possessed (were granted) the freedom to express their own will in becoming all which they chose to be.

Just as matter in the universe—through gravity—forms groups and associations, so too do conscious entities—through love—form into groups. These group consciousnesses would possess a singular consciousness of its own, while still allowing the individuals to retain their own. Like the cells within our physical body which form tissues within organs, these group consciousnesses could join with others to form ever larger and more complex aspects of consciousness. They might also be compared to galaxies, solar systems, planets, and moons.

By joining together through associations, conscious entities gain the advantage of being able to perceive of their selves as being something more, while still retaining the ability to know their selves as being unique. In some ways this could be perceived as being a paradox, yet it's a very real state of consciousness which some of us (myself included) have experienced. It can be experienced in a more limited way by identifying oneself with some group; it could be a sports team, a religious or social group, or a nationality. The difference being, though, in the degree to which one truly identifies self with the group, for there are always degrees to which individuals in these groups differ in their perceptions.

The way in which God—as a "God-head"—expresses Its will throughout the many aspects of Its consciousness (throughout all groups and subgroups), is most likely similar to the way corporate CEOs express their will throughout the corporation: by delegating authority. This—I believe—is why there have been so many different descriptions of God throughout history, in our various religions. That God works through others is readily accepted by most people who believe in a God; and we observe this in ourselves when we find occasion to be of assistance to those whom we perceive to be in some need.

We might write to the President of a company requesting a certain product, and fully expect that he will not design, fabricate, pack, and deliver the product to us personally, but that he will respond to our request and direct others to fulfill these functions for us. I believe that it is the same with God. The difference being, of course, that with God, all the agents involved are manifested aspects of It; so it could be said that God did indeed "personally" fulfill our request.

This concept, however, is also rather impractical to us, since we—the recipient—are also aspects of God. For this reason, I will try to refer to the God-head only as God, and describe the levels and groups of consciousness that have been granted free will to act as agents of God's will as "Higher Consciousness". It's just too confusing to describe the different manifestations of consciousness that act in the capacity of facilitating God's will, as also being God; even though—in the most real sense—they are.

To illustrate this, consider the man caught in his home during a flood. While the water was threatening to rise, a police car came by to evacuate him, but he refused—stating that God would save him. Later, when the water was at his door, a boat came by with rescuers; but again the man refused—again stating that God would save him. Eventually the waters were so high that the man fled to his roof. When a helicopter arrived to rescue him, however, he again refused; so he eventually perished in the flood. When he finally met God, he asked why "He" didn't save him; to which God replied: "I sent a police car, a boat, and a helicopter; but you refused my help each time."

Throughout mankind's history, God has been continually active in facilitating Its plan for our growth and development; and It always uses agents to accomplish Its will. Sometimes these agents are what we call Alien Beings, and at other times they are spirits from higher levels of consciousness (angels as an example) who mostly appear to us in dreams or visions, as it is more difficult to lower their vibrations enough to appear in the flesh. But most of the time God uses us to assist those in various types of need. And if you're like me, you've been both amazed and humbled when someone whom you've considered to be unspiritual or even base turns out to be the one to provide what it is that you needed.

So, if you've prayed for some need, and you receive help through a dream or a friend, you may rightly thank God; the initiator of the process or plan, which is intended to guide you. And, when your need is for some type of redirection or learning experience, you might also thank God for the source of your pain or upset.

Consciousness as cells within God's body:

When we consider that we are essentially consciousness, then it can rightly be said that as long as we are not conscious of being a part of God, then we are not. Since I've previously stated my belief that we are all a part of God, I hope that this doesn't confuse you. I'm essentially suggesting, here, that we are what we perceive ourselves to be; that if we perceive of ourselves as being separate from God, or from any other group consciousness, then that is what we are—at least until we come to the awareness of being more.

Stated another way: It may be said that we are—in consciousness—separate from God; and through a process of spiritual development (in consciousness), are growing in awareness toward an eventual realization of our oneness with God. At that point, then, we would have the consciousness of God, and fully know ourselves to be that which we have always been without being conscious of it. It is only in consciousness that we can separate ourselves from God.

God's plan, as best as I can conceive of it, is to grant us great freedom to pursue our individual wills; and when joined with (or in association with) others, to pursue a mutual goal. But since this expression will lead away from a consciousness of being one with God, It has provided a means for our eventual return in consciousness. Since many religions refer to the agent of this return as "The Holy Spirit", I will use this term as well. It is—to my thinking—an active expression of what I've called ILP. It acts like blood within the human body; flowing throughout all aspects of reality, and touching (inspiring) every cell or soul or conscious entity. Also, like blood within the human body, it provides certain qualities which we require: love, health, energy, intuition, and a deep desire to become more than we presently are. These qualities will eventually lead us back to our source—in consciousness—to God.

I also suggest that God has provided a communication system—also a manifestation of the ILP—which acts similar to the human body's lymphatic system. This force acts to bring information from every cell of the body—from every conscious entity—back to God. It is this which I believe people refer to as "the Akashic Records", or "God's Book of Remembrance". This field of energy retains a record of every action performed by entities—be they a thought, word, or deed—and makes it available (potentially) to every other aspect of consciousness which is able to attune to it. It's like a library which allows God and Higher Consciousness to know our needs, and provide us with the opportunities or learning experiences which we require for our growth and development. This record also provides a source of useful information to all others who have achieved the capacity to "tune into" it; hopefully for constructive purposes. Edgar Cayce—as claimed by the A.R.E.—was one individual who possessed this ability.

The Journey through Realms of Consciousness:

I've made a sketch (adopted from the Association for Research and Development [see Introduction]) which provides a reasonably accurate picture of the way in which I view the journey of conscious entities in their sojourn away from the Source, and back again. It is intended to show various paths which individuals (consciousness entities) might choose to take in their journeys through time and experience. Of particular note is the frequency at which they might function: the higher the frequency, the more divine or spiritual their expressions; the lower the frequency, the more human or materialistic. On the right, I've defined approximate frequency ranges which would correspond to life-forms in various realms of existence.

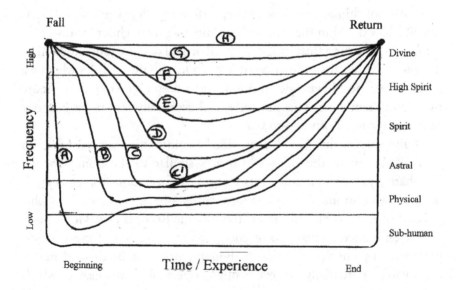

The top left corner of this chart represents the point at which God brought all individual conscious entities into existence, granting them the free will to choose their own path; represented by the curved lines identified with letters. Obviously, the top right corner is the point at which all "souls" eventually return—in consciousness—to oneness with God. At that point they will retain memory of their experiences, and thus their individualities, while sharing in the consciousness of being God: a truly wonderful goal to pursue!

The Fall

Referring to the chart, line A is intended to represent those souls—as described in the previous chapter (under *God is the Creator*)—which chose to enter into physical expression through the universe of their own creation. According to the A.R.E., these souls dove deeper into physicality than was expedient, and became stuck. Line B is intended to represent those souls who chose to come after them in an attempt to rescue them, and lead them out to higher consciousness. And line C is intended to represent the path that subsequent souls took in order to help both A and B entities to raise themselves up in consciousness. I believe that those of us who are on earth at this time, are represented by these three lines.

I also drew line C with a fork, whereby C^1 represents those who came down for a very short time and—in failing to get stuck—were able to lift themselves back up. I believe that many of our world's prior Masters, Sages, Prophets, and Saints were among these; and that many of the world's religions sprang up as a result of their influence or teachings.

In lines D, E, F, and G, I intended to depict souls or entities of higher consciousness who chose experiences in higher non-physical realities. Particularly those in E and F could be thought of as guides or spirit helpers. Finally, in line H, I intended to depict those who chose not to fall, but to dedicate themselves to sustaining the highest vibration, assisting those in D, E, F. and G in their development.

Reincarnation:

The problem which many of you will certainly note is that this chart infers that there is no death; that consciousness continues without interruption for perhaps millions of years. If this concept is troublesome for you, just consider your present physical life; you sleep for about 8 hours every night, and arise again each morning to face a new day, and another period of consciousness. I believe that this is how it is with consciousness in general.

When I was a child and youth, I had a lot of problems in trying to integrate the many teachings from my religion. This was because so many of them just seemed to be in conflict. As I previously mentioned, these were resolved for me when I considered the belief in reincarnation. It made perfect sense to me, and provided a way for life to be both fair and just. In fact, I came to the ultimate conclusion that; "the way life should be, is the way that it is".

I fully realize that some religions reject the idea of reincarnation, believing it to conflict with some of their most basic teachings. Hopefully in the chapters to follow, I will be able to address these teachings, and show how they are mostly true, but in some ways misunderstood; so with a clearer understanding, followers of all religions may understand how reincarnation not only doesn't detract from their religion's value, but rather augments it.

What I consider to be the fact of reincarnation, is also something that can never be proven to everybody's satisfaction. There are so many stories of children remembering people, places, and events that they otherwise couldn't have, unless they were truly there, that one would think that reincarnation was a proven fact. But it's easy to discount another's professed experience. When one has their own experience, however, that's a different matter. And this is true for the subject of ESP and Out-of-Body experience as well.

One of the arguments against the belief in reincarnation is that populations have gradually increased over the years, inferring both that there weren't enough lives for present people to have had in the past to validate that people of today all had prior lives, or that new souls must be coming into incarnation for the first time in order to add to the population. My answer to this is first, that population growth has not has a steady increase, but has gone up and down as civilizations such as those in Lemoria and Atlantis rose and then fell; second that souls are multi-dimensional and can project aspects of themselves into more than one body at a time; thirdly that more than one soul can project into a given body; fourthly that waiting times between incarnations have gradually decreased over time; and lastly that indeed new souls are coming in all the time. This latter fact is one of the reasons why so many are psychopathic or sociopathic; they are new souls acting very much like intelligent animals, who have not yet developed the capacity for empathy or compassion. But don't take this explanation as an intention to prove the validity of reincarnation; what counts as proof is different for different people.

Stuart Chase has been quoted as saying: "For those who believe, no proof is necessary. For those who don't believe, no proof is possible." This can be said for the subject of reincarnation; so I will not try to offer any proof for it (the proof—if people are willing to look for it—is already there, to my thinking). I will instead state it as a reality that I have come to accept, and leave it to you to make up your own mind.

Many lives, many experiences:

In awakening more of Its "sleeping" body (ILP) into consciousness, God provided both Itself, and a multitude of individualized conscious entities, with the ability to experience as many types of expressions as imagination and choice could provide. Each conscious entity would be able, through its connection with its Source, to go out and freely pursue life experiences, and gain the benefits that such experiences provide in terms of both pleasure and learning.

I can little guess what life is like on the higher dimensions of reality, so I won't make the attempt to describe it. But I sincerely doubt that they are floating around on clouds and playing harps. Even life on the dimension of reality just above ours is beyond my capacity to fully guess; though I would venture to say that all levels or frequencies of expression center around the ability of consciousness to be creative. For the ability of consciousness to "awaken" ILP or give it form and expression (creation), seems to me to be the most wonderful and fulfilling expression of any conscious entity. Whether there is a type of death and reincarnation on higher planes, then, I can't say for sure. But if the Biblical account in

Genesis is correct, then it was in entering into a physical expression that death (as we perceive it to be) became a necessity. For this reason, I will assume that reincarnation—the process of returning to physical form in different bodies—only exists in this physical dimension and the one (or ones below it).

It is this capacity to enter a variety of physical incarnations that allows consciousness the ability to experience physical life in a wide variety of ways. Each conscious entity would not be limited in having to choose only one life experience before returning to God; which would give it a very limited freedom to pursue life. But with the ability to enter again and again, souls could experience life in a very balanced way; experiencing pleasure and pain, wealth and poverty, sickness and health, high intelligence and mental challenges, a long life and a very short one.

Agreements and Contracts:

Since life experiences are dependent upon interactions with other souls, reincarnation allows one or more souls the ability to cooperate among themselves in providing all souls with the experiences that they desire (or need) to have. This raises the subject of soul contracts or pre-birth agreements, which seem to be obviously necessary in order for any conscious entity to gain the experiences which it requires. One can't, for example, experience the pleasures associated with a lifetime of great power and wealth, unless others are willing to choose a life of servitude and lack; and neither can one experience a life as an invalid unless others are willing to provide the necessary care that such a situation would involve.

Since individuals retain free choice while they are alive, agreements or contracts may receive some alteration once entities become incarnate; and though this may lead to some degree of hardship, accommodations can be always made and adjusted to as necessary.

The Purpose of Life:

This raises the question of hardship in general. After all; who in their right mind would want to experience a difficult or challenging life? I believe that the answer to this relates to the very purpose of life! In my previous book—*Dawn of Unity; Guide to a New Prosperity*—I suggested that the purpose of life was to grow and become all that we are capable of becoming. Now I will be more specific. If we are—in reality—a part of, or expression of God, then the purpose of life is to grow in consciousness until we actually come to share the consciousness of God. Rather than a physical type growth wherein we become bigger, more mature, or wiser, this is a growth in self-awareness, whereby we come to identify ourselves in ever-expansive ways until we finally come to view ourselves as being a part of that only Oneness which we call God.

Love is the antithesis of Fear.

Perhaps the most important thing I learned in my life is that feelings of love Love cause an expansion in consciousness. This is why so many philosophies and religions stress the importance of love; love of God, love of self, and love of others. This is so vitally necessary in order to fulfill our purpose in living that some people propose that the very purpose of life is to learn how to love unconditionally.

Fear, on the other hand, causes a person to seek power over others, and become greedy in seeking to obtain more and more of those things which they feel will provide them with greater security. Fear causes consciousness to withdraw into itself, becoming increasingly selfish and ego-motivated; and the actions performed through these motivations cause entities to become increasingly guilty which leads to more guilt, creating a vicious cycle of cruelty and pain.

Fear is also contagious. Not only can one fearful person stimulate fear within another, but actions performed out of fear—such as those that harm others—create fear in the minds of those so harmed. This often leads to acts of retribution, which increases fear in the violator; leading to defensive actions which can cause additional fear in the one previously harmed. This too creates a vicious cycle of pain and suffering.

Acts of love, however, can heal the pains of abuse received from those who, in ignorance, act out of fear. And love is also contagious. Those who exercise loving acts are loved in return, and this love received empowers the one to become more loving in return. This creates a cycle from which all benefit, and the benefits extend outward to embrace others, who likewise become motivated to act accordingly.

Life is for Learning.

William Shakespeare was quoted as saying: "All the world's a stage, and all the men and women merely players:". Though he obviously had a different intention in expressing this view, it very well describes the back-drop for learning that this world provides.

Virtually every experience that we encounter in life provides us with an opportunity to choose an action based upon either fear or love. Think about it. We receive a solicitation in the mail for a donation to some charity, and out of fear for our own financial security we toss it in the trash. Someone asks us to spend some of our time to provide help or assistance, and we decline out of fear that we won't have enough time left to accomplish our own goals. Though these are relatively petty examples, and ones which do have a degree of validity to our saying "no" on occasion, they point out how very often we are asked to choose.

More serious choices involve those where we are enticed to actually cause harm to others, or seek to gain power or some advantage over them. And these choices are not always obvious. When we shop, looking for the lowest priced item, we are encouraging the producer of the item to offer less compensation to the people actually responsible for its availability. There are many under-paid workers in the world who could stand to benefit from our being more discerning in our choice of purchases. Buying "made in America", for example, may help Americans (or those in Guam), but it doesn't help those in third world countries, who are often victimized by their desperation for employment.

Perhaps the most difficult occasion to choose between acting out of love or fear, however, occurs when we either perceive ourselves to be threatened with harm, or were actually hurt by someone. The desire for defensive actions or retribution is motivated either directly or indirectly out of fear, and can only perpetuate that which we intend to avoid with our action. But to love in these challenging situations can be very difficult for us. So these "lessons" become opportunities for our greatest learning.

We learn through experience.

In the chart I provided, the horizontal axis represents both time and experience; for it is through many experiences over many different lifetimes that we finally come to learn the lessons necessary to set aside our fears and act out of love toward others. This is one of the reasons why I embraced reincarnation when I first heard of the concept. Before that consideration life seemed unjust, and I couldn't conceive of God as allowing such a state to exist. But by recognizing that all people will have all types of experiences, I came to perceive seemingly unjust events and circumstances as opportunities for balance and learning; and therefore spiritual growth. In essence; we start out in ignorance (or the need for love), and, through experience, gain wisdom.

It seemed to me to be quite simple. We make a choice and experience the result of that choice. If we later regret the choice we made, then the next time we make a different decision, and hope for a better result. Once we learn what choices produce the better end result, we become better equipped to make similar choices in the future; and the quality of our life improves accordingly.

Though this might sound good, there are often complications. What happens when we perform some action that benefits ourselves at the expense of another, and we don't perceive ourselves to have suffered from it? And what about the times we unselfishly give in some way and perceive ourselves to have been punished for it; or at the very least, not rewarded? The answers to these questions lie within the subject of karma.

Karma is for Learning; not Punishment.

The term "karma" originates from Eastern religions which teach reincarnation; providing the justification of later lives of suffering and pain. For that reason (and because the teaching of reincarnation is also rejected) it is often rejected by Christianity and Judaism (among others). But Judaism incorporates the concept within their laws; such as "an eye for an eye", and Christianity refers to it as "the law of sin". In the New Testament of the Christian Bible, it is expressed as "reaping" what one "sows"; referencing the fact that seeds planted will bear like fruit. A more contemporary version of this law states that "what goes around comes around". These all pretty much say the same thing. I prefer the more scientific version: the law of cause and effect. This states that "every action produces an equal and opposite reaction."

However one chooses to perceive of this law, it exists to bring balance to life's expressions, and provides us with opportunities for learning. It's too easy to be unmindful of the consequences to others of our selfish expressions (those based upon fear). But when we later experience the same consequence from some other person's actions, we begin to become more aware of the hurt that others had to bear from our prior choices.

I believe that one very obvious example of this phenomena today, is in the low self-esteem often experienced within members of the African-American and Native-American communities. I feel that many individuals, who were bigoted toward these groups of people in the past, have reincarnated into these groups; carrying with them their own prior bigotry. For this reason I fully support appropriate measures to instill "black pride" or "native pride" in these groups of people. All people must one day come to recognize that there is no justification for deeming others—regardless of race, religion, sexual orientation, or anything else—as being less worthy of receiving love and acceptance.

The law of karma also provides a reason why some may be born into poverty or with certain handicaps; but just because one is born into such situations, doesn't mean that they are paying for some prior "crime". I want to repeat this, because it's so important. Upon recognizing that errors in judgment can lead to future experiences of pain or lack, it is too easy to generalize and conclude that all those who live such lives—or experience such hardships—are paying for prior mistakes. The truth is, though, that many individuals choose such lives or such experiences for totally different reasons! And one of these is to provide opportunities to others to show mercy or compassion. Yes; some entities willingly accept lives of even cruel torment in order to assist others who are touched by them in some way. These individuals deserve our love and respect; not our disregard or judgment. And where the ultimate lesson in life is to learn how to love unconditionally, to try to discern who deserves judgment and pity over gratitude and love, is an error in itself. Let your respect, gratitude, and love go out to all who suffer.

I titled this section "Karma is for learning; not punishment", because I wanted to place the emphasis where it was most appropriate. God does not will that any entity suffer; but It does require that all entities learn. One might say that suffering is the "default" means of learning. If one is unable to learn from other means, then appropriate suffering results. This—as expressed earlier—is an expression of God's "tough love".

46

A good example of this change in emphasis can be found in a Christian New Testament story wherein Jesus was asked why a certain man was born blind. Jesus response was that it was so he could learn mercy. When—as a child—I heard this, I was really bothered by it. It seemed to be totally unfair to this man; for we all need to learn mercy. Why pick on this man so cruelly?! My minister's explanation didn't help much either. He said that the man was used in order to teach the world (through the story) about Jesus' healing ability and capacity to forgive. When—years later—I read the same story in "The Aquarian Gospel of Jesus the Christ" by Levi, I was much more satisfied; for in that gospel, Jesus stated what the man's prior error was, and his parents' as well. Unfortunately, this gospel—regardless how highly I liked it—failed (in my opinion) to put the emphasis on learning where I feel it should be. As a result, I put both accounts of this event together in my mind. (On my website www.dawn-of-truth.com I offer a free download of a cross-reference I made, so that those of you who are interested may compare passages and stories from The Aquarian Gospel to the New Testament gospels.)

Positive Karma:

Since all "seeds" aren't "bad" and "cause and effect" can also be quite enjoyable, I want to say something about the results of performing "good" deeds. All actions produce corresponding results, and acts of kindness and generosity will certainly produce benefits. But it must be recognized that it is the motivation behind the action that is most important. Simply put, God can't be bribed. It could also be said that "God reads the heart." (And this latter statement relates to negative karma as well. Motivations behind actions are always considered.)

Positive actions, in addition to producing positive results, can do a lot to counter-balance prior negative expressions, but only—in my opinion—when relating to the original error. It's just like with us in our social relationships. I accidently put a dent in your car and you're angry. I compensate you in a way that appeases you, and you're no longer angry. Making a large contribution to some charity is not likely to do anything to appease your displeasure. And though it might appease you to some degree, allowing you to put a similar dent in my own car will still fail to provide the type of appeasement or reconciliation that would be most satisfactory.

In my prior book: "Dawn of Unity; Guide to a New Prosperity", I devoted a chapter to the subject of our criminal justice system wherein I emphasized the need to replace punishment with learning. I suggested that when a crime is committed, the offender receive an opportunity for true rehabilitation, and the victim(s) receive appropriate compensation and counseling. This is what I feel God desires in Its exercise of justice. What we may perceive, to be punishment through the law of karma, is intended—I believe—to be an opportunity for learning; so that the offender will not desire to repeat the offense.

The appropriateness of Guilt, Remorse, and Repentance:

After any expression of harm to another, karma will result unless action is taken to appease or mitigate the harm done. But even if this is done, karma will still result if the corresponding lesson isn't learned. To illustrate this, let's use the prior example of the dented car. If, after appeasing the owner of the car for the damage done, the offender continues to drive in a careless manner, so that damage could occur to another person's car; then some experience will be necessary for "educational" purposes. It even could be that the offender uses justifications or excuses to avoid recognition of guilt, and escape any feelings of remorse that would certainly result.

It's a very common error for a person to overlook one's own guilt for engaging in some inappropriate action, but to fully judge others (as being guilty) for similar expressions that they perform. Often we become so used to our own weaknesses or short-comings, that we over-look them or find justifications for excusing them. But when we see these same failings expressed by others, especially when they cause us harm, we readily pass judgment upon them, criticizing them for their actions.

This judgment is then reflected back upon ourselves, and we become accountable for our own denied guilt. Many people suffer the karmic consequences of actions or expressions of their own as result of their subsequent judgment of others. Also by justifying or refusing to recognize their own failings, many people never experience the degree of remorse necessary in order to bring them to repentance and subsequent changes in behavior.

It must be recognized that without a feeling of remorse for one's inappropriate actions one cannot come to repentance, and is unlikely to change the undesirable behavior. This will cause as many karmic lessons to befall the individual as are necessary for the desired learning and subsequent change in behavior.

Because of this, recognition of guilt can lead not only to feelings of regret or remorse, but also to fear of consequences. To a degree this is helpful; in that it can motivate one to repent and change one's actions in the future. Unfortunately, excessive feelings of fear can replace or displace the motivation for repentance, and the lesson isn't really learned; instead the offender may be inclined to become defensive, and cause additional harm in attempting to avoid any consequences.

On the other hand, a person can judge self to be guilty far beyond that which is appropriate, and cause undue stress in the form of remorse to bring about more suffering than is truly necessary or desirable. Even when the degree of guilt is justified, feelings of remorse—if not brought to conclusion through repentance—can chain a person to feelings that are both harmful and inappropriate.

The solution is to be honest and discerning in judging one's own actions with regard to the degree of guilt, and to then use one's feelings of remorse as a motivation to repent, and therefore to dedicate one's energies into making changes in behavior or attitude. And this is best followed up by some constructive action to demonstrate the correction. Repentance has been defined as "going the other way"; and some action in the direction of that "other way" can be most helpful in affirming to self that the lesson has truly been learned.

Grace absolves Karma:

Grace, to my understanding, is a mitigation of karma by forces of Higher Consciousness. It <u>may</u> come about after one has repented of one's prior actions, and it <u>may</u> come about after some reconciliatory action is taken; but one cannot earn grace. Grace is the granting of absolution from karma, when Higher Consciousness considers that a lesson is sufficiently learned, repentance is sincere and substantiated, and no further benefit would be achieved with an action of karma. This release from karmic debt is often referred to as God's forgiveness.

I used to be conflicted with regard to the act of forgiveness when I was taught to forgive others for the harm they caused me. I was led to believe (as I'm sure some of you may) that if I forgave someone, that they wouldn't suffer any consequences for their actions; they'd be "getting away with it", and would likely go on to do the same thing to others, or to me again. I since came to realize that this was a misunderstanding; that there were essentially two types of forgiveness: God's forgiveness, and our act of forgiveness.

When one of us forgives another, we absolve the karmic debt that they "owe" to us; but this does not mean that they won't still be required to "learn their lesson". Through our forgiveness of others, we are only able to mitigate the karmic bond which is established between ourselves and them. This not only frees them, it frees us as well. And by freeing others of their debts to us, we allow for the possibility of receiving Divine Grace for our own similar failings.

On the other hand, when we refuse to forgive others for the harm they cause us, we deny the possibility of receiving grace or forgiveness for our own failings of a similar nature. Many people affirm this truth every time they recite the "Lord's Prayer", when they ask to be forgiven "as" they forgive others. And many people, who believe themselves to be forgiven of their failings (sins) because their religion tells them that they are, still suffer the karmic consequences for the mere fact that they aren't forgiven. They might have judged others—denying them forgiveness, or they may have failed to bring themselves to repentance for their failings.

I'm sure that everybody who has come to feel remorse for some personal weakness or short-coming has also met with frustration over the difficulty experienced in trying to change. And though I've suggested that true repentance leads to a change in behavior, I'd like to make it clear that this often takes a long time to accomplish. In fact, one may never become able to escape some personality patterns or traits in the present lifetime. What passes for repentance in such situations—based upon my own personal experience—is a sincere desire to be reformed. Essentially, it's the fervent desire and sincere attempt that is accepted as proof of learning. After all—it's learning that God wants from us. What occurs, in my opinion, is that at the conclusion of life, when we (or God) review(s) our prior actions, the sincere effort—though met with failure—is counted as success, because that is what we were trying to accomplish. And this desire to be different will carry over into the next life wherein we <u>will</u> be different in that regard.

From Ignorance to Wisdom:

At the beginning of our existence, as individualized conscious entities, we possess incredible capacities for creation and both the freedom and desire to express ourselves as unique beings. For some, this brings the desire to become as gods; powerful and full of self-glory. It is this illusion (that we <u>can</u> be both individuals and like God), that leads us into the denser frequencies where emotions and sensory stimuli are most manifest. But it is here that we lost the capacity to recall our origin, and we (like the story of the Prince who became the Pauper) became stuck in our own creation, believing that only this realm of density was real.

The result was that we became more desirous of obtaining power, self-glory (through the attainment of possessions), and sensory stimuli; competing with others in the effort. This perceived need to compete for the things we desired brought fear into our experience; fear that we wouldn't survive, and fear that we would suffer from any type of lack. As a result of this fear, we became even more consumed with the desire to gain power over others and competition led to conflict and injury. The threat of pain or suffering added to our feelings of fear, and we eventually reached a density of vibration which was difficult to endure. As a result, we began to reconsider our ambitions and look for a better way to become satisfied.

Through the process of reincarnating—life after life—into lives of various qualities, we came to experience how it felt to be both rich and poor, both weak and powerful, both intelligent and mentally challenged, both free and enslaved, etc., experiencing life from many different paradigms. And with each new experience we grew more and more in wisdom. Without the balancing effect of karma, we could have remained in our deluded thinking that we were capable of being like God if only we could amass enough power. And this could have prevented us from ever returning to the higher frequencies where love and the consciousness of oneness abound.

Each life lived, though, presented us with a gift of identity and perception which carried over after death. Lessons learned, together with remembered experiences of both pain and pleasure, helped to enable us to empathize in (later lifetimes) with people in all life situations. We began to see ourselves in the poor and disabled, and empathize with them as a result. From the unconscious recollection of the types of pain which people in difficult situations experience, we even began to show compassion for others, and perform acts of service and kindness in order to help mitigate their suffering. And, so, little by little we grew in our capacity to love others.

At first we extended a conditional type of love, based upon the expectation that we would receive some benefit or reward for our actions. Also, we withdrew love from those whom we feared: those whom we perceived to be threatening to us. And eventually we came to see all others—even the most dangerous or despicable—as worthy of our respect and love. This change in attitude came as a result of our having grown from ignorance to wisdom, and with future learning, we will finally come to love all others unconditionally, and share in the consciousness of God which has always loved without restraint.

The path from ignorance to wisdom is not an easy one, but the rewards make the trip well worth any suffering we encounter along the way. It's one that we have been traveling for a very long time, and which we will be on for a long time yet. Where it leads us, though, is purely up to us, for each time we make a choice we set the universe in motion to respond to that choice. So let's be wise and choose expressions based on love; and refrain from acts motivated by fear, which hurt others. If we can accomplish that, we will have no cause for worry; and can spend our days in joyful gratitude for the many blessings that only love can provide.

WHAT ARE WE REALLY?

The Grand Paradox:

I've previously expressed my view that all that exists is God; that therefore we are an expression of God. This makes it difficult to then describe life as a process of ever drawing closer to God until we gain oneness with It. The answer lies in our state of consciousness; wherein we are—in consciousness—what we perceive ourselves to be. So until we truly perceive ourselves to be one with God, it can be said that we are (in consciousness) apart from God; but this is only an illusion—actually a delusion.

Edgar Cayce (reference the A.R.E.) once confirmed to a questioner that Cosmic Consciousness (or Christ Consciousness) was the recognition of being oneself and yet also being the whole. I believe that the reason this state of consciousness is also referred to the Christ Consciousness, is because Jesus—during his period of teaching—was in this state. Several of the comments he made reflected—in my opinion—this paradoxical state of awareness.

When Jesus stated that what we do to others we do to him, he wasn't saying "it is <u>like</u>" doing to him; I believe Jesus truly felt oneness with all people. Later when Jesus stated that he and "the Father" are "one", I believe that he was again expressing from this state of consciousness; I don't believe that he was trying to say that he <u>was</u> God in the way that Christians interpret it. I furthermore believe that when Jesus spoke of "the Kingdom of Heaven", he was referring to this state of consciousness, and not a place where the "saved" go after death.

Coming to a realization of our true Oneness with The All is the goal of every soul on this planet; whether this is realized or not. All the hardship and suffering that mankind experiences, is a result of perceiving self to be separate from the Whole; even in competition with other aspects of the One we call God. When we finally realize who (or what)—in fact—we really are, our attitudes and expressions will change remarkably, and we will finally find a peace that defies human understanding, which sets us free to be the creator beings that we were intended to be.

This higher (or exalted) state of consciousness comes about when we find ourselves able to love ourselves completely and without reservation; something that's impossible to do when we carry unresolved feelings of guilt. This is not to say, though, that we need to become perfect; rather, far from it. What we need to do is to be honest with ourselves about our weaknesses, accept them, and express a sincere desire to remedy them; whether we are able to actually achieve the goal in this lifetime or not. By knowing that there will be future opportunities to resolve even the most challenging quirks in our personalities, we can affirm that in time we will achieve our desire. On this basis, then, together with acknowledgement of our willingness to pursue self-improvement, we <u>can</u> forgive ourselves for our present weaknesses and set aside all those attitudes that prevent us from loving ourselves fully and without condition.

Once we have achieved this state of unconditional love of self, our "cup" will truly become "full to overflowing", and this feeling of love will quite naturally flow out from us to others. And in this unrestricted outpouring of love toward others, our consciousness will expand to include these others. It's as though our consciousness is restricted by our capacity to love fully and without condition. The more encompassing our love for others, the more our perception of self expands to include others. When we eventually allow ourselves to love All, our consciousness will expand to include All, and we will finally come to a realization of our oneness with God.

And the wonderment is that we will not lose our awareness of still being self. It's an incredible state to be in, one which I've long desired to return to since I first experienced it many years ago. In describing my experience, together with what preceded it, and how it changed me there-after, I hope to provide a guide which you might use in your own pursuit of a higher consciousness: a higher awareness of self, others, and God.

An Experience of Cosmic Consciousness:

I mentioned in the Introduction that as a child I had a lot of questions with regard to seemingly inconsistent and illogical teachings of the religion in which I was raised. These were finally answered when I was introduced to the teachings and philosophy of the A.R.E. which arose from the "readings" by Edgar Cayce. This motivated me to begin an active attempt to put what I was learning into practice, and the main theme was that we grow to heaven as we develop ourselves, rather than go to heaven upon death because we accepted a particular creed.

I began a process of introspection whereby I considered my many faults and weaknesses, and made attempts to become a better person. Quite naturally I found this difficult. Those of you who have tried the same will know what I mean. To obtain help in this endeavor, I often prayed for guidance and assistance; sometimes asking to be released from what I considered to be bonds. Instead of receiving a magical transformation (as I had hoped), I was left with my struggles.

Eventually I found and joined a small group of people who met with an individual gifted with insight into human nature; and through this group came to understand myself better, and recognize some of the key areas of my personality which contributed to my failings. One of these was a difficulty in being open and honest about my feelings. After I became able (by trusting this individual) to open myself up to him, I felt a sense of release from long-held feelings of guilt and unworthiness; and this served to open my heart a bit more to others with respect to their own challenges. I even began to extend love to others—strangers I would meet or pass by—by visualizing myself throwing sticky balls of love at them, which would remain with them as a type of blessing.

At the same time I was doing this, however, the more domestic side of my life was in a state of restriction. I had recently started my own business, and it wasn't bringing in enough money to meet all my needs. Of particular concern to me was the apartment I was living in. I was having problems with the landlord who didn't want to keep up with necessary repairs, and I felt trapped—unable to have the financial resources to find a better place to live. Unpleasant as this situation was—this feeling of financial restriction—I later found it to have been a blessing.

One day I received a phone call from a business client informing me that he wanted me to perform an extensive amount of work on several of his machines. This news caused me a great deal of joy, for the income I would receive from this job would—in my opinion—meet the needs of my financial situation, and set me free from that bothersome restriction. I remember sitting down at my kitchen table just reveling in the great feeling of freedom and joy that I felt.

As though to test my feelings, I then thought about other issues that might bring me down from this "high", and I could find none. This added to my joy. I thought of faults that I hadn't resolved, but I fully accepted that since I was motivated toward self-improvement, that these would eventually become corrected; that I didn't need to be concerned about them now. And the more I thought about it, the more I realized that I could find no reason why I couldn't just love myself fully. This recognition produced a profound feeling of love within myself; so real that I could actually feel myself being filled with it. In fact, it came to a point where I just couldn't hold any more of this feeling of love—as though I would burst—so I began to mentally project love out into the world to whoever could use it.

I'd never been in such a euphoric state before; feeling so free, so accepting of self, and so full of love. I reached for a cigarette (this is not an endorsement of the habit) to calm myself some, but it didn't help; so I decided to go out and buy another carton as I was running low. As I was still feeling this flow of love through myself when I arrived at the department store, I naturally began to send it out to all the other shoppers I could see. And this is when my consciousness shifted. Until that moment I was feeling freedom, joy, and love; but as soon as I was in the presence of others my consciousness expanded to include them.

I came to fully perceive that they were me; that we shared a oneness of being. Words from a poem I had once heard came immediately to mind: "No man is an island, entire of itself;" and I realized that this poet (John Dunne) must have gained the insight that I was now experiencing.

Looking around at all the other shoppers, I also became fully aware of something far greater—more divine—that surrounded them. I couldn't see it, but I was keenly aware of its presence; even feeling that I had a rapport with these (which I thought of as over-souls), as if they knew what I was experiencing. I recognized that a deep and total relationship existed between these "over-souls" and the person they surrounded, yet the person was totally unaware if its presence. I thought of the analogy of a parent holding the hand of its child, as they walked along; yet the child was totally oblivious to the presence of the parent which guided it.

I saw a mother responding with emotion and frustration to a screaming child, and I felt compassion for them both; feeling strange about it as well, for I was also feeling that they were also me; it's hard to describe. Let's just say, I felt no judgment, though I recognized that neither parent nor child were acting in harmony with the other; and I felt that their over-souls felt the same as I did: totally compassionate and understanding; that this was all a small part of a much greater process.

I realized that what I was perceiving as an over-soul was, in fact, the true self, and that the consciousness of individuals—like the woman—was like that of a teacher. It was this teacher—what we tend to think of as our self—that performed the role of educating the subconscious mind, which acted very much like a small child. This "child" needed to be educated for the benefit of the parent (the over-soul—the true self), and it was the teacher's role (our role as a conscious entity) to educate it, by teaching it how to act appropriately through the installing of beliefs. I recognized that it is belief which determines action, and through experience the conscious mind formulates and later alters or adjusts existing beliefs held by the subconscious mind, until it becomes better suited to the needs and desires of the greater soul—what I was perceiving as the true self—an over-soul.

As I walked further down the aisle (I'd only progressed about 20 feet at this point), I was brought to realize that the over-soul guides everyone through life, from situation to situation, to experience opportunities for learning. How we respond to each situation determines where we will be led next; as every time we make a choice, the universe moves in appropriate response to that choice. For me, at the time, this was a novel and most profound realization. It was validated when I came close to the checkout counter of the grocery department. I viewed an argument between a customer and cashier; and realized that they had both been led to the situation, so that they would have an opportunity for resolving some prior issue that was in need of resolution. And again, without any feeling of criticism—only compassion—I knew that they would need additional opportunities if they didn't work this one out to a satisfactory conclusion.

When I finally got to the cigarette counter to make my purchase, it was a really strange feeling to be talking with and interacting with someone I recognized as being so much at one with, and for whom I felt so much love and compassion. That she didn't know it, made it seem as though I was keeping a secret from her; yet I knew that I couldn't even begin to describe my perception to her if I tried, and that it wouldn't be appropriate to do so.

As I began to leave with my purchase, I began again to look around at the people, recognizing the presence of their over-souls. I felt that they were aware of me, and that communication was possible, but not necessary; sort of like giving a nod to someone you know as you walk by. This recognition caused me to more fully realize my relationship with them, and to God.

It was then that I became fully aware of God—the All in All. I could feel that It was aware of me, and with this awareness I became aware of the source of the love which I had long been feeling. In fact, by placing my attention upon it, the feeling of love became much more intense. I was then fully aware of being like a cell in God's body, and of being nourished by Its intense love for me. I thought how much our own bodies are reflective of the body of God which I was—at the moment—perceiving myself to be a part of. I thought of each soul as being like a cell in God's body; whereby a finer nourishing substance surrounds the dense nucleus of a cell in the same way that the over-soul surrounds each of us. I also thought of the flow of love, and how it was like the blood-flow within a body; touching every cell. I also realized that the outpouring of love from God is there for everyone, and at all times; but that we just aren't aware of it because of our limited state of consciousness.

I also likened God to a cluster of frog eggs; whereby we are the black dot in the center of each individual clear jelly-like egg. In this analogy, the clear eggs represented the whole soul; where the over-soul was not sufficiently recognized because of its clarity. It was, however, the part of the egg that nourished the nucleus and aided in its development. The focus, for one viewing the eggs, though, was instead placed upon the tiny black dot in the center, which—like us—would slowly develop into becoming a tadpole and eventually into a frog.

As I was nearing the exit to the store, I looked back once again in recognition of the profound fact of my feeling of oneness with everyone. I marveled at the dual perception that I had; of being both self, and also All. Looking at one person in particular, I thought that if that individual were to be in some way diminished, then so would I; my perception was that total.

After leaving the store I lost my reference to others, and began a process of thinking about what I had been experiencing. I don't know when I actually left that state because I was using my heightened state of awareness to consider my own life and involvements. Obviously I began to think of the group I was involved in, and the things the facilitator had said. I realized just how true something else he has said was; that I expected too much of myself, and therefore of others. And I thought about how this was evidenced in my personality. I also gave greater consideration to my tendency to be more analytical rather than feeling; whereby I too often "act from my head, rather than my heart".

Later in the morning after my experience, I had a chiropractic appointment, to address problems in my lower back (one of a series I had agreed to). When I laid down on the table, I was still in such a mood, that I totally relaxed under his care; trusting that no matter where he pressed or pulled, I'd be OK. I guess you could say that I surrendered my body to him. When he began his manipulations, and began to make adjustments, he stopped. He said that I was so relaxed and loose, that I didn't need any adjustment; that he was afraid that if he tried, he might actually hurt me.

Three days later when I met some friends at a social gathering, I felt no need to be my normal "verbally active" self. I was relaxed and content to just "go with the flow" and appreciate those I was among. More than one person commented upon how different I was; how at peace I seemed to be. What could I say? I was. There was nothing I wanted from them or the encounter that I wasn't already receiving.

It took about two weeks before I was close to normal again. I say "close" because I don't think I ever came all the way back "down". I was left with an almost constant recognition of the presence of a higher consciousness in my life. I suppose it's the over-soul's presence that I'm still aware of most of the time. Yes, there have been times when I've been very down and felt alone and abandoned; even angry. But those times soon fade when I return my awareness to the reality that I was allowed to get a glimpse of.

The experience also allowed me to be more humble; for I can't help but know that we're all in this together—so to speak, all a part of the same whole. It taught me that there is no greater or least. We are all learning our lessons as best as we are able at the time; and we will all eventually get to where we are being led toward. It's only a matter of how much time and trouble we want to put up with during the journey.

I came to conclude that the consciousness which I experienced is a level of awareness that all people will eventually come to in time; when they're ready to set aside their guilt and fear, and refrain from acts of judgment and condemnation of others, in favor of expressing unconditional love through their forgiveness and acts of mercy.

Reflections on the Experience:

In looking back, I realized that the steps I took, which led to my experience, were very similar to the ones enumerated in Alcoholics Anonymous' 12 step program. Without realizing it, I had taken the first few steps. I later learned that there was also a course called EST which accomplished something similar. In fact, many religions incorporate some of these same steps in their dogma or religious format. I don't intend to list any steps, for I believe that they might be unique somewhat to individuals. I only know what led me to where I was at, and this I have described to you—the reader—for your own consideration.

What does stand out from the experience, though, is the nature of our own soul's consciousness. Until now, I have presented the concept of consciousness as being something of a single entity, which exists within groups, and groups of groups, until ultimately it is a part of the All or God. The experience I just described, however, presented a conscious entity as actually being a unit of three parts or aspects: the subconscious mind needing an education, the conscious mind performing the role of teacher, and the over-soul as parent, over-seeing and guiding the entire process; even to the point of determining the lesson plans.

The Multi-dimensional nature of Soul:

There were three main aspects to the experience I had, which I want to put together into a model which can be used to give a clearer understanding of what I perceived as true. These were the oneness we all shared, our relationship with God, and the triune nature of consciousness.

If you recall, one of the first impressions I had, was in remembering John Dunne's reference to islands. Ironically, islands wouldn't be perceived as being separate if there was no water surrounding them. They would merely be perceived as mountain (or volcano) peaks. I believe this closely parallels our relationship to each other. The shift that I experienced in consciousness, allowed me (metaphorically) to see through the "waters of illusion", so that I could recognize that we were not separate islands, but rather peaks of mountains joined to a oneness we call planet Earth.

To better portray both our oneness with All, and include the truer nature of our consciousness, I'd like to reference again the description of a cluster of frog eggs. Perhaps I can also interject my much prior description of a hierarchy of consciousness within the totality of God, in the process.

Using the analogy of the cluster of frog eggs, these could be perceived as representing a group consciousness within a hierarchy, if one could consider clusters of clusters, and clusters of them, etc. This would be much like clusters of cells in the human body which form tissues, then clusters of tissues which form organs, etc. In this analogy, as already stated, each egg would represent a soul, with the aspect which we are familiar with (and identify as self) as being the black nucleus in the process of growth.

What I want to interject, though, is the three-fold nature of each of these cells or eggs. What I perceived as the over-soul being the parent, the middle self—which we perceive as our conscious mind—as being the teacher, and the subconscious mind as being the child in school, are aspects of consciousness which I have not addressed before. Their relevance, however, is crucial to our understanding of who and what we are; and to understanding the greater portion of our purpose for being here on this planet (in this school of life).

I'm sure that most of you are familiar with the concepts of subconscious, conscious, and super-conscious minds; for they were theorized by Carl Jung, and have become rather common place descriptions of our consciousness. They also coincide with my experience, whereby the super-conscious mind would be that which I perceived as an over-soul; the only variance being that I perceived the super-conscious mind as being the true self, or the soul mind.

All of the New-Age or metaphysical groups that I have been involved in, also recognize a number of bodies within our total being; calling these physical, astral (or emotional), mental, causal, etc. I'm not really interested in defining these or giving them names, because quite frankly, I have no personal experience to suggest that these definitions or classifications are valid. I have, however, obtained validity of the fact that a number of ever-finer or less-physical bodies do exist within our soul substance; so without trying to define or number them, I will present them in a general way that is useful to my intentions here.

The following diagram is—like the one in the prior chapter—derived from material which I was exposed to through my involvement with the material presented by Edgar Cayce through the A.R.E. I have made some modifications to their model in order to better make some points of my own. My intention is to better portray our multi-dimensional nature and connection to God; as well as to visually depict the obstacles that we confront in attempting to deal with our personal limitations and expand our consciousness. The divisions are not intended to be accurate; for I have no way to know what is truly accurate from my own personal experience. It is as close, though, as I can conceive of it as being; and it suits my purposes in presenting it.

Divine Plane

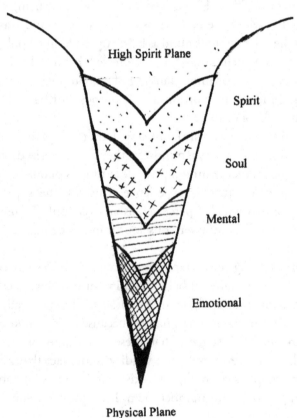

High Spirit Plane

Spirit

Soul

Mental

Emotional

Physical Plane

This diagram is intended to depict the multi-dimensional nature of our soul's consciousness. The shaded areas within each segment are intended to depict beliefs or attitudes that have been "learned" for better or for worse. Some of these will need to be adjusted, and some removed entirely in order for the physical consciousness to be able to make contact with the higher levels. It's difficult to depict, since the diagram is rigid, but the consciousness with which we normally perceive reality—perhaps what I could call our ego's consciousness—can reach up into the higher levels. We often do this when asleep, or in some other altered state.

At the very top of the diagram, the triangle is funneling out to connect with triangles representing other souls. One might consider the type of cloud layer from which tornadoes originate; and think of each tornado as representing a soul coming down into the physical plane for expression (hopefully for much kinder expressions!). One might also consider some funnels as descending only part of the way down, and not actually contacting the earth; these would represent entities that instead chose to express themselves on higher planes of consciousness. These could make direct contact with incarnate beings by essentially directing their point of contact to the relative location on the multi-dimensional triangle.

It's all about Frequency:

I don't know to which level I reached when I had my experience, but I do know that it was because I raised the frequency of my consciousness to a higher level; so that I was able to make contact with one of the higher planes of consciousness. The perceptions and insights were then reflective of the state of awareness existent on that higher plane. It was like temporarily clearing away the hindrances, so that a beam of light (or higher awareness) could filter down to me, who was still functioning on the physical plane.

First the feeling of freedom, then the feeling of joy, and then the self-forgiveness which allowed for the profound feeling of love, brought me finally to a high enough frequency of consciousness, that I made attunement to the level of awareness present on that plane. If you think about it, you will realize just how much our vocabulary infers that various states of consciousness are measured in frequency. Higher frequencies cause a feeling of enlightenment, while lower frequencies are described as states of depression. One lightens one up, while the other presses one down. Serious concerns relate to things that <u>matter</u> (relating to density), while states of bliss are described as feeling <u>high</u>.

This is why people who are depressed, or who are focused on dark subjects such as those relating entirely to material pursuits, find it so difficult to feel empathy toward others, or a connection to God. Others who are generally happy and optimistic find it much easier to feel love for others, and a connection with God or higher powers. I have come to realize that my relative state of consciousness determines the quality of my dreams and other night-time experiences.

When I'm depressed, I find it difficult to recall dreams, and when I do they are often unclear or disjointed. When I'm feeling optimistic or happy, on the other hand, I find myself remembering vivid dreams, flying dreams, and lucid dreams. I sometimes even get the impression that my awareness is functioning somewhere outside my body, even if I'm just perceiving that I'm in the yard or in some other part of the house. Dense feelings seem to keep my consciousness grounded in my dense body, while lighter feelings seem to allow for a type of freedom, whereby my consciousness can become free from the body and experience other states of being. What's actually happening at those times I can only speculate; all I can relate is the perception that I possess at the time.

Another phenomenon I occasionally experience when feeling generally happy and optimistic, is that of ESP of one sort or another. It's as though dense feelings close me off from information or perceptions that are otherwise available if my state of consciousness were to be operating at a higher frequency. I only wish I were able to obtain control over this type of phenomena, for the experiences seem to just arise at random occasions without my intending them to. Only rarely have I been able to produce an experience of that type. Perhaps one day we will all learn how to control this expression of our consciousness which Edgar Cayce said was a quality of soul which we all possess.

I've met and talked with others who've had all the types of unusual experiences that I have, and many of them had them more regularly and more superior in other ways. I've also met other people who have experienced states of consciousness like the lengthy one I described earlier. They seemed to vary in length and in scope, but the feeling of euphoria and oneness was there; and it always seemed to be preceded by a feeling of freedom which brought elation. I look forward to the day when we all begin sharing our similar experiences; believing it to be the ultimate destiny of us all to reach such higher states and remain there—not settle back down as I have done. It is my hope and intention that this book can be a guide in helping you—the reader—to raise your own state of consciousness out of the realms of fear and doubt, and into states of unconditional love; with hope for a far greater reality to come.

We are Creator Beings:

We are by nature creator beings; and without the influence of outside agents such as aliens from other worlds, and enlightened individuals from other continents; we would—in my opinion—have evolved into a pagan society. We would be scientists; studying the forces of, and patterns within the cycles of nature, so that we would be better able to adjust our choices in harmony with them. We would also, quite likely, have assigned names to these forces and patterns in order to aid communication when referring to them, but we would not naturally have believed that we could influence them in any way, unless we actually found that we could. Also, we would not have thought that disease could be remedied by eating certain herbs or drinking certain potions. That these practices eventually became a part of pagan culture, indicates that people at some time found out that they could influence the patterns and forces of nature through the use of ritual, and that they could receive information from these forces to guide them in obtaining remedies for their ailments.

In studying the forces of nature, and in having needs, it was only natural that some pressing need be addressed toward the relative force that had been assigned a name. If a positive benefit had not subsequently resulted from such an expression, there would be little motivation for people to create elaborate ceremonies or rituals in order to continue the practice. So, in my opinion, it was only natural for people to discover their innate creative powers, and their ability to exercise a degree of control over their lives through such use.

We are Social Beings.

It's also natural that social structure would have evolved out of our needs for survival, and that those who were the strongest and most dominant would have assumed positions of power over others. This would have allowed societies to develop whereby people could gain advantages from each other and share in others' innate talents or abilities. People working together as a unit, is after all, the most practical way to live.

And a part of this would be philosophy, were those gifted in the quality of reason, would impart their conclusions to the society for all to share. But religion—as practiced today—wherein teachings with regard to an afterlife of either pain or suffering, would not likely have come about unless there was some strong outside influence present to validate the teachings. This leads me to support those who give credence to the influence of powerful alien beings on early cultures; for these entities—upon being recognized for their extraordinary abilities—would have been afforded great respect or fear.

I believe that those who study ancient culture are finding that religions actually had a dominant role in creating social structures; and not the reverse—as previously theorized—that religions sprang up as a result of a successful society. It's only natural that a god-like being would be able to use its power and knowledge to influence social structure; even to the point of laying down rules or laws for people to follow, under the threat of dire punishment.

We are not alone.

Besides the probable (I think obvious) influence from alien beings upon our cultures, there is ample evidence—in my opinion—of the existence of and influence from more spiritual sources. I already mentioned the natural tendency to assign names to forces of nature; but there are undoubtedly other lesser forces active within our lives. That primitive cultures would include beliefs about, and practices involving spirits or demons, gives credence to the fact that such entities exist; and that they have a degree of influence in our lives.

Beliefs in an after-life can also become validated when people report experiences involving those who have previously died. Other types of phenomena could also be explained by attributing them to the existence of disincarnate entities. These phenomena could include visions or dreams, whereby helpful information was provided by some spiritual agent.

Validation could also occur where people to be bothered in some way by seemingly unearthly powers.

Putting it all together:

The reason I make reference to what "seems to be", based upon logic and what seems to be natural, is to make a distinction between what is more natural for us as we truly are, and what we are told that we are by either science or religion. Too often we fail to think for ourselves, and consider from our own experience (and exposure to others' reported experiences), just what seems to be true or valid.

On the one hand we are taught in schools about the findings of science, and in accepting their proofs, go on to also accept their beliefs as well; which are not proven. A scientist cannot prove, for example, that realities that they can't measure or test, don't exist. So, any claims by science that aliens or ghosts or psychic phenomena and the like don't exist, are themselves invalid; for neither can their claims be proven.

Religions present us with a different set of beliefs, and bolster them with threats of punishment if we refuse to accept them. And in opposition to the strategy of science which demands proof, religions require faith or unsubstantiated belief. Religions obtain the validation that they require through examples of personal experience, and by providing some quite valuable benefits. But there is also a limit to their wisdom and teachings, which they attempt to cover up by demanding compliance based upon blind faith. So, as with the scientific approach, we are left in a state of uncertainty over a number of important subjects. These are the subjects that I've tried to address here, for your consideration.

THE ROLE OF RELIGION

Necessary for Social Structure and Learning:

As conscious entities, unaware of either our multi-dimensional nature or our creative abilities, we require both assistance and guidance in order to better learn what we need to, in order to grow into becoming what we are capable of. It's the same as with the animals in the wild, which rely upon the example of a parent to teach and guide them, so that they can survive and prosper in a challenging environment.

Without the structure that religions provide, people would need to look elsewhere for answers to life's challenging questions, and for guidance in making necessary decisions. They would become dependent, then, upon structures of governments with their rules and regulations, and become easily victimized by those with greater power. This is not to say, however, that religions haven't heavily influenced the practices and policies of governments; or that people with power haven't used religions to further their own ambitions. Religion can be, then, both a benefit and a detriment to society at large. Yet even when religious teachings and practices have been used against people's best interests, they have provided experiences through which people can learn and develop as spiritual beings.

Inspiration toward achieving Excellence:

In providing a framework for connecting with God (or a higher power), religions have inspired people toward achievements of great excellence. Consider the impressive structures created by mankind in order to appease or impress their Gods. Consider also the arts; the great works of music, sculpture, paintings, and mosaics which are valued and respected today because of the fervent desire to create something worthy of God's approval. The very idea that we owe our existence to a Divine source, moves us to want to express gratitude and praise to our Creator in the most demonstrative way possible.

And when we credit God with acts of assistance in our personal lives, we quite naturally seek to express our gratitude in return. We might even perform great deeds in the hopes of receiving future benefits in return. In any situation where mankind perceives of a much greater power, it is a natural instinct to seek favors from it, and offer thanks in the best way we know how. This "looking up" to something incomprehensively greater, is a source of inspiration that guides us into both "reaching up" (in terms of extending our capabilities), and into "growing up" (as we develop spiritually) through our association with religious doctrine and influence.

Religion is like the surface of a Suspension Bridge.

By far the most vital role of religion plays out in its ability to provide a reliable structure for our return (in consciousness) to God. And whether our perceived separation is due to the biblical fall from grace, caused by a devil in the form of a talking snake; or due to our soul's own desire to experience the density of material expression, the results are the same. We need a format or protocol which we can use, in order to raise our consciousness back to the heights from which it descended. Religions provide that structure in a multitude of ways, and this aids us in our spiritual growth: our growth in consciousness into ever higher frequencies of expression.

I once watched a video of a primitive society constructing a suspension bridge across a wide and deep ravine. This ravine could represent the chasm between us, with our limited awareness, and that higher state of awareness which we are trying to reach through growth on this physical plane. It could also be thought of as the gulf between humankind and God.

The first thing the society did, in preparing to make the bridge, was to have a group of their members get to the other side, so that they could help to facilitate the construction from that side. Obviously, this was not an easy task for this group to achieve (without the benefit of a pre-existing bridge), so these individuals' efforts were greatly appreciated. The same could be said for those pioneers of religious doctrines who found their own path to God, and then made the effort to teach others; showing them the way in the best way that they knew how.

It also helps to know that forces of higher consciousness are also actively influencing us seekers, inspiring us to persevere, and providing feedback to aid us in our learning. These—together with the pioneers (or prophets)—perform a vital role in assisting us to build a useful bridge to higher wisdom.

The first effort to bridge the chasm is accomplished by shooting an arrow, attached to a very fine rope—the thinnest rope they can make, across the ravine. This is a crucial step which often meets with failure, because if the rope is made too light, it breaks in the process. But if the rope is made too heavy, its weight prevents the arrow from reaching the other side. Here is when those on the other side, as well as helpers on the archer's side, play a vital role in encouraging repeated attempts.

It is the same with those first attempts of a person seeking contact with the Divine. Here the teachers—whether prophets, ministers, or gurus—play a vital role; for it is often their encouragement and guidance which motivates seekers to keep trying though initial attempts may fail. Assistance is also provided by the higher forces of consciousness which inspire one to keep trying; perhaps even to try new methods, until success is made.

After the first small rope finally reaches the other side, it is secured, and used to pull across a slightly larger rope; and again failures are possible. For this first rope is feeble, and sometimes breaks in the attempt to pull across a larger rope; requiring the process to begin once again with another arrow and another fine rope. But through persistence, and the continual encouragement of others (and lots of rope making), eventually larger and larger lengths of rope are pulled across; until finally a rope strong enough to bear the required load is successfully anchored on the other side.

First attempts, by anybody seeking communication with the forces of light and higher consciousness, often do meet with some moments of failure; and there one must always keep on trying. Here is where religious leaders and inner guidance from higher realms, together with fellow seekers, aid and support those making the attempts until a strong connection is made. And once one truly establishes a reliable connection with Divinity, the way is open to begin using that bridge for one's own benefit as well as for the benefit of all.

But one strong connection is not enough to be truly practical; so one strong rope is used to pull across more lengths, so that a structure can be built that will allow one to carry heavy loads without fear of falling off. And often this structure includes pieces of wood planking to act as a walkway over which animals and supplies can be moved.

These structures can be likened to the rituals and practices of religions, which aid the aspirant in building a life centered upon this Divine connection. This is where religions have served societies quite well throughout history. And though the wood planking and other parts of the structure don't aid the connection, they do provide a degree of ease in allowing one to use the connection in a more beneficial and practical way.

This is like saying that it doesn't really matter what religious practices or rituals are used to assist one in using their Divine connection to God. The very fact of there being many religions today, each providing people with the means to establish a living relationship with God, proves that point. It's just disappointing to me, though, that there is so much fighting and conflict among religious groups who compare the walkway on their bridge to the walkways on other bridges; and in finding fault with the style or appearance of the walkway, deem the bridge to be unsound or unreliable.

Because the type of bridge I just described has no anchors to support it in the center, it has a tendency to sway back and forth, and this can lead to fear on the part of those using the bridge. In the example I gave of building the bridge over a ravine, such supports are not possible. But when the bridge is made wide enough, and constructed over a river—not too far from the ground beneath it—then supports can be made to secure the walkway so that is more secure, and not prone to movement.

These supports or anchors can be likened to beliefs within religion which are presented to support the basic teachings, rituals, and practices, so that people will accept their validity without question; for it is in questioning that people can become fearful and might avoid using the bridge. Examples of these supports may relate to the credibility of religious texts, of the person responsible for establishing the religion, or for the individual(s) around whom the teachings center. Supports might also exist in the form of stories; which validate the rites and ceremonies, or the reliability of the teachings.

Though there is great benefit provided by these supports, it must be remembered, though, that they do not provide the connection; they do not even support the bridge itself. For were these supports to break away, the bridge would remain; the connection to the other side would not be lost. The only damage that would occur would be to the stability or quality of the walkway built as a convenience. And this walkway could be built and rebuilt many times without affecting the connection through the ropes or cables high above. Also, if the walkway that was made was it turn properly supported by the connecting ropes, it also would be undamaged by any loss of the anchoring supports; their function being only to provide stability.

It's difficult for me to express my feelings about the way different religions view other religions; as it is so clear to me that all religions serve the same basic function: to assist people the world over—from different cultures and times—to establish a closer connection with the higher forces of Divinity and so be able to raise their own state of consciousness to higher levels. I guess it's like hearing my close friends fight over what I perceive to be petty differences, when I appreciate some elements of the differences, while accepting the short-comings I perceive all to possess; myself included.

Bridge Maintenance:

Let's go back to the analogy. Once the bridge is completed, and the walkway properly anchored, care must be given to maintain the continued soundness of the structure. This is because with weather and usage, the ropes and their connections to the walkway, can erode. Though the strong heavy ropes which span the bridge last for a long time, if properly made and anchored, the smaller ropes, extending down from them which attach to the walkway, must be frequently inspected. For if these fail to support the walkway, those on the bridge could become lost to the waters or the chasm beneath.

This is to say that members of religions must be constantly aware of the integrity of their relationship with God; regardless which name they give It. They do this by questioning their own actions and the motivations behind them. It is too easy to justify practices that conflict with higher principles; and religions are not immune to this possibility. Through the reading and contemplation of sacred texts, prayer, meditation, and study with other seekers, people affirm and strengthen their connections to the divine. And when they question policies and practices adapted by their particular religion, in considering how well these are supported through a connection with God, people are giving due attention to these critical elements of the bridge.

On the other hand, when people put all their attention on the anchors which support their religion of choice (or heritage), the stories and beliefs which support their religious practices, then they risk losing their precious connection to Divinity. And it is easy to do this when there is a lot of tension between people of different faiths, for the focus continues to be upon the uniqueness of the religious practices, and those beliefs or writings which validate them. Often people become very fearful of attacks to these supports for their religious practices, for they may have come to believe that these are necessary in order for them to reach God. The fact is: they are not. One needn't even be a member of a religion, or believe in God, to draw closer to higher consciousness; for it's truly the love that one expresses toward others (a high frequency of vibration of consciousness) that lifts one—in consciousness—to oneness with the Divine. It is the unconditional love of God for us which forms the strongest bond between us; and religious practices which demonstrate unconditional love toward others, which help to form the connecting ropes between the heavy cables and the structure of the walkway or religion.

A big problem for me, is that I perceive sincere individuals, truly desirous of establishing a closer connection with God, actually letting their own connections wither away through neglect or misuse; because the uniqueness of their own religion or their own religious views become so important to them, that they begin to put all their attention there; believing that this is the only way to reach God. By failing to look up to the ropes or cables that support them and their religion, they look only straight across at the dogma which their particular religion provides as a path to God. Then, when others (like this book) challenge the validity of certain beliefs or practices (as this book is doing), they become fearful and defensive; believing that others (or this book) are attempting to prevent them from reaching God.

What's truly ironic is that by challenging the integrity of these supporting anchors, or the value of religious dogma, the focus can also shift to the supporting ropes and cables that truly do support ones path to Divinity. After all, what do you do when you're crossing a foot-bridge, and it starts to become unstable? You reach for the ropes! So by challenging or questioning the elements of one's own religious faith (as I did as a child), while at the same time holding fast to one's personal connection to God (as I did as a child), one can become led into a much surer relationship with Divinity. Then one needn't become fearful about attacks to accepted facts or stories which form the basis of any particular practice or belief. In fact, one can construct their own walkway, using planks resembling those used in other religions, to create their own unique path toward God, as they perceive It to be.

I've had the pleasure of experiencing a connection to God while worshiping in a variety of churches, temples, synagogues, and mosques; just as I've felt a connection at home or in nature. I've even felt a connection to Divinity when visiting the ruins of ancient sites, and when becoming involved in rites and rituals practiced by pagan religions. And the only time I've felt uncomfortable was in a situation when curses (prayers for someone else's ruin) were ignorantly extended by the fellowship.

This occurred, surprisingly enough (since I had previously experienced such a high vibration of love), during a meeting of "born-again-Christians". For some reason, they felt it necessary to ask for God's judgment upon a woman who started a business practicing astrology, and offering "readings". They ignorantly believed that this was "from the devil" and needed to be attacked by them (they "prayed" that she lose her business). I never returned to that group, but heard from a friend shortly thereafter, that their group had disbanded and was no longer meeting. The message I'm trying to stress here, is that no matter how close to God a religion or group can come, if it fails to pay attention to the highest of principles, it risks losing its own connection to the Divine. God—by any name—is Love; and it is the expression of unconditional love that God requires of all who aspire to gain a closer connection to It.

Religion as a Teacher:

If life is a school wherein we grow from states of ignorance, through a multitude of various experiences, into attaining wisdom, then religions offer us the variety of lessons and opportunities that are instrumental in teaching us what we need to learn in order to grow and expand both our capabilities and consciousness. Religions perform this function, not only by being a constructive influence in our lives, but also when they motivate us to do things that are "less than best". And as contradictory as it may seem, even when religious teachings and practices have caused great harm to people, these too have been opportunities to learn about ourselves.

I've come to recognize that there is a lot of good that can be said for the world's various religions: their beliefs and practices. But there are also beliefs and practices that should be questioned by those who truly desire a closer connection to God and Its Truth; and these areas of question exist—in my opinion—within all religions. I've been taught that "God inspires", but I've also concluded that "mankind corrupts". Part of the reason for this, I believe, is that assumptions are made that are not valid, that people misunderstand the teachings of the one (or ones) around which the religion was established, and that the leaders or authorities within the religion attempt to create a structure suitable to their own goals and ideas.

Rather than faulting religions for this (at this time anyway), I'd like to stress that these failings or short-comings provide important lessons for us to both challenge us, and aid us in our spiritual growth and development. Life is indeed a school where we grow from states of ignorance (wherein we make lots of mistakes) to states of wisdom (wherein we become able to help others). If religions didn't provide us with challenges, they would be of little use to us. They would exist in the form of over-zealous parents, insisting upon doing our homework for us, and telling us what to do in every situation. And from their influence, we would find it difficult to learn anything for ourselves.

After all, God didn't have to grant us the gift of free will. It could have made us perfect little automatons, going about vibrating beautiful energies all the time, without a thought to do otherwise. Yet through our capacity to make free-willed choices, we are susceptible to error; for out of ignorance we often fail to consider the validity, value, or detriment to certain expressions. The example I gave of the cursing prayer being just a minor one. Many people have suffered and died over the ages, and many wonderful cultures put to ruin, under (what I believe to have been) the misguided intentions to promote good. The message here is that we need to constantly question ourselves and the practices which we support and believe in. This is the aspect of life that is so important to our own growth and development toward higher consciousness.

Religious Misconceptions

Childhood Questions:

In the Introduction to this book I said how as a child and youth, I had many questions with regard to the teachings of the religion in which I was being raised. In this chapter I intend to answer some of them, and add to that other conclusions that I have come to which allow me to make more sense of both Christianity and some other different religions. Part of that is making comment on practices and beliefs which are based upon teachings which I have come to believe are misunderstood, or based upon erroneous assumptions. Please don't take this chapter as a critique or criticism, but rather as an attempt to clear up what I believe to be misconceptions based upon my own feelings, thoughts, and experiences. I leave my comments with you to consider in light of what you know. Also, since I was brought up in a Christian faith, please understand that this is why so many of my comments relate to beliefs held by that particular religion. I just don't feel qualified or able to make more than a few comments about other religious beliefs and practices.

Exoteric vs. Esoteric:

It is my opinion that much of the confusion or misunderstandings with regard to subjects in the Bible stem from the frequent use of metaphor in describing certain truths. This is, I believe, because many readers of the texts (which were assembled into the Bible) weren't ready to properly understand some higher truths, so they were referred to cryptically or in parable form. To accommodate them, an outer (exoteric or more literal) meaning was provided to satisfy their desire for some degree of understanding. Those who possessed a higher awareness of truth could find value when looking within the literal words and meanings for a deeper or hidden (esoteric) truth. This chapter, in part, is my attempt to reveal the esoteric meanings of some scriptures which I believe have resulted in confusion when considering only the exoteric or more literal outer meaning.

The Nature of God:

In the first chapter of this book I delved into the subject of God, and described my opinions with regard to concepts commonly held about "Him". The idea that God is a "being" with many human qualities, who is trying to fight evil in "His" efforts to provide "His" favored with a happier, more rewarding life experience, just isn't so in my opinion. This description of God as being jealous and vengeful is a significant example of using metaphor to put a point across without having to go into details about higher truths.

In my opinion, the misconception resulted from the law of karma (cause and effect) being personified as a God fighting evil and rewarding good. In truth, it was rather that God laid down laws to guide our spiritual growth and development; and the balancing law of karma serves to fulfill Its purpose in providing our learning experiences. This characterization of karmic law as being God has led to a lot of misunderstandings about God; particularly when the law of Grace is later introduced. Since I've already devoted two chapters to this important subject, I won't elaborate too much here. But I believe that this false perception of God has led a lot of people to conclude that God doesn't really exist. I feel that they might have seen the illogic in this belief and in rejecting the belief, also rejected the idea of God; not considering that there could be another explanation for the inconsistencies. A quote from Epicurus, I believe, speaks clearly about this misperception of God:

"Is God willing to prevent evil, but not able? Then he is not omnipotent. Is he able, but not willing? Then he is malevolent. Is he both able and willing? Then whence cometh evil? Is he neither able nor willing? Then why call him God?

Epicurus (Greek philosopher, BC 341-270)

Though I feel that I've already provided my answer to these questions, I'll make a summation here. The answer is that God has given us a great gift; that of free will. It is up to us to prevent ourselves from being malevolent or committing evil acts. God will not interfere; instead It (not "HE"—I don't believe that God is an anthropomorphic being with genitals) has provided laws (particularly the law of cause and effect—Karma, and the law of Grace) which will eventually lead us into learning that expressions of love demonstrate a far better way to live.

In my opinion, God allows suffering for the very same reason that parents of babies allow them to soil their diapers, wake them up in the middle of the night, and spit up their food. God loves all of us, and recognizes that we are in the process of learning. I also believe that in most cases, those who appear to be the victims of other's actions, are learning lessons themselves; possibly even experiencing the pain that they ignorantly imposed upon others in the past. I say "possibly" because there are other reasons why a soul would agree to accept an experience of suffering. I'm certain, though, that in virtually all cases of evil done, the victim had agreed (on the soul level) to have the experience.

Reincarnation as a cycle of rebirth:

As a child and youth, I too was bothered by the seeming unfairness of the world; wherein some people would be born into lives of relative hardship while others seemed to have been blessed. Of particular bother to me were children born with serious handicaps, or who died very young. Also, since I was taught that only Christians could go to heaven after death, it bothered me that those who died without having an opportunity to hear of Jesus would be punished. In fact, it bothered me that anybody should experience an eternity of suffering for any error.

The idea that souls are immortal and live different lives at different times and in different life situations made perfect sense to me; for herein could life become truly fair and just. Unfortunately, my minister couldn't share my view, even though I pointed out references in the New Testament that I thought to be supportive of same. I referred to John the Baptist's being a reincarnation of Elijah (or Elias), and to Jesus comment to Nicodemus about the necessity of being "born again". He (rather the church) had different opinions about these references. Even when I pointed out that some Jews at the time obviously believed in reincarnation, because of comments made with regard to whom they though Jesus was, and that Jesus' own disciples must have believed the same when they asked what sins the man blind from birth had committed, my pastor brushed it off as erroneous beliefs held by others. He referred me to a verse in the book of Hebrews that clearly stated that man lives only once and then dies; and to him (or the church) that was proof enough. My reply was that the author wasn't addressing the subject of reincarnation, but rather making an analogy to support the assertion that Jesus only had to die once for our sins. Besides, I said, man does (usually) only die once; it's the soul which reincarnates; not the "man". Well, as you can imagine, he wasn't dissuaded from his conviction. Allowing himself to be convinced, would have put him in the position of disagreeing with the church's doctrine. Besides, I already had my opinion, and he couldn't present any argument to make me change my mind. You may, of course, have your own.

What I have come to conclude is that reincarnation is a process where souls continue to return to life in the physical world until their lessons here are properly learned. After successfully completing that part of their "education" they can move on to life experiences in the immortal realms; in "incorruptible" spirit-bodies.

What is Heaven?

I could say so much about this subject, that it could be a chapter by itself. So, I'll try to be brief and to the point, leaving out a lot of reasons for my opinions; they don't really matter anyway. The belief, that we live once, are judged, and then spend the rest of eternity in a state of perpetual bliss because we chose to accept the correct religion, can be a very desirable belief to hold onto. It may be why the idea of reincarnation is so illogically (in my opinion) rejected. I think that one of my sisters (though she'd probably deny it now) summed it up very well for me. She said she wouldn't even consider the subject; when she finished with this life, she wanted to believe that she'd spend forever in heaven; and that was it. She didn't want to even consider believing that she might have to return again and again.

I've come to the conclusion, then, that the misconceptions with regard to heaven have a lot to do with people's rejection of the thought of having to reincarnate: they just don't want to consider otherwise. Unfortunately, I don't think heaven is quite as people expect it to be. And even among those who do believe in reincarnation, and accept that there are a variety of different states of consciousness which we may ascend to after death, I hear different views of which one heaven is supposed to be.

Regardless of others' opinions, it's the church's opinion I intend to address here. I believe the misconception arose for a number of reasons; chiefly as a result of Jesus not having given a detailed description of it. He spoke mostly of "the Father's kingdom", and this was later decided to be a place where one spends eternity after death. So, when Jesus spoke of "my Father's house" as having "many mansions", it was decided that he was talking about some place with lots of living quarters. When on the cross, Jesus spoke of Paradise; and this too was decided (by the church) to refer to heaven. Also, in the Book of Revelations, when reference was made to a "new heaven and earth", this too was decided to refer to this same place called heaven, where everything would be blissful.

My opinion at the moment is that different states of consciousness or realms of existence are being referred to here, and since there was little elaboration on any of them, they were all assumed to be referring to the same thing. I think also, that the early church may have felt that the promise of an eternity of bliss for accepting their religion without question would be a pretty easy sell. And corrupt governments would have liked the assertion as well, because the people under their rule would be more inclined to accept hardships in life, if they felt they'd be greatly rewarded afterwards.

My conclusion is that heaven is <u>not</u> a final destination in consciousness that those deemed to be worthy ascend to after death. In referring to the graph I presented in the third chapter, I described a number of states of consciousness above this one, which we rise to as our consciousness expands to higher frequencies. This would relate to Jesus assertion of there being "many mansions" (states of consciousness or dimensions of reality) in his "Father's house"; the house referring to all higher planes, dimensions, or states of consciousness. In referring to heaven, then, I'd describe it as a range of non-physical realities or realms of consciousness that are above this physical dimension. In fact, for reasons I'll go into later, I'll suggest that the realms of heaven are above the astral plane as well. In reference to the chart, I'd say that they include the spirit, high spirit, and divine planes. Remember, though, since I have no good knowledge of what planes truly do exist, I just approximated them as "spirit" and "high spirit"; there are most likely very many distinct planes of reality contained in heaven.

When Jesus referred to his "Father's kingdom", I believe he was talking about the state of consciousness which he himself was in, because he stated that his "kingdom is not of this world". I believe that he was using the word kingdom to refer to his state of consciousness; which I earlier referred to as cosmic or Christ consciousness. I believe that Jesus was—through his example and teachings—trying to show "the way" whereby people could achieve this state of consciousness for themselves; thus why he said that if people followed his teachings and did the will of "the Father" that they could do the miraculous things that he did.

In reference to Paradise: I believe that Jesus was speaking of a place of rest where people go after death, so that they can rest for a while and recuperate from their ordeals hear on earth. This opinion is substantiated, I believe, by reports of "near-death experiences" wherein people describe finding themselves in a peaceful and serene place. I believe that souls who still have lessons to learn on this physical dimension of reality, will eventually leave this "paradise" to return once again—reincarnate into another physical body—by entering into an appropriate (pre-chosen) baby's body at birth.

And finally I believe (as Edgar Cayce suggested) that the Book of Revelations is a meditation guide or description of how people can personally reach higher states of consciousness. In referring to the Genesis story of the "fall", where Adam and Eve ate from the tree of knowledge, and the tree of life was cut down: I suggest that life in this physical realm, living under the law of karma and suffering the cycle of rebirth known as reincarnation, is represented by the tree of knowledge. In the book of Revelations, I believe that St. John is describing a vision—metaphorically speaking—of the tree of life. He is describing the tree that was cut down, so that we would have an idea of how we can obtain that fruit and live forever.

The A.R.E. offers a couple of very good books on the symbolism that is used in the text of Revelations; and I suggest that those interested pursue that source. In regards to heaven, I'd say that the Book of Revelations does describe how to "get there"; but the events described are descriptive of an internal process of spiritual development, rather than prophesies of world events to come.

In summary, my view is that, in the beginning God created many souls who were granted the freedom to choose expressions on any frequency of consciousness that they desired. Some decided to create and express themselves in dense form in a material reality, so that they could experience the five physical senses including sexual expression. This has been called "the fall" wherein they metaphorically ate from the tree of knowledge of physical reality. This brought with it the need to know good and evil and therefore suffer and die through the laws of karma and reincarnation; needing to continue in a cycle of rebirth in corruptible physical bodies until they were able to escape their carnal desires. The removal of the tree of life represented, then, the loss of higher attunement which would have allowed them to remain in incorruptible spirit bodies, living in realms of higher consciousness which were collectively called heaven.

When God was credited with having created the heavens and the earth, I believe that (esoterically speaking) the author was referring to these planes of consciousness: the physical one (earth) and the spiritual planes (heavens), not the earth and the physical universe (which would be the exoteric view).

In spite of all that I have said about the Book of Revelations, and prophesies of a new world to come, with judgment and all that; I do believe that there is great truth there. I just don't believe that these prophesies (like those found in other parts of the Bible) are attempting to describe heaven, or life on higher planes. Instead I believe they are referring to a new creation which I will try to describe (as best as I understand it) in the last chapter of this book.

What are Purgatory and Hell?

What I have expressed with regard to karma and reincarnation, to some extent describes my view on these realms. In adding to the previous assertion, and in again referring to the graph at the beginning of the third chapter, I'd say that Purgatory and Hell relate to a number of states of consciousness that exist on this physical plane, as well as the astral plane above it and subhuman planes below it. I certainly do not accept the accepted view that those judged as "goats" be damned to an eternity of suffering and torment. In my opinion, such a sentence would be totally out of character for a God of Love. I can understand, though, how there could have been a misunderstanding.

Jesus occasionally made reference to the "eternal flames" and spiritual "death". In the prior, I believe he was referring to a low state of consciousness wherein one suffers for their sins—much like Purgatory. But I take this "place" metaphorically as a state of consciousness which could become evidenced in a future physical incarnation, or be experienced in an appropriate astral experience. It is my understanding that many realms of reality exist within the astral realms; astral referring to emotional. When you consider the very strong emotions that accompany "evil" acts, you might perceive why a life in a predominantly emotional reality could serve as a punishment or purging experience.

The movie "Pirates of the Caribbean" portrayed a group of pirates who were suffering in a state very similar to what could occur in some astral realms. Lacking a physical body, yet remaining alive, they were unable to satisfy their desires for food or drink. They expressed how frustrating this was, and how desirous they were of regaining a physical form. Any person who dies with overly-strong compulsions could find themselves in a purgatory of sorts where their desires remained, but where they were unable to satisfy them; or perhaps on the contrary, where they were doomed to experience a reality where that particular indulgence was overly abundant. Perhaps they would have the opportunity to regret having so much of what they desired.

Generally speaking, though, I believe that Jesus was referring to the results of karma when describing judgment and punishment in hell's flames. And if that is true, then he could be describing life again on earth, wherein one experiences the suffering that was ignorantly imposed upon others.

Whether as a lifetime on earth, or as an experience in the astral realm, the stay in hell is neither eternal nor apart from God and Its love. Recall, if you will, that "the Psalmist" wrote that "even there" God is present to help. In the "Aquarian Gospel of Jesus the Christ" by Levi, Jesus explains that hell is a place of refinement, whereby the dross is burned off and the gold survives. This is in reference to a place (in consciousness) of purging one from inharmonious attitudes and tendencies. In reference to astral realms: though the "place" may be eternal, one's stay there certainly is not. Once an entity is sufficiently purged, or comes to recognize their errors, they are provided with a means of escape or deliverance. It's much like the concept of Purgatory; in fact I believe that purgatory is a better description of the state that people call hell.

Much confusion has arisen, in my opinion, from Jesus' reference to death—meaning death of the soul—and by warning people that certain expressions would lead one there. This "death" I equate to the very bottom of the graph, which I presented at the beginning of chapter three. It's not a state that a soul would ever reach, however, but more of an absolute used to indicate a direction. It's an absolute which certain expressions or attitudes would draw one toward, but never quite reach. The greater the guilt, fear, selfishness, and lust for power over others, the more one would descend toward that extreme. The more one expresses love, however, the more one will ascend into higher states of consciousness toward total oneness—in consciousness—with God.

Another reason for the belief in a sentence of eternal damnation in hell is that it follows from the belief in the reward of an eternity in heaven. If the church is going to present one view as being valid, then for consistency's sake, the opposite must also be presented. Perhaps also, the teaching is also an attempt at manipulation; intended to more easily obtain converts: absolute judgments upon death.

How does one escape karma, suffering, and the cycle of reincarnation?

There's a lot I'd like to say here; but simply put, it's to learn the lessons from the "tree of knowledge" and apply the "fruit of the tree of life. Put another way—as will be discussed more fully in the last chapter—one stops acting out of fear, and starts acting on the motivation of love.

There are two key elements involved in the lessons derived from the "tree of knowledge". One is to lose one's strong attachment to physical "fruits" which consist of earthly pleasures, and the other is to absolve all karma obtained by causing harm to others in the pursuit of these "fruits".

The remedy to the first is to realize that carnal pleasures don't truly satisfy, and therefore, to not become a slave to their appealing nature. This is what is referred to as "subduing the earth"; it means overcoming the carnal or physical cravings (lusts) for earthly pleasures (as relating to the five physical senses). To "subdue the earth" <u>does not mean</u> to ravage the world's natural beauty and resources or to unnecessarily harm plants and animals out of greed for greater financial profits.

Eastern religions put more focus on this than middle or western religions. And though I've found great value in some of their practices, I tend to feel that they sometimes go over-board in their attempts at renunciation (of physical pleasures). To me, it sometimes seems that in fearing a wrong answer to a school assignment, they choose to avoid the class altogether. Another analogy would be to essentially lock oneself in one's room for fear of enjoying the outdoors too much.

For a person with an addiction, though, this is actually a good policy though, as one recognizes one's inability to be moderate in the relative expression. A lifetime of renunciation can also be a good life to balance a prior life in which excessive pleasures were indulged in. Every religion has both advantages and disadvantages, so religions which offer extremes do have their place in this world; though they might not be best for everybody.

Lusts of the flesh, so to speak, are not the only things people need to let go of. As a result of one's fear, in addition to one's carnal lusts, people often hurt others. This particularly occurs when desires for power predominate. These acts of harm to others incur what I've previously called karma; the natural result of cause and effect in motion. This is the law of sin referred to in the Bible; the fruits of which bring on judgment and consequences. It is also the accumulation of karma that produces the necessity of future lifetimes on earth through reincarnation. By harming others, one incurs karma and gets stuck in the physical reality through repeated cycles of rebirth until all lessons are learned and all debts (karma) paid.

The "default" means of paying off karmic debt is through meeting what one sows, so to speak. This is the "eye for an eye" type payment.

It's the most painful of the means of absolving karma, but it's also (unfortunately) the way most of use make payment. This is because it operates automatically when we do not use a better method.

A better method of resolving karmic debt is in performing acts of service to others; especially those whom we may have harmed in the past (a prior lifetime perhaps). This means has the additional benefit of allowing us to feel good about what we're doing; as opposed to becoming angry over our need to suffer. The third way is similar to the prior; it's in giving love to others without condition. Here the act of service is less defined and tangible. Jesus stressed this method when he encouraged people to love their enemies and bless those who persecuted them. It's not always easy to do, but there are tricks or techniques that can be helpful.

Viewing others as like a young child who doesn't know any better, is one attitude to take that can help one express love to someone who is either threatening or hurtful. Jesus used this method when he forgave those who crucified him: "they know not what they do". It also helps to consider that we are all a part of God, and on the same path toward a full conscious awareness of that fact. Acceptance of the instructional nature of karma also helps, as one considers that the pain we receive is payment of a prior debt of our own, and if this particular individual didn't harm us, then someone else would have; and for our own good. Jesus once said; "it must be that offenses come, but woe to them from whom they come". This can be taken as an affirmation that the pain we experienced had to be experienced from someone, so there is no point in blaming this one. Also, in recognizing that the person who harmed us is also going to require a lesson sometime in the future, we can recognize a benefit for that person by our blessing.

How does one become Saved from one's sins?

The ultimate means of salvation is through what could be called magic or alchemy. This is a sudden change in consciousness brought about by some appropriate ritual. Jews practiced forms of this technique in laying their sins upon a goat, and then freeing to goat, which took away their sins. Sacrificing an unblemished lamb was also, I think, intended to accomplish this function, but it could have degenerated into a mere act of trying to pay off one's debt if there hadn't been a sincere intention of laying one's sins upon the animal before slaughter. Obviously Jesus allowed himself to take the place of the lamb in this ritual, so that those who placed their sins upon him could, through his guiltless death, receive pardon. This is where the idea of faith alone is accurate. Unfortunately, the type of faith required for this to work is sometimes difficult to attain if one possesses too much of a sense of guilt.

In the ritual that Jesus provided us with, we needed to consciously place all of our guilt upon him, retaining nothing in reserve. When we find ourselves too burdened with guilt to be able to possess the degree of faith required to lay all of our sins on Jesus, we continue to feel guilty and to project that guilt onto others; judging them, and refusing to forgive them. When we do that, we make Jesus' sacrifice of no effect for ourselves (at least to the extent that we hold back). What we are left with instead, is an example to follow in our lives which assists us in the process of using the lesser means of escaping karma. Fortunately Jesus also acted as a role model for us to follow so that we can eventually come to the point where we are able to set aside all of our guilt and accept complete forgiveness. He did that by teaching and demonstrating how we might be able to forgive others.

Jesus' teachings very heavily focused upon forgiveness of others, as it is through the act of forgiving others of the harm they caused us, that we become free ourselves, so that we might be able to accept Jesus' sacrifice for our sins. By bringing ourselves to the point whereby we <u>can</u> forgive others, we also bring ourselves to the point whereby we can forgive ourselves as well. And when that happens, then we are able to accept God's forgiveness. In essence, our ability to forgive others and our ability to forgive ourselves are essentially the same; one being a reflection of the other. (Remember what I said about others truly being self? This is the truth that our soul knows and responds to.) It is, then, when we are able to forgive others and self that we are able to possess the faith necessary to receive the grace of God which forgives us of our sins and saves us from the law of karma and the wheel of reincarnation.

When we are not able to truly lay our sins upon Jesus due to excessive feelings of guilt, the sins held back cannot be forgiven through faith. We have essentially denied Jesus' saving grace to some extent, and we will remain under the yoke of sin until our karmic debt is paid. If we can't recognize a feeling of guilt remaining within ourselves, then we can see its evidence in the way that we treat others. If we find ourselves being angry, judgmental, or condemning of another for some wrong, then we can be sure that we are still holding onto guilt for a similar type error that needs to be let go of and "laid at Jesus' feet" for forgiveness. Once we find ourselves able to forgive others of their particular crimes, then we can know that we hold no feelings of guilt for the same type of crime, and that this error can be—or was—forgiven.

According to Edgar Cayce, (I'm paraphrasing), Jesus' act of atonement is only significant to the extent that we apply it in our own lives by forgiving others. Jesus spoke of this condition many times; even providing parables to clarify the law. When Jesus said that in condemning another, we took him off the cross and made his sacrifice as nothing, I believe that he meant it. I also believe he meant it when, after giving us the Lord's Prayer, stating that if we forgive not others, then neither will our heavenly Father forgive us. There's a lot that Jesus taught that the Christian church is unable to accept due to its insistence that there is no rebirth. After all, it's virtually impossible to forgive everyone like Jesus did in only one lifetime; so if this is the only life we have, then God can't be requiring the impossible of this life, and therefore can't really mean it when he expects us to forgive everyone and cease from condemning or judging.

Within the Christian religions there is disagreement as to whether one is saved through faith alone, or if good works is also required. I've partially answered this already; but since very few of us are able to possess the type of faith required to receive a total and absolute remission of guilt, one could say that something akin to good works may also be required. But good works, in order to be of any benefit must be performed with the appropriate motivation, and by themselves do not qualify one to receive grace. Instead these acts of service pay off karmic debt more slowly.

If "being saved" applies to being saved from the consequences of one's earthly sins, so that one can move on (ascend) into higher realms of conscious existence (heaven), then what is truly required (besides losing one's strong attachment to carnal pleasures) is that one ceases to judge others for their actions, forgives others for acts of harm to oneself, truly repents of one's own errors to the extent that a sincere effort is made toward self-improvement, and finally ceases to judge oneself, forgiving self for one's yet unresolved weaknesses. This is what allows one to become able to ask for mercy/grace and have an expectation that one can be forgiven. It isn't easy to do; and that's why most people spend lifetimes on the slow-turning wheel of karma.

It must be remembered that grace is not earned; it is not good karma. Through the law of grace, karma can be resolved when higher consciousness (God) determines that the respective lesson has been learned, and that acceptable efforts have been made to essentially return good for evil. This is where the idea of good works gains validity. It must be remembered, though, that through good deeds one does not earn grace; one merely demonstrates one's change of heart. For this reason, the motivation behind such actions is more important than the action itself. It must also be remembered that if one refuses to forgive others for a failing that one's self possesses, then that failing cannot be forgiven through grace. One cannot receive what one is unwilling or unable to also give.

What counts as good works, are, generally speaking, expressions of love toward others: acts of service or of kindness. For it is in expressing unconditional love toward others that we open ourselves to receiving love from above in the form of grace. But again, I repeat: it's not earned. Through sincere expressions of love toward others, God may—if It feels it to be appropriate—grant us grace and forgive one or more specific karmic debts.

Grace is for all people, not just Christians.

In my opinion, the faith that saves, has very little to do with claiming to be a Christian. In fact, I believe that since Jesus claimed to have died for the sins of all people, that people of any (or no) religious affiliation can receive grace by laying their sins at the feet of either Jesus or God, and demonstrating by their forgiveness of others that they have indeed let go of their guilt. If a person from a religion other than Christianity can believe that this is possible, then for them it is; this is how "faith alone" saves. It's faith that one's own sins <u>can</u> be forgiven. And it's in grateful appreciation for having received this grace that one goes on to be gracious and merciful toward others.

I understand that Lord Krishna also—like Jesus—allowed himself to be an atonement for sins; so Hindus could lay their sins at his feet. There are also Gurus which offer to take on one's karma (sins) and offer Shakti pat—a type of blessing that similarly changes consciousness. Jews have long had the tradition of placing their sins upon a lamb, and offering up their sins with the lamb in an offering to God. This can also bring people to receive grace if they are able to truly do this in their heart. One cannot afterwards condemn others, hold grudges, or declare any to be "sworn enemies"; for this would invalidate the act. When one receives grace, one <u>must</u> be able to extend that grace to others.

I believe that people of any religion can even lay their sins at Jesus' feet, claiming the atonement that he promised to all. I recognize that this assertion might anger some Christians, but I believe that this is what Jesus meant when he said that he died for all. So one could be a practicing Buddhist or Moslem and without changing their religion, or even admitting to others what they have done, can indeed partake of the grace which is freely offered to all <u>who can receive it.</u> I must emphasize the last part of this statement, because it isn't easy sometimes to really let go of one's guilt. This is demonstrated or proven in the way that we find ourselves able to extend that grace to others; forgiving others of any harm they might have caused us.

I also feel comfortable in asserting that one needn't even call upon Jesus' promise to receive forgiveness (if one also goes on to forgive others); though it could help in being able to believe that one could receive grace. The truth, as I feel it, is that God—by any name—is Gracious and Merciful, and will forgive sins (bestow grace to) anyone of any or no religion who truly repents, makes a sincere effort to improve, and who forgives others in return. If you're of a different faith, just try it, and ask your God for confirmation in some way. I cannot believe that anyone who goes to God asking for mercy will be denied it if one truly goes on to forgive others of sins committed against them. After all, this is the example which Jesus set for us all.

I can well imagine that most Christians will disagree with me about that, citing Jesus' assertion that Jesus is the only way to the Father's kingdom, or that only through Jesus can one be saved. So, in reply I'd like to add that Jesus is within all people, regardless of religious affiliation to the extent that they emulate his example of extending unconditional love to others. After all, Jesus said that one cannot love except he be in them.

The Name of Jesus, or In Jesus' Name:

The exoteric or outer, literal view of these phrases is that the literal name is what is significant. The esoteric or inner meaning refers instead to the nature of Jesus. In Judaism, as in many other cultures, names had meaning; they corresponded to one's nature. So the above phrases—from the esoteric viewpoint—are saying that only through the nature of Jesus can one ascend to the Father, or be saved, or have prayers answered. Reference to the name of Jesus, then is a reference to following his example; recognizing him as the way to God by virtue of following in his footsteps. This was confirmed by Jesus when he said that one must pick up their own cross and follow him. The example he set, and the pattern that he followed, is one that we all must follow to reach the higher planes; whether we believe in Jesus or not. One can be a Hindu, Buddhist, Moslem, Jew, or Secular Humanist, and still be following Jesus to the Father.

To those who insist upon the literal meaning of the word, I'd like to suggest that Jesus wasn't even Jesus' name. It's a Greek name assigned to the Nazarene called Yeshua (or Jesu or Jehashua, or any of the other names people have attributed to him). In fact, some even suggest that the one called Jesus was really a collage of two or more individuals; that sacred writings from several sources were combined into one to create the persona that is identified as Jesus. This is not an important detail to me, but it may be to others of you, so I won't make any solid claims about these assertions. As far as I'm concerned, they're all here-say.

As far as praying "in Jesus name", I'd also like to point out that doing something in somebody else's name, indicates that one is acting as an agent of that named person; acting in their interests as they would do if they were present. So with this understanding, again, reference to the name of Jesus is a reference to Jesus as the way, an example to emulate. This is true whether one is seeking a way to the God, or seeking an answer to prayer. And with regard to prayer; anybody who has ended their prayer, saying: "in Jesus name", must know by now that these magic words don't guarantee the positive result that Jesus promised. Prayer in the name of Jesus should be a prayer for the best for others; an act of love and compassion, devoid of selfish interest. It would be the type of prayer that Jesus would have asked had he been present.

How to Pray Effectively:

Jesus gave us two conditions under which prayer would be answered (and not with a "no"). The first is that we pray "in Jesus name", and the other that we ask in faith; "believing".

94

In praying in "Jesus name", we ask something that Jesus would have asked; something that's the best for all concerned; not something just for self, to improve one's own quality of life. This is a prayer, generally, for someone else's welfare; something that we would have no reservations about asking. The requirement that we be able to believe that the prayer can be granted, means that we must be able to feel—on a subconscious level—that the prayer is worthy of being granted, and that there are no reservations or doubts held by our subconscious mind in regard to its being answered.

As an example, I'll relate a prayer request that was granted to me when I was on a fishing trip with my uncle and a couple of his friends. This was during Spring break during my senior year of college, when my friends were going to Florida. My uncle invited me to join his friends on an ice fishing trip; a "coming of age" invitation I didn't want to pass up. The trip was for a weekend in the cold North, and we tried several of my uncle's favorite spots during the first two days, but without any luck. On the final day, I could empathize with his disappointment, as he really wanted to show me a good time, and to demonstrate how capable as fishermen they were. At the last spot, close to our base camp, I prayed that we would finally find success. My plea was for my uncle; that he be able to salvage his pride and make the trip a success. Actually, I was having a good time, regardless; but I could feel his disappointment and wounded pride in not being able to find where the fish were. In asking that I catch the biggest fish, I felt that this would be what he would have liked as well; as it would have been his gift to me; something he would have taken pride in.

While praying, I searched my heart to perceive if I had any reservations as to why the prayer could not be granted; and feeling that there were none, continued to pray until I felt that the request would be granted. I called on Jesus' promises, and affirmed that I wasn't totally asking for myself, but mostly for my uncle and his friends. I continued to pray until I felt that I had received an assurance that my request would be granted. Essentially, I prayed until I could feel the faith that was required.

Within five minutes of completing my prayer, I hooked onto a 5 pound Lake Trout, and soon after, the others also started catching fish. It seemed as though a school of them had come by. By the time we quit that evening, all but one of us had caught our limit of 3 fish, and that one went out the following morning to catch the final fish to achieve his limit. It turned out just the way I asked; with myself catching the biggest, and my uncle—as well as his friends—being proud that they were able to show me a good time, and demonstrate that they knew where to go for a successful fishing trip.

The key to the prayer's success, I believe, was in gaining the cooperation or consent of my subconscious mind. I had no reservations that my request wouldn't be granted; as I was not being selfish, but instead was asking for others' welfare. I also prayed until I could feel within, an assurance that my prayer would be granted. Belief is not a mental activity; it's not something that we can obtain purely from a desire to have the prayer granted. Faith comes when the unconscious mind agrees to the justification for the request; and in giving its consent, allows us to know it.

Jesus as "The Way":

When Jesus said that he was "the way", he was saying he was an example; that we must pick up our own crosses (karmic debts) and follow his example of forgiving others, just as he forgave those who crucified him.

I often wondered, as a youth, why it seemed that Jesus was so often wrong (from the church's viewpoint) in what he taught or in what he told people were necessary things to do. By "wrong" I mean that what he taught was not what the church taught. An example is the rich youth who asked what he needed to do to be saved. Jesus didn't say; "believe on me"; instead he pointed out an area of difficulty for the lad: his wealth. This assertion of Jesus' contradicted the teachings of my church, essentially making him wrong. The church of my youth taught that all Jesus' teachings were essentially trumped or over-ruled by the fact of his later dying on the cross and rising again. When I pointed out that Jesus said sins wouldn't be forgiven if we don't forgive, I was told that Jesus' sacrifice even forgave us for that; essentially invalidating Jesus' teachings. Now; did Jesus not know that he was wrong, or was he a liar?

It bothered me, too, that Jesus dedicated most of his ministry to telling people to forgive others, to love others, to help others, and to refrain from judging anybody; but then the church declares that these are just good guidelines to follow, not something we really have to do to be saved. The belief that faith alone saves, makes a mockery of so much of Jesus' teachings that one wonders if he even knew what he was talking about. I think that it was rather the church that misunderstood Jesus' teachings.

I raised the question to a minister when I was a young adult; raising the question of whether we're truly forgiven if we continue to perform the same sin over and over again. He said that the church uses the two truths to keep people in line. If people start feeling too guilty, they preach the gospel of grace to them. On the other hand, if people get too lax in curbing their expressions, then he throws the law of sin at them. By using this technique a person can never feel totally secure in receiving atonement for sin. This admission helped me to recognize that even the church doesn't clearly understand the path to "salvation".

Jesus was very clear that we not judge others or else we would be judged—faith or no faith. He was also very clear that if we failed to forgive others, then we could not be forgiven. Unfortunately, by holding to the claim that upon death there is only two places to go, and no rebirth or opportunity to continue the process of meeting Jesus' requirements, then of course one has to toss out all Jesus commandments; taking them as requests maybe.

If people were to truly recognize Jesus as the way, then they would try their best to follow his teachings, and use him as an ideal in conducting their own lives; he would be the pattern to follow, the one to emulate in life. People would, then, cease judgment, forgive others, and patiently accept the challenges that they must bear.

Remember, though; the voice calling for repentance preceded the arrival of the Savior. This was to demonstrate that before one can be able to forgive, one must first repent of one's own failings; and commit oneself to a program of self-improvement whereby all past sins can be washed away.

Non-judgment and Forgiveness:

Since forgiveness and non-judgment are so crucial for us, and so difficult to master, a bit of a commentary on the subject may be helpful. Jesus actually gave us some really good tips on how to be able to accomplish these necessities of life; but the church gives them little emphasis because they place so little value on actually becoming non-judgmental and forgiving. In my opinion, these are the two most important subjects contained in the Bible; and for that matter, the most important subjects contained in this book. Mastering these can truly set us free. In fact, I believe that they can set anyone free, regardless of religious belief, if they are truly followed.

Through Jesus' ministry, he provided us with some very helpful tips on how to come to be able to forgive self and others; and these generally consisted of helping us to gain a different attitude toward the subject. At the end of this section I will describe these as best as I have come to understand them, and add several insights of my own. But before I do this, I want to clear up some misunderstandings with regard to what I believe forgiveness and non-judgment really are; and are not. And most important, I hope to show the interrelatedness of self forgiveness and forgiveness of others; they are so interconnected that I believe it to be virtually impossible to be able to forgive others unless one is truly cognizant of one's own failings, and sincerely desirous of remedying them.

Every soul is predestined to return—in consciousness—to God; how far the soul chooses to delve into the lower realms (frequencies) determines the range and scope of lessons that must be learned in order to re-ascend. People cannot, then, escape the necessity of experiencing the consequences of their choices; and this is usually accomplished through the law of karma, whereby individuals are given the opportunity to experience for themselves the results of choices that they made in the past. This relates not only to physical actions, but to attitudes or beliefs held. As an example, a wealthy individual who lacks compassion for the poor will be given the opportunity to be poor, and learn how it feels to have compassion denied. The intent is not to punish the offender, but to educate; to show—in the most demonstrative way—the way others are affected by one's own poor choice or expression.

Forgiving another of an action against self, dissolves the karmic bond—of cause and effect—that would otherwise lead you into needing another relationship with the individual, so that you would have the opportunity to cause the other the same type of pain you received prior. So essentially, by forgiving, you set yourself free as well. You do not, though, absolve the individual of any harm committed against others; nor do you remove the necessity of that individual's learning the appropriate lesson. They just won't be learning it through you.

By forgiving another, you are not, therefore, letting that person "get away with it" in the over-all sense; only with regard to the singular action involving you. If that person is causing the same pain to others, or that individual's action toward you is a result of some area of ignorance, then the person will be provided with as many opportunities as are necessary to replace the ignorance with wisdom.

I must say, though, that if you do choose to forgive a person of their action against you, and you do it with the feeling of satisfaction that the individual will receive "their just rewards" from someone else, or in some other situation, you should ask yourself if you are truly forgiving. It could be that you are still seeking retribution; but just don't want to get involved yourself. The test, I suppose, is with regard to how compassionate you feel toward the one who hurt you.

The attitude toward an offender that feels most appropriate to me is the recognition that if I was harmed, then the offender is probably harming others and has a difficult lesson to learn. This recognition causes me to feel compassion for the offender, for I know from my own experience how difficult life's lessons can be. This feeling of compassion, then, leads me into desiring that this person suffer as little as possible in order to learn the required lesson. I don't desire that this person suffer any more than is necessary, and I don't desire that any pain come as a result of retribution on my behalf. This feeling of compassion stems from a feeling of empathy I have for the offender; because I have learned for myself just how painful some learning experiences can be, and I wouldn't want another to have to suffer as I have.

Now, having the attitude that I just described, though close to ideal, is not likely to be felt by a victim unless the victim has already learned the specific lesson involved. You have to remember that experiences of pain are almost always karmic lessons. This should lead those who find themselves to be victims of others' actions, to consider whether or not they are truly innocent themselves, or whether they are learning a lesson. And if it's a lesson, then one should more appropriately thank and bless the "teacher", rather than desire retribution. This is why it is so necessary to recognize that the law of karma (unless absolved through grace) is always active, and always providing us with lessons until we truly learn the most harmonious way to live with others.

Now this makes it sound as though one can't really be able to forgive another until one has already learned the appropriate lesson; and that's very close to being true. The best reply to this is to consider that this injustice experienced is the final test in this particular course, and that if the correct response is provided, that this type of pain won't have to be experienced again. With this attitude, one can then put the emphasis upon one's own state of consciousness, and perceive the offender as someone who will have to pay a price for providing this most welcome gift. I say "welcome gift" because it provides a victim with the opportunity to give the "right" answer to the test, and therefore become free of this particular karma or lesson.

To better illustrate this, let me give you an example from my own experience. My first job after graduating from college was in a small company that's owner had a fiery temper. This didn't affect me until I made a significant mistake that cast doubt upon my loyalty to the company. The owner called me to task for it in a fit of temper, and I was so affected by his demeanor that I was unable to satisfactorily stand up for myself and communicate to him that the accusation wasn't warranted. As a result of this I was fired.

Fortunately I had already gained the respect of an individual who had recently left the company to start his own business with a partner, and he offered me a job working with him that held a lot of promise for advancement. Unfortunately, though, this man's partner also had a bad temper which was very problematic for me; because, where I had a college education this man only had an 8th grade education—he had learned the business from experience alone. As a result, he was constantly looking for excuses to prove that he knew better than I, and couldn't accept that at times I knew better than he. This led to many occasions when he would blow up at me, and this was a constant irritant to me. On one occasion his outburst got me so angered that I couldn't keep my mind on what I was doing and almost blinded myself. My unease and anger built until after another of his tantrums, I quit the job. I was so angered at this man that I couldn't even focus on writing a resume, much less seeking another job.

When my unemployment benefits were coming to a conclusion, though, I took a step down to work for a small company in a slightly different field of work. And you've probably guessed it; the owner of this company also had a nasty temper. It was while working for this company that I learned about life lessons, and started the process of considering what it was that I needed to learn from this type of experience. I realized that I too had a temper at times, and that it was a very immature means of achieving control and of defending oneself against the possibility of disagreement. I began to see it as an immature indication of insecurity; quite the opposite of what it appeared to be on the surface.

The next time my boss flared up at me, not only wasn't I bothered by it, I had a hard time keeping myself from smiling; I could see through his façade! Well, it wasn't long after that when I realized I wasn't going anywhere with that company, and had an opportunity to start my own business, so I gave him notice and left under good terms. Having my own business, though, didn't shield me from people with tempers, though; as two of my clients were men who used temper tantrums to control their workers. But the surprising thing is that neither of them flared up at me, even when we had a disagreement, or they didn't like the way I was servicing them. For some reason they restrained their unhappiness and we were able to work out our differences in a more mature manner. But these were only two; most of my clients had excellent personalities, and I never had to deal with tempers again.

The fact is, I was able to see the cause of my own tendency to have a fit, and in recognizing why I would occasionally blow up, was able to curb that expression of my own. Now, I'm not perfect—far from it—and I've even used temper since (sorry dad), but when I have it's been with an acknowledgment that I was acting out a role to produce a specific desired response. In other words, I wasn't being victimized myself by this unconscious impulse; but rather chose to use the expression because I consciously felt that it was the best way to accomplish my purpose. The most important part of this story I haven't revealed yet; and that's the most important part.

Over the years I had held onto anger towards my prior two bosses; especially the second one. I felt hurt and cheated, and was so angry at him I could hardly think straight when I thought of the pain I had experienced from him. It wasn't just the temper; there were a lot of issues that made me angry toward this man; and I didn't even consider the possibility of forgiving him. After I learned what I needed to with regard to temper tantrums, though, seeing them as expressions if immaturity and insecurity, I felt totally different toward this man and my first boss as well: the one that fired me. I was finally able to forgive them; and I didn't even think of myself as having done so. It's more that all my anger seemed so unnecessary or uncalled for. These men were no longer victimizers in my mind, but rather teachers; and rather than be angry at them, I owed them gratitude for providing me with the experiences I needed in order to learn a necessary lesson.

Now, this isn't the only lesson I've needed to learn in life. I've had others far more painful. But what helps me to deal with the pain I experience from others' actions, is the recognition that I'm not a victim as much as a student, and that those who hurt me would have to pay a price for the benefit that they provide to me; and this produces a feeling of indebtedness to them, and compassion for them as regards lessons they will need to be learning. Forgiveness is then rather easy to do. In fact, I don't even think of it as forgiveness. I just lose the feeling of judgment. After all, one cannot forgive unless a judgment has already been made. In changing my perception, I have begun to perceive those who hurt me as teachers who are assisting me. And how can I find fault with that? And in recognizing that their expression is a good indicator that they have lessons to learn, I can feel compassion for them out of a feeling of empathy; for I know how much I don't like to learn hard lessons.

In describing my own experiences and feelings I don't intend to be boasting about any of my achievements (that's a good way to set oneself up for a humbling experience), but rather to express how so many different facets of the subject all tie together within the subject of forgiveness. The alternative is a detailed analysis which I'm not sure I can communicate well enough to be clearly understood.

There is an obvious connection between the necessity of looking honestly at one's own attitudes and expressions when bothered by someone else's. This is because the other's is a reflection of one's own. If this were not so, it wouldn't bother one much. In fact, I'd suggest that the degree, to which another's actions bother one, reflects the degree to which one has a personal shortcoming of one's own to consider and resolve. This consideration, though, should not result in a feeling of guilt, but rather of understanding and acceptance. This can only occur, in my opinion, when one is humble enough to admit that one isn't perfect, and does have issues in need of adjustment. With this attitude, one is more open to being grateful for the experience which revealed an area of one's life that could stand for improvement. And if one can become grateful on the basis of having a true desire for self-improvement, then forgiveness is almost automatic; in fact one may not even make a judgment at all. And if one does, it certainly shouldn't be harsh, but rather mixed with a feeling of compassion.

There are many tricks or techniques a person can use which can aid one in being able to set aside anger for being harmed. This anger is, after all, the emotion that causes one to judge another and desire retribution. It certainly prevents a person from being able to forgive.

Jesus offered a very helpful suggestion when he suggested that one turn the other cheek. What this does is take part of the blame off of the other person and place it on oneself. It's difficult to continue to be angry at another for hurting you when you ask for it again; for now you'd have to blame yourself as much as the one who hurt you. It's also an affirmation to oneself that the injury wasn't such a big deal if you can accept a repeat.

Jesus suggesting that you give a cloak too when someone asks for your coat, or going two miles when someone asks you to go one, are further examples of this same strategy. When one willingly allows oneself to suffer, it's more difficult to blame someone else for doing the same.

When I was fired from that first job, I had been angry at a co-worker who would keep bumming cigarettes, and never bought me a pack to compensate me. He had also borrowed a book from me and never got around to returning it. After I left and moved out of state to my next job I kept thinking of this man's injustice, and would get angry. And now that I was a distance away it seemed that he would get away with what he took from me. When I finally realized that my anger was hurting me more than the loss of a book and cigarettes, I decided to turn my other cheek. I took a similar book of mine, and an amount of money equivalent to the cost of the cigarettes he had bummed, and mailed them to him. And guess what. I was free! I was never again bothered by his lack of consideration.

Years later I had another friend who kept borrowing money with the promise of repaying me. Well, after this turned into a couple thousand dollars, I realized I would never get it back; and I hated being used as a chump as much as I hated losing the money. Years later, though, I thought I had a really good investment tip, and put all my available funds into it. Well, the tip wasn't so good after all; in fact it was horrible. I lost practically everything. But you know what? After that I was no longer angry at the friend who made me a chump. I had just made myself a chump and lost more money than my friend took. In fact, had my friend repaid me, I'd probably have invested and lost that as well. So, though it wasn't an intentional turning of the cheek, it accomplished the same result. I believe that this technique works because we often don't perceive a fault in ourselves that is being reflected by someone else's behavior. And if the fault originated in a prior life, it would be very difficult to recognize it.

It may well have been that I had known this man in another life and the tables had been turned the other way, whereby I failed to repay a loan that he extended to me. This is how personal karma often works out. I wish the Bible contained references to this type of karma (The Aquarian Gospel of Jesus Christ by Levi does.), but I believe that it was what Jesus was hinting at when he said to pick up one's own cross and follow him. In this case, the cross to bear was the karmic debt. Recognition of this need to resolve past issues through karmic results also provides a helpful way to become able to forgive. This is because the recognition of an error within self, or a lesson to be learned, helps to adjust one's attitude so forgiveness is possible.

By considering that present unpleasant experiences can be karmic repercussions of actions performed in an earlier life (debts that need to be paid) one's attitude can likewise change; by changing the paradigm from which the experience is viewed. It would be helpful to remember, though, that the present experience isn't intended to be punishment (though it does serve to mitigate subconscious guilt); its primary purpose is to allow one to forgive oneself—in this case the self that lived some life in the past—for the type of expression now being experienced by another's poor choosing. Once the current offender is forgiven, the prior self's expression is also forgiven. Truly we do forgive self when we are able to forgive others. And when we are truly able to forgive ourselves, then forgiveness of others becomes much easier. In fact we may find ourselves not even judging them as having need of forgiveness.

Also, when finding ourselves able to forgive some act of harm from others, which occurred as a result of karma, or as a lesson to be learned, we can experience a significant feeling of freedom. This is because we can recognize that our debt has been paid, and that by demonstrating that we've "learned our lesson", maybe we won't have to have this type of experience again. It provides a sense of invulnerability, then, to that type of experience in the future.

When on the cross, Jesus asked his Father's forgiveness, for those who were crucifying him, on the basis that they didn't know what they were doing. Here Jesus offered us a justification that we can use to adjust our own attitude toward offenders of any type. By recognizing that people cause harm to others out of ignorance because they just haven't yet learned their lessons, one can begin to perceive less need for blame. We don't blame our children for failing to succeed in something they haven't yet learned how to do; so the same attitude can be held for others who cause harm for the same reason. Even premeditated acts of harm to others, where it is known that injuries will result, are acts of ignorance. These people just haven't yet learned that we are all a part of the same whole; that their ultimate happiness can only come through expressions of love; and that they will eventually have to meet the consequences of their actions.

This perception of those who intentionally harm others can be most helpful in allowing one to feel compassion for them. And with the feeling of compassion (love) there is no desire for retribution. And the judgment is rather in the form of recognition that they have something to learn. In fact, they could be doing the very best that they can at the present moment. We just can't know what problems or challenges another is facing when they cause us harm. When we can successfully shift our viewpoint in this way, our attitude toward them will also shift making forgiveness that much easier.

In one of Jesus' sermons, he is credited with advising us to pray for and bless those who use or harm us. This is an outgrowth of the recognition that others will have to pay a price for their ignorant acts. Our prayers and blessings will be helpful to them, so that they can more readily learn their lessons and move on; ceasing to harm others in like fashion in the future.

Jesus said; "It must be that offenses come, but woe to those from whom they come." In this, he was pointing out the need we often have of being on the receiving end of some offense for our own learning and growth, and how it takes others to provide us with these needed experiences. It also emphasizes that these "teachers" or "lesson providers" will have unpleasant experiences themselves as a result of having fallen victim, so to speak, of our need for the lesson.

On this basis, we should pray for them, and grant them a blessing; even (if it is possible) out of a sense of gratitude for the service that they have provided for us at their own personal expense. This view can also help us to be able to forgive more easily. It helps us to lose the desire for retribution.

Perhaps the most important thing to consider when desiring to escape karmic debt and learn our lessons is that it's often easier to forgive others, than it is to forgive ourselves. This is because we usually have higher expectations for our own conduct than we do for others'. Self-forgiveness is a vital necessity if we are to move on and grow into higher states of consciousness. One cannot fully love others until one is truly able to love one's self. And to do this, we need to be honest with ourselves, and recognize that we aren't perfect, and that some of our short-comings will have to be accepted and lived with our entire lives.

Yes, some tendencies or attitudes are relatively easy to change. But some others, especially compulsions, may be very deep seated into our subconscious through childhood programming, and very difficult to resolve. Though counseling can help, often we need to just accept our weaknesses, do the best as we are able to mitigate them, and rest in the hope that they will not follow us beyond the end of this life. This is where the serenity prayer can be most helpful:

Serenity Prayer:

God grant me the serenity to accept the things I cannot change;
courage to change the things I can;
and wisdom to know the difference.

The tendency to judge people for their actions also interferes with our desire to be forgiving. When we judge someone's action to be "bad", we tend to judge the person to be bad as well. This can lead us to act inappropriately to the person in the future, causing the individual to treat us accordingly. The solution is to separate the action from the person who performed it. There is a saying that goes something like this: Love the person but not the act. After all, there is a lot of good in the worst of us; and a little bad in the best of us. But I have another suggestion.

One doesn't need to label anything—people or actions—as being either "good" or "bad". One can just see things for what they are. A murder cuts short a person's life, preventing them from being able to enjoy a longer life. A theft causes a person to suffer a loss that can be painful. An assault causes injury to a person, hurting them physically and emotionally. A judgment makes it difficult for a person to respect and esteem another, inhibiting one's ability to love the other.

God *does not* show Favoritism:

Perhaps the most difficult misconception held by religions is their belief that God favors their own religion over others; or worse yet, that God will punish those who accept other faiths. This belief not only interferes with people's ability to forgive and be forgiven, it severely inhibits their ability to love others as God commands in every major religion.

It's understandable how the misunderstanding can occur, though. Religions are social structures that depend upon the loyalty of their followers to function well and survive. Also where beliefs among religions exist, each religion is inclined to discourage people from considering the alternate view. It then becomes a matter of self-survival to convince followers or possible converts that their product is the only acceptable one. They might even make threats to keep their followers loyal. These beliefs, then, are most often based upon self-interest, rather than upon ultimate truth.

When one accepts the notion that people reincarnate into different lives, it can then be recognized that each major religion has its own unique qualities which may make it more or less desirable for a specific individual who comes into the world with specific lessons to learn. It could be, for example, that a person very wrapped up in material pursuits and desires might choose to come back as a Buddhist, and spend much time in meditation; in renunciation of physical possessions. A Christian who paid little attention to obeying God's laws might choose to come back as a Moslem or Jew; and if there was prejudice toward either religion, then that would be the likely one to choose. On the other hand, a Jew or Moslem who became excessively focused upon trying to obey strict laws might choose to return as a Christian and learn tolerance and forgiveness. And members of any religion, who held strong animosity or prejudice toward any other religion, would most likely reincarnate into the religion so that they can learn to appreciate and respect that religion as well.

Every religion has its strong points and short-comings. If there is a religion that has it all, I haven't become acquainted with it yet. Perhaps a non-sectarian religion that offers the best qualities of all the religions would appeal to me. But it would have to be very open-ended, because there is still so much about reality that I still want to understand. A focus upon meditation and dreams would be a requirement; as would a de-emphasis upon any leader or teacher. I think everyone has something to teach, that nobody has a monopoly on wisdom, and that we don't need to go through an intermediary (particularly an incarnate one) in order to reach God.

The Origin of Religions:

If one were to look back toward the time when today's major religions came into being, they will find that an enlightened individual recognized significant failings in the existing beliefs held by the culture, obtained inspiration with regard to new understandings, and set out to teach those to the populous. The result was the formation of a Divinely Inspired religion to displace the existing beliefs <u>of that particular culture at that particular time.</u> And on that basis it was both true and appropriate that the religion teach that their way was the only way to God; for it was the only way for those people at that time.

Returning to present time, when advancements in communication and travel have brought cultures out of isolation and into contact with each other, there becomes a situation—as we have today—whereby these superior religions begin to clash when they each continue to declare that their own religion is the only way. This is most unfortunate; for though it may have been true at one time, it is no longer true.

Consider an analogy whereby people living in Chicago feel a need that they can't satisfy. Somebody realizes that what they seek can be found in Wichita Kansas, and gives them driving directions to get there. They take these instructions and print them in attractive fonts and bind the pages in gold-leafed leather booklets, and distribute these throughout the city. Soon word spreads and soon people obtain this vital information and praise the man who provided it. They write stories about the man, write songs praising his great wisdom, erect statues in his honor, and even build architectural wonders adorned with gold and precious stones, within which they worship the man. And though many of the people start out on the journey proscribed, only one or two of them ever complete the trip to receive the benefit of the information he gave them.

Now, about the same time, people living in New York City also felt a similar lacking; and they too didn't know where to find resolution. A woman in their midst, however, remembered from her childhood that what they needed could be found in Wichita Kansas, so she spread the word and wrote out driving instructions, which were also printed and bound in beautiful booklets which became circulated among the NYC residents. And as in Chicago, people wrote stories and songs, erected statues and built monumental structures in order to worship and praise this woman; but though many started out on the proscribed path, only one or two actually finished the trip to receive the benefit she provided.

This same situation also developed in Houston and Los Angeles with identical results. After a number of years, through advances in communication, the people from each of these four cities began to share the great wisdom that they had received from their respective enlightened teachers whom they adored, and were angered to learn that there were three other cities making the same promises; yet the holy books which these other cities were circulating gave different messages, and were telling people to do things contrary to that of their own sacred texts. This resulted in great conflicts among them, for each group feared that the others' instructions were not only faulty, but intentionally misleading.

Eventually the residents of Wichita heard about the fighting and accusations, and even obtained copies of some of the various texts; but since they had lived in the city and never found the remedy that was proclaimed to be found there, they dismissed the whole thing; concluding that all the teachings were false, and that those who promoted them were obviously trying to mislead people. It's a shame too, because had they compared and studied the instructions contained within the four different texts, they would have found a commonality that would have led them to the prize that had been in their midst all these years without their even realizing it.

Those who did persevere in studying their various texts, and followed the guidelines that they contained to the very end, came to make a most unexpected discovery; for in the midst of a large public park, in a seldom used area of the park, they located a deep crevice in a rocky ledge. And lodged deep within the crevice, as though lost by someone many years ago, they could see a small golden ruler with one small word inscribed upon it. That word was **Love.**

After contemplating this, they came to realize how simple and yet profound, the remedy was; then their hearts fully opened and all their prior fears and unhappy feelings just melted away, dissolving into nothingness. Anxious to share their discovery with their neighbors back home, they each set out to return to their native cities and share the wisdom that they had found.

But because their message was so simple, nobody would listen; the people were so caught up with the rites, rituals and practices that they had developed to honor the one who gave them the directions, and so preoccupied with defending the legitimacy of their instructions against the challenges from those who were declaring their own to be the only valid ones, that they couldn't even start to consider something so simple. They couldn't even bring themselves to take the trip themselves, because in order to do that they'd have to leave behind all that which they had dedicated themselves to building, and which had given them a small measure of satisfaction with their lives. They dared not lose that now in a pursuit for truth; they promised themselves, instead, that they'd go there after they retired, or at the end of their life.

Though it is not my intention to be offensive or critical, this story (though presenting an exaggerated situation) reflects to an extent what I feel to be a reflection of religious attitudes around the world. I do recognize that the great majority of people of religious faith do follow their own religion's teachings and practices as much as they are able, and as it relates to the previous story-line, may feel that they are on their way to Wichita, or have indeed found what they were directed to find there. My only reply to this, then, is: What have you found? For if you have not found yourself able to love all others unconditionally, and to apply the wisdom contained in "The Golden Rule" (Do unto others as you would have them do unto you.), then perhaps you are still on the path; or that you—as the story suggested—followed it for a ways and then turned back as did those in the story.

Too many people, in my opinion, seem to put more emphasis upon worshiping the teacher than actually applying the lesson, and many well intentioned people, dedicated to their particular faith, fight with those from different cultures who were brought up to accept different religious beliefs and customs. I consider it to be very unfortunate, when a close inspection of the teachings of all religions point to the same destination. Why is it so hard for people to set aside their differences and love each other unconditionally? Is it really so hard to forgive?

Yes, people can always compare details of any other religion to their own, and find areas of conflict; but though there can well be room for improvement, there is still very much that is of value to those who are inspired to accept that faith as their own. If there wasn't value for them, their own spirit (soul) would inspire them to seek elsewhere (as I was inspired to do during my youth). Hopefully, if and when this happens, the seekers will hold fast to their personal connection with God, so that they may be open to following Its inspiration and guidance during their search.

I don't intend to infer that I oppose the act of evangelism; whereby people actively try to gain converts to their own religions. If it isn't overly intrusive, it can be of great benefit to many. Exchanges in ideas and opinions can motivate people to consider different options. I do not, however, support acts of violence in the exchange; and neither do I believe threats that invoke fear should be used as a selling technique. In all expressions, I believe that acts of love should dominate. Hopefully this book will be considered to be among these.

When Jesus sent his disciples out into the world, asking them to teach others what he had commanded them to do (love, judge not, resist not and forgive), I believe that they did a pretty good job in following his request. Many years later when the Christian (Catholic) Religion was established in Rome, the founders made what I consider to be some major errors. These could have resulted from simple misunderstandings, their intentions could have unknowingly been corrupted by an overly zealous attempt to do what they thought to be God's will, or there could have been some baser motives involved. One can only speculate. Regardless, the teachings that they ended up promoting and emulating in their methods, were—in some respects—at variance with what Jesus had taught or commanded. Incredibly horrible acts of genocide resulted; and over a long period of time, affecting civilizations around the world. Now, this is all in the past now, so I don't intend to dwell on it; but I do want to use it as evidence that mankind can very easily corrupt some very pure teachings. And though this can occur for a number of reasons, the desire for power and control is certainly an influence that must be watched out for, when considering any religious policies, teachings or practices.

The Origin and Purpose of Religious Law:

In the beginning of soul's expression in human form, there were no laws or rules to guide them in their expressions. In primitive states of being, people conducted themselves very much like animals. Lacking guidance they competed with each other in pursuit of their pleasures and desires, and the strongest dominated over the weak causing suffering and pain.

In order to provide a way out of this state of chaos, forces of higher consciousness (or God) inspired enlightened beings to provide order through the creation of civilizations united under a set of laws. Stories accompanied these laws in order to provide them with validation and interest; also a hierarchy of leadership was established, and given the authority to maintain order and ensure the survival of the society; functions of government and religion were provided by the same social order.

In looking back into history, the above pattern seems to have prevailed throughout the world within various racial groups. I find it particularly interesting in recognizing, in fact, that there were several different races, inferring that the origins of humankind were biologically influenced; perhaps by the same agents who provided the social structures. This supports the assertions of the Genesis story that races of people were made in the image of their creators, and validates the early laws forbidding one to marry outside their group.

It's very likely that at the time these laws were written, there were indeed human forms that were little more than intelligent animals; so that sexual unions with these could adversely affect the integrity of the favored race: the race created and chosen by the god-like entities to become the dominant society.

Virtually every early civilization around the world had its own racial type, own set of laws, and own unique stories which together identified the group, the society, and the religion. And as long as these diverse ethnic, religious, social groups retained their own isolation from other groups, they survived well and functioned to provide a viable and satisfactory society. Each seemed to have been inspired by their religion to build monuments and structures to honor their god(s), which provided them with their needs and social order.

Central toward the success and survival of these early civilizations, were sets of laws which affected virtually every aspect of their living. These covered health issues as well as rules of conduct; and almost universally set a double standard with respect to relationships with those outside their social group. These latter laws were very likely put into place to ensure the purity of the race and ensure that their own society would have dominion over any others; a necessity for their own survival during these primitive and vulnerable times.

Since early mankind was ignorant with regard to appropriate foods to eat, and other health-related issues, many laws were written for guidance in these areas. The enlightened beings that created these civilizations had far greater knowledge than their people, so it was their responsibility to ensure that the ignorant were raised to follow sound principles and guidelines. These higher entities or lesser gods (acting under the will of God, and through Its inspiration) performed a role for their respective civilizations that can be likened to that of present-day parents in raising their children.

When children are very young and ignorant, like the early civilizations, strict rules are necessary to protect them from harm: stay away from strangers, don't handle knives, don't play with fire, go to bed and take naps when told, don't eat this or that, and don't hurt your siblings. These rules that were created for early civilizations, as with those for young children, were very necessary and appropriate then; but what about later? What would happen if the ones who gave them their laws and social order were to leave them, or die?

Children, like civilizations, eventually begin to mature; and within that process it is most appropriate that the strict laws become more flexible so that more responsibility can be given to children to further their education and prepare them for adulthood. There must come a time when children are allowed to establish their own rules of conduct within a less restrictive framework of higher laws. Certainly laws with respect to causing harm to others need to be retained firmly in place, but other laws need to be relaxed or set aside; so that children, like civilizations, will have the opportunity to grow in wisdom on the basis of their own learning and experiences.

This need for entities to grow spiritually, based upon their own unique set of life experiences, makes it difficult for them when old laws are held rigidly to, long after their usefulness has been accomplished. In this I am referring to laws which restrict the freedom of women, keeping them under the dominion of men. Since the reasons for these early laws were not passed down with the laws, a discussion of this subject is appropriate here.

Male and Female Relationships:

Before souls "fell" and required a physical existence for their spiritual evolution, they lacked a sexual identity; they possessed the qualities of both sexes as we know them. This is reflected in the Genesis story wherein

"Adam" was first created in a state of being "alone". When "god" was said to have decided that it was not good that man be alone, it was in reference to the recognition of the need for the androgynous beings (represented by Adam) to be sexually oriented in order to better assist their development. The "rib" which was removed from the androgynous soul was rather its feminine nature; the androgynous "alone" soul then becoming two separate sexually polarized entities. The masculine male was expressive in nature, acting on the basis of mental reasoning (left brain), while the feminine woman was receptive in nature; her purpose being to inspire (not nag) the masculine man into courses of action. This relationship is expressed by the fact of "Eve" being the one tempted, and "Adam" following her suggestion to eat.

It is because the receptive nature is susceptible to all forms of temptation, including influence from astral beings, that the rational or mental faculties were so much needed to be stronger and more in control of the decision-making process during the early years of humankinds earthly experience. This is why laws were written in such detail, delineating virtually every aspect of one's life. Mankind just was too lacking in personal wisdom to be able to make good decisions on its own. Without a number of lifetime experiences, souls lacked the capacity to make sound moral choices on their own, so they required a set of laws covering every aspect of their life, in order to successfully navigate early lifetimes in this physical dimension. The intuitive/receptive nature of early mankind could not be trusted to provide reliable guidance; it was too innocent and naïve, lacking in the variety of human experiences necessary to allow it to eventually learn how to discern temptation from inspiration.

I want to make it very clear that I'm not only speaking of early men and early women; I'm speaking of the early masculine and feminine nature of early mankind. The confusion arises from the fact that at the early stages of our evolution, they were essentially the same. At the time souls first began to incarnate in this realm, and religions were first established, the male was very masculine in its expression, and the female was very feminine in hers. The man could only act on the basis of reasoning, and couldn't trust the judgment of the woman who received impulses and urges, but lacked the ability to discern a proper course of action to take.

It was for this reason that the institution of marriage was established, and why the woman was put in a submissive role. The couple represented the split androgynous soul which incarnated, and by living and working together, they would—through repeated lifetimes and experiences—eventually come to a point whereby both men and women would be equally balanced in their masculine and feminine qualities.

Also, through repeated lifetimes and experiences of a wide variety, souls (both men and women) would grow in wisdom and understanding, so that they would be better able to discern which impulses or desires from their receptive nature would be better ignored or acted upon.

No longer Children:

With men and women both increasing in wisdom, it must be recognized that it isn't best to treat them like children any more. And with the balancing of people's masculine and feminine natures, as a result of lifetimes of experience, the early laws have become both unnecessary and inappropriate with respect to the subjugation of women in general. There was indeed a time when they were necessary, but that was then and this is now—thousands of years later. In fact, there are both men and women alive today who possess more of the qualities of the opposite sex; and this makes such early laws actually detrimental to continued spiritual growth.

These early laws not only applied to the dominance of men over women, and the established roles which men were allowed in society and denied to women, but they applied to the institution of marriage, and the nature of sexual relationships as well. These laws too are no longer necessary and could compromise individual's ability to grow as spiritual entities. With respect to legally recognized relationships and personally defined relationships, it is best for each couple to make their own best choices; no longer relying upon a social structure or order to make decisions for them.

Governmental bodies which write laws for human conduct with respect to male/female rolls should separate themselves from the influence of antiquated religious codes; and allow for greater freedom for individuals to make their own choices with regard to most relationships of an interpersonal nature which involve mature adults.

Mature people of today are much different than the men and women who lived thousands of years ago when early religions were established to guide people into establishing a healthy society. Today the children are becoming mature and it is detrimental to continue to treat them like children. Now, maturing souls need to be allowed the freedom to act upon the basis of the laws that (through repeated experiences as both men and women) they have come to believe are most appropriate for them at this time. People of today are much more like young adults than children. Though there is still a need for laws to guide them, they need to become more self-reliant, so that they will eventually be able to know from the basis of their own experiences and wisdom what is most appropriate for them under each situation which they encounter in life. And when they finally learn to say "no" to their ego's influence, and listen instead to the inspiration that comes from higher consciousness, it will no longer be necessary for laws to be written in texts or carved into stone; for they will have become written into their very hearts and souls.

This process will require the maturing individual to eventually step through their own fears and sense of loyalty to the teachers of their youth; but if they are sincere, and have learned well, they will find that they can receive inner guidance by listening to their own heart and reaching up to higher consciousness for guidance along the way.

A spiritual development course I took part in, offered by a church that was established through C.A.C., following the suggestions of Cosmic Awareness, contained a very profound assertion. Cosmic Awareness indicated that every god or deity that mankind can comprehend has its reflection within each of us; that if this were not so, we would not be able to conceive of them.

I believe that the validity of this principle is evidenced by the fact that all people who aspire to establish a personal connection with God, regardless of which entity (or lesser god) may have actually been the initial inspiration for the desire, do in fact have the capacity to realize that most rewarding goal. I believe that God has inspired various entities of higher consciousness to fulfill Its will in cultivating civilizations around the world; providing various sets of laws, backed up by stories, to guide entities on lower consciousness levels (such as we on the physical plane) into realizing their divine nature, and so to inspire them to let go of the comfort of the old and reach upward for newer and higher principles, laws, and ideals to live by.

This is not an easy thing for many people to do, especially souls who are new to this earth experience; but for those who have learned most of the lessons that this world provides, the path toward God and higher consciousness can be a most rewarding one. Those who do not allow themselves to do this, and who become too wrapped up in the dogma of their own religion to actually follow the course that their religion offers them, will find one day, that all paths lead to the same place: the same realization. And that realization is that we are all One; all parts of the same Whole which we call God.

Enjoy your trip; it will lead you into experiencing a love far beyond human comprehension; will dissolve all feelings of guilt and fear, and set you free to experience the ever higher states of consciousness found within the many mansions of God's kingdom.

The Messiah:

Soon after the fall of Adam, God promised to send a Messiah to save people from the consequences of the fall (karma and repeated incarnations) and lead them to God. Virtually every major religion that exists today is either still waiting for that Messiah, or has identified it with some entity or prophet who was here for a while and then died, promising to return. As a result, virtually every person seeking a closer union with God is waiting for something or someone outside of and apart from their own self to come and save them.

I would like to stress, once again, that every deity or personage that people can comprehend is a reflection of something within their own greater being-ness. Take a look at the funnel of your own soul's consciousness which I presented in the fourth chapter. The highest funnel can be interpreted as being that Messiah which many look for.

It's ok to look for others to teach, guide, and inspire us during our seeking to draw closer to God; but in failing to recognize the true source of the higher consciousness that saves—the Messiah within—one fails to find the only true Messiah. It is a part of our own soul, a level of higher consciousness or awareness that connects us directly with God.

Take some time in meditation and open yourself to this source of love and higher consciousness. In alignment with the diagram I offered, you might even imagine it to be in the form of a funnel or sphere of brilliant light a foot or two above your head. Imagine its light radiating down into your head and body, or as radiant water pouring down into your body and filling it. Use it any way that feels appropriate, but don't locate it so far above you that you begin to perceive of it as something distant and apart from you. It's a part of your own divine being, patiently waiting for the time when you are able to give it full expression in your life.

And once you set aside your fears, and animosity toward others, and learn to absolve your own guilt through forgiveness (of self and others), you will find your consciousness expanding until you fully realize that you and it are one. And when that day comes (and one day it will), you will find yourself exemplifying the Messiah; giving it expression in your life.

The Taskmaster

Challenges:

It's rather safe to say that life in this physical realm is challenging. Whether or not it was the Supreme God's intention that higher forms of consciousness enter into physical expression, or even that a physical reality ever be created, is a moot subject in my opinion. Since we do have a physical universe, there is obviously a Higher Consciousness that is God of this realm, and the same question might be asked of It. Since many people and religions consider souls' incarnation into physicality to be a "fall" from grace, I can accept it as such; but I also recognize that this type of experience provides many blessings which far out-weigh any difficulties we experience here.

Once we finally return to higher states of consciousness, we will take with us wisdom gained from a collection of experiences unavailable to those higher souls who never "fell" so far. And these experiences, together with the wisdom that they provide, will add to the collective consciousness of all higher levels of consciousness above us; we will have made a significant contribution to the total consciousness of God Itself. And this, I believe, will make it all worthwhile.

While we're still struggling, though, with all the temptations and false illusions that exist within this realm, it's quite understandable that some may feel otherwise and despair. May you all soon find hope, though, in the assurance that there are indeed many in realms of higher consciousness that are reaching "down" to us; trying to assist us in our upward climb.

A Dark Force?

One of the most troublesome and misleading misconceptions promoted by various religious teachings is the concept of a force of evil fighting against the force of goodness which we call God. This idea has been further popularized by the *Star Wars Series* written by George Lucas (original book series written by Oliver Simon). Though religions generally claim that God will eventually defeat the "Devil", the *Star Wars Series* claims that there must be a balance in "The Force"; a notion which I whole-heartedly disagree with. That said, I want to commend Mr. Simon and Mr. Lucas for presenting us with a very constructive view of the positive side of "the Force", which is available for everybody—not just Jedi Knights—to attune to and use for the benefit of All.

The idea that there exists an evil force to balance the good force reminds me of a *Hagar the Horrible* (Chris Browne) comic strip in which Lucky Eddie and Hagar are in a boat on the sea at night. Lucky Eddie is holding a lit candle, and one of them (I forget which) comments about how dark it is. Then the candle goes out, and one of them makes a further comment: "Now that's Dark!" The obvious suggestion was that the darkness was so dark that it could actually put out the light. As a comic strip the idea is funny; in a movie the concept is entertaining; but within religious teachings, the concept is very troublesome; even dangerous to accept. It has very little basis in truth; disregard the entire idea.

As creator beings in a reality partly of our own creation, we need to be very careful as to what ideas and concepts we direct our energy (attention) toward. Our collective creation of the Consciousness known as Santa Claus is a quite beneficial use of our creative abilities. That Spirit's influence can be felt by millions the world over; and influences many thousands into performing great acts of generosity, appreciated by millions more. Parents debate with their children as to whether or not Santa is real; I say that he's very real. And to the extent that people embody the consciousness of Santa, and exemplify its spirit, they too are Santa.

Likewise Jesus was a perfect embodiment of the Christos (or Logos), the consciousness of God, as a result of his having raised his consciousness (through lifetimes of experience starting with Adam) until it was high enough to be a vehicle for the Christ Consciousness to express through. This is another way of saying that Jesus attained the Christ Consciousness and became the only son of God. We too, when we raise our own vibrations high enough, can also embody the consciousness of God, and we could also be considered to be true sons of God or Christs.

The collective creation of an evil consciousness which we identify as the Devil is something that we should not continue to energize; its creation has resulted in needless suffering for thousands of millions. The misconception of the Devil being a fallen angel that is at war with God and trying to bring people down to hell by performing acts of evil, may have been largely true a long time ago, but it hasn't been true for a while. And it never tried to lead people into accepting religious faiths that are not "the right one"; it never had to. Satan (a personification of the human ego) has been perfectly adept at corrupting all religions; so that none of them are totally valid, or absolutely true in their teachings.

Present day belief in a powerful enemy of God identified as "the devil" is something that we all need to look at very carefully, so that we can find ourselves able to remove attention from, and belief in, this creation of religion, ignorance, and fear. Let's work to assure that its days are numbered on this plane. It only exists now to the extent that we give energy and attention to our belief that it exists.

Now, I don't intend to infer that there haven't been some very real entities from realms of spirit conducting themselves in ways that we could label as evil. Nor am I suggesting that some very troublesome entities aren't trying to lead us away from "the Light". What I'm trying stress is that these entities are just that; they are not gods, and they are not permanent forces created by God to maintain some balance.

The best symbolism I can think of, to describe the source of evil in God's reality, is that of darkness. Not a force in and of itself, it is a lack of light. Put another way; it's ignorance. And ignorance dissolves with wisdom gained, just as darkness dissolves with the light. There is no dark force anywhere in God's creation other than those put into motion by conscious entities acting out of their own ignorance.

Early in this book I described an un-awakened aspect of God which I described as an Infinite Living Potentiality (ILP). This potential force can be put into expression by any consciousness. It's like a piano upon which any kind of music can be played. Until a person gains the wisdom required to play the piano well, though, some pretty unpleasant sounds can be heard. These discordant musical numbers could be likened to "evil" expressions, performed by "evil" spirits or people. But since all consciousness is on a path of spiritual growth and evolution, eventually we will all learn to play most beautiful music, and there then be no darkness or ignorance to detract from our joy.

The Lucifer, the Devil, and Satan:

When discussing misconceptions with regard to heaven, I expressed my view that different words and phrases were later assumed to be referring to the same thing. It's my view that the same misunderstanding has occurred with respect to the negative forces identified as Lucifer, the Devil, and Satan; which some religions have described in their teachings.

While I agree with the standard opinion that Lucifer was an "Angel" (entity of higher consciousness) which rebelled against God, leading others with him, where I differ is in the use of the phrase: "rebelled against God". I consider it misleading. Lucifer, like all entities of higher consciousness, was given the gift of free will; and he used that freedom to delve much deeper into realms of density than some people believe that God had intended for souls to go. In Lucifer's choosing, then, it can be said that he rebelled against God's will. It's also my opinion that he initiated what could be called a battle of evil against good, in trying to motivate other souls to indulge in the low vibrational energies associated with power, fear, greed, and lustful indulgences in defiance of God's will. I believe that Lucifer even departed further from God's plan in creating the half human, half animal forms that were described in various legends. In this respect only, could he correctly be identified as the Devil, as depicted in particular by the Christian Religion.

The hell which Lucifer and his fellow "fallen angels" were "cast into", as a result of their "rebellion", refers—without doubt—to the same realms of consciousness that exist on this and astral planes where one may be said to meet one's karma. I have already discussed the subject of hell, so I will not elaborate on that here. Suffice it to say that there are many "mansions" of hell, just as there are many mansions of heaven.

I also agree with religion's view, that in its fall, Lucifer became essentially a force of evil which inspired many to indulge in very base and carnal pursuits, and in that context was rightly thought of as "the Devil". I also concur, that from this hell (the astral planes) Lucifer, as the Devil, did have followers which were considered to be demons; also tempting people to indulge in carnal lusts so that they could feed off of the energy of their emotions and passions.

It's my opinion, though, that Lucifer did not remain long in these lower realms of consciousness, but eventually repented, and began the process of ascension in consciousness, along with many of his followers. While he was active in his "rebellion", though, he very closely did fit the given description of a tempter, acting in opposition to God's will.

I feel it most appropriate, however, to point out that Lucifer's rebellion occurred very early in the earth's history; long before the first human forms were caused to become evolved here. It was intended that human bodies, created "in god's image", would be appropriate forms for these fallen souls to use in order to eventually work their way out of their hells and return eventually to higher levels once again. For more on this subject, you can contact the A.R.E. According to Cosmic Awareness (the source for the C.A.C. material), Lucifer has already made his way back to God; so I'll assume that many of those who followed after, have also left this realm of density, and are not in hell any more either.

With regards to the other fallen souls who followed Lucifer, I'd suggest that though some of them may remain in the astral realms (hell) some of them could be us. I believe that the use of the word "angel" is also misconstrued when used in the ancient writings. It's my opinion that these fallen "angels" were instead conscious entities that possessed free will; and on that basis, are more appropriately called fallen souls. An angel, in my opinion, is a form of higher consciousness that either lacked the free will to lower its state of consciousness, or chose to remain on higher planes. Since I have no strong feelings about the subject of angels, though, I haven't tried to investigate it, so won't try to say more here. I only wish to stress my opinion that I believe that those who followed Lucifer in the fall, were conscious entities such as we are; souls who are in the process of incarnating time and again until they finally raise their vibrations sufficiently to move off from this dense plane.

The "devil", in my opinion, was initially more of a collective term to refer to demonic entities that resided in the astral (emotional) realms of reality. These were non-physical entities which attached themselves to humans in order to feed off of their strong base emotions. These entities were, I believe, were prayed to or conjured up by some groups of people in order to use their power to aid them in satisfying their own carnal passions. Though Lucifer may at one time have been the dominant force as a devil at one time, he has not—to my understanding—been so, for some time. Though many demons or devils certainly do exist to plague those susceptible to very base passions and emotions, there is not—in my opinion—a chief devil existing now that is at war with God; as promoted in current religious teachings. There are rather a host of lost souls trying their best to feed off of human emotions; and they accomplish their ambitions by trying to stimulate strong passions and emotions within people.

My suggestion is that people do not give attention (and thus emotional energy) to these entities. I further suggest that one avoid any attempts to draw these lower forms of consciousness to them for any reason. They could become quite troublesome. I believe that these entities are also attracted to some rituals that utilize strong emotional energy—particularly sexual energy. People who seek power and control over others are also prone to be influenced by these. The over-indulgence in drugs or alcohol can also attract these devils or demons, and when one's consciousness is impaired and weak as a result of the use of these, the spirits can use that as an opportunity to establish an attachment or even a possession.

I believe that the idea of a singular Devil, which is Lord of hell, the force behind all evil, and leader of all demons, is a construct of religions who felt that they needed to create the idea of an adversarial being strong enough to war against God. I believe that they used this in an attempt to cause fear in people in order to motivate them to join their religion. The image of the goat/man for the devil was actually the image used by Pagans in the past, to represent their highest male deity. By using that image, the church no doubt hoped to demonize the god of that pagan religion, and thus aid them in discouraging its continued popularity. Unfortunately, by creating the idea of a Devil with powers like God, and by giving it an image and form, they inadvertently gave existing demons more power.

In conclusion I'd say: pray for the well-being of the fallen "angels", sending them light and love to aid them in their evolution; but do not give attention to the Devil or any demons. Any emotional energy directed at them can only serve to draw them toward you or strengthen them. And to the best of your ability avoid any strong base emotional energies when intoxicated or under the use of drugs. In fact, it would be better to avoid strong base emotions at any time; they're not good for you.

Satan is another word used by religion to refer to the devil; I believe this is an error in understanding what Jesus was talking about when he used the term. Unfortunately, with usage, the term has stuck in human consciousness in reference to Lucifer or the Devil. It has particularly been used by those who worship "the devil" in attempts to gain benefits from demonic forces, and attack religions for one reason or another; these groups call themselves Satanists. My suggestion is to not become involved in any way with these people or groups.

As I understand the way Jesus used the term "Satan", I believe he was referring to the human ego. It is a part of the consciousness of each one of us residing on the physical plane. In saying that one is tempted by Satan, one is acknowledging the influence of the carnal passions of this plane, influenced by the illusion that we are separate individuals, and not a part of the Oneness. I believe that this ego "mind" is a natural result of our living in this physical dimension which gives us the illusion of being separate from God. I do not believe that the promptings of Satan or ego come about solely as a result of the influence of some external evil power.

In "the Father's kingdom" (realms of consciousness above the physical and astral planes), soul is aware of its union with the All (at least in my opinion). In saying that Satan tempted eve to eat the apple, the meaning is that souls had lowered the vibratory rate of their consciousness so low that they lost the awareness of being a part of God. These were then given an opportunity to experience density through a process of incarnating on the physical world; and through repeated lifetimes, in learning to distinguish between good and evil, would finally be able to grow in wisdom and "be like God" as the "serpent" promised.

The ego is a term used to describe the sense of self being self (and generally self only). Some people and groups consider the ego to be the enemy; and in many respects it acts that way. It tempts us through various carnal desires, and instills in us the feelings fear, guilt, and desire for power over others.

In my opinion, then, Jesus was essentially talking with himself (his own ego) when he was tempted in the wilderness. His consciousness had just risen to the level of Christ Consciousness, and he wanted to take some time alone to think about it, and consider how he would use it to fulfill his ministry. He probably had a lot more to consider than the three temptations recorded in the bible. He realized that he could turn rocks into bread; meaning he could manifest all the wealth and worldly goods he wanted. He realized that he could have all the power he wanted, represented by the vision of all the worlds being his. And he realized that he could receive praise and adoration from the people by showing off his miraculous powers. These are all very familiar temptations which naturally arise from the ego mind.

In my opinion, Jesus—throughout his ministry—represented the conscious mind of humanity, his disciples represented 12 aspects of personality found within the subconscious mind, Satan represented the immature ego, and the resurrected Christ represented the mature ego (the level of selfless-awareness that exists on higher realms).

In subjecting himself to crucifixion, I believe that Jesus was in essence putting his immature ego (with all its desires & fears) to death. When Jesus referred to putting Satan under his foot, he meant under his power. The reference to Jesus over-coming Satan, crushing its head, and all similar phrases, are ways of saying that he overcame the temptations of his ego that relate to the physical experience. The cross he carried either represented his own karmic load, or the karmic load of those who surrendered their sins to him. He set a pattern for us to follow in overcoming the desires of our own flesh; our own ego's influence.

I also believe that the word Satan is derived from the word Saturn; the planet that is believed to possess the quality of restriction, and which causes us to meet our limitations. In Astrology, it is Saturn's influence which brings our karmic lessons to bear. Saturn, or Satan, then, can be thought of as the Taskmaster. It tempts us and tests us like the predators in nature; weeding out the weak and devouring them. In nature, predators ensure that the weak, sick, and inferior animals are killed so that only the strong survive to mate and propagate the species. This is the role that Saturn plays in our lives; it challenges us just like Satan.

The planet Saturn puts us in conflict with our own personality weaknesses and makes us stronger as a result; because we are forced to deal with the challenges and restrictions that it presents to us in life. Satan, as the carnal force within each of us, tempts us to indulge our senses and desires for self-interest; and here is where it serves as a taskmaster. When we are weak and give in to inappropriate expressions, we suffer the consequences, and hopefully learn not to repeat the action. In this way it tests us; putting us to task for our mistakes, and indirectly helping us to grow in wisdom and spiritual development.

Self-Righteousness leads to Judgment and Guilt.

One of the most obvious expressions of our ego (personified as Satan) is in the act of self-glory; especially when we boast to others about our accomplishments or qualities. Ironically, one can even boast about one's humility. Within the area of religion or religious belief, ego manifests as a boasting that one has pleased God, and is being blessed by God for fulfilling God's demands; whether they be of good deeds done, laws obeyed, or possessing the correct set of beliefs.

The big problem with expressions of self-righteousness is that it leads people into judging others to be inferior to themselves; less worthy, less loved, and more deserving of punishment. Self-righteous people often point to other people's problems and pain as evidence of God's judgment upon them, and perceive their own blessings as evidence that God loves them more.

This arrogance will eventually produce a karmic backlash; because in judging others, we judge ourselves, and the faults which are perceived in others, being a reflection of our own weaknesses, will cause us to receive the fruits of our judgments.

Self-righteousness infers more than superiority over others; it also infers that one is more favored (for some unknown reason perhaps) by God; for they believe that it was God that allowed them to have the capacity to become obedient and faithful in the first place, by sending the Holy Spirit to them. This notion is especially troubling when people believe that God only predestined a select few to become saved; and in feeling themselves to be among those selected to be saved, considers that they must, therefore, be better or more worthy than others because the Holy Spirit gave them the capacity to "believe". I mentioned this misunderstanding before. The notion of 144,000 "foreknown" who were predestined to be saved, was a reference to a group of souls who came into this plane to help the fallen to escape the "hell" they had put themselves in. Because this would be a risk for them, other souls in realms of higher consciousness, promised to look out for them to guarantee (predestine) that they wouldn't get stuck themselves; that they would be saved or rescued, if necessary, should they forget who they were and why they came.

The reality is that all souls will eventually become saved and will return to higher states of consciousness. And those who boast about how worthy they are, are only yielding to the ploys of their ego, and will bring karmic repercussions upon themselves as a result. The consciousness that Jesus possessed—as already described—is a humble one which recognizes that we are all part of the same Whole called God. None or better or more loved than another. Eventually all will come to recognize that fact; and the sooner people learn to restrain the impulses of their ego, the sooner they will be able to cease the judgment of others which will only result in judgment of self and the corrective experiences that this will require.

Guilt leads to Hell.

My assertion that guilt condemns one to hell may seem overly harsh, to those who hold to the belief that hell is a place where people burn for eternity. Properly understood, hell is a state of consciousness wherein people reap the consequences of their prior actions; those for which they believe themselves to be guilty of. It is the ego which motivates a person to commit an error, the ego's judgment that one is guilty, and the ego which causes one to suffer in order to appease the feelings of guilt. In this way "Satan" tries to pull souls down to "hell".

Jesus' intention was to provide a way for people to set aside their guilt, so that they could become saved from the painful consequences of their judgment. He was not entirely successful, however. As mentioned before: most people carry too much guilt to be able to accept grace. Even so, the way toward redemption has been shown, so that people anywhere—and of any religion—can receive atonement to the extent that they find themselves able to set aside their guilt and cease judgment of self and others; forgiving self and others without reservation.

One might ask: why would one's ego want to suffer? I believe that it provides self with the opportunity to focus upon one's identity. The ego arises from the illusion that it is separate from the Whole, and as a result perceives itself to be all-important. It craves as much of anything as it can get in order to add to its experience, and validate its realness or identity. All lusts for carnal pleasures arise from this; so too do desires for power and glory. And though it may seem masochistic, the ego takes pleasure in being a victim; wallowing in its own pain and torment allows it to feel more real and alive.

If you think about it, you may even recall some friends or acquaintances that seem to keep wallowing in their own pain while still doing the same things that caused it in the first place. Their continual focus on self feeds their ego's desire to be recognized. Even negative attention or attention to pain is still attention, and if they can cause others to give them attention in this way, their expressions are rewarded. If a friend tries to draw you into this game, try to redirect their attention to others; it will help to free them from the grip of their own ego (Satan). You might also try to get them involved in some community activity or service organization which will help them to focus on assisting others with similar problems.

The ego craves anything that validates its perception that it is separate from the Whole, and special; it's a survival technique. Any idea that leads to a feeling of unity with others is perceived by the ego as an attack, because it detracts from the feeling of self-importance. This is why the ego must be "put to death" or "crucified" in order for one to return to God. People must allow themselves to be "saved" from the influence of their own egos because its very survival depends upon remaining separate from the Oneness found in the higher planes of heaven; a state of consciousness that all souls are striving for.

Fear leads to Hell:

Fear also stems from a failure to believe that God will provide for one's needs. Part of this results from ignorance, or disbelief in God as a force of love. Most fear, however, results from feelings of guilt. Once a person judges self to have committed some error, the resulting guilt produces a subconscious need for correction, and fear results. Subconsciously we all know that cause will produce results; this is the law of sin or of karma. Though there are better ways to resolve prior errors (acts of service, expressions of love), the only way that we can ever hope to totally escape the consequences of "sin" is to forgive ourselves and others.

Fear also stems from misunderstandings with regard to what God's laws are. If one believes that God commands that we not sing or dance or laugh, then these expressions would also lead to judgment, remorse, and fear of God's punishment. Though most would not now consider these expressions to be sinful, there was a time when they were; and people were punished and rebuked for engaging in such frivolities.

Mistaken notions with respect to conduct deemed to fall under God's laws, are still—in my mind—very evidenced today; leading to a lot of fear, judgment, condemnation, and all the results that such ego-based expressions produce. Perhaps I should have pointed out some of these in the prior chapter where I referred to the origin of religious laws within the subject of religious misconceptions. But because since they invoke inappropriate fear, and are sustained by ego-based feelings of self-righteousness, I felt it best to describe them here. They include all occult subjects, such as ESP, Parapsychology, magic, communication with spirits, and the like.

Fear of the Occult:

The word, "occult" actually means hidden, and nothing more. People often associate the word with "cult", though, or more specifically, with evil cults; and this is why the misunderstanding is often perpetuated. The subjects included under this label, are—metaphorically speaking—some of the fruits on the Tree of Life, because they are expressions of the greater soul.

When souls chose to express themselves in this physical realm, they metaphorically ate of the Tree of Knowledge; its fruits were the five physical senses. Because humankind was ignorant at that time—like babies—the metaphorical Tree of Life was cut down, or hidden from them. This is because of the great power that these fruits contained. Like a parent hiding knives, matches, and chemicals from its children, occult wisdom was hidden from humanity.

Some souls (like overly-curious children) were able to discover some of these truths and apply them to their peril because they hadn't yet learned the difference between good and evil, and used the higher wisdom in inappropriate ways. This is why God (or the agents of God), at the time, forbade these practices; threatening dire punishments for violating the laws. Wise parents apply this same policy in protecting their young children from possible harm.

After Jesus' resurrection, and to an extent during his ministry, some occult wisdom was taught to his disciples who used it, describing them as "gifts of the Holy Spirit". In reality they are attributes of the soul (of all people) which are (hopefully) hidden from them until they are spiritually mature enough to use them in a constructive way. Some references to occult subjects are contained in the Book of Revelations; these dealing with the interconnectedness of the soul's body with the physical body (the chakras), and how they operate through the path to redemption.

In order to clear up some inappropriate fears, I'll try to give a brief account of various occult expressions which I feel warrant some better understanding.

*Astrology was actually a science in the past which described influences upon people throughout their lives. This became problematic when people put too much emphasis upon these influences, using the wisdom as a substitute for religion. Today it can be used as a psychological tool whereby people can better understand themselves and the issues that they are dealing with in life.

Misunderstandings about the science occur in part because the stars (which make up the signs) themselves do not produce the influences. The creators of this physical universe placed energy fields within or around the universe, which—from our perspective—originate from those locations where the various constellations can be seen. It's not, therefore, the constellations themselves that produce the influence.

When a souls enters the physical plane at birth (not conception), it enters the newborn baby during a specific time when the energies, which correspond to signs, produce a type of pattern which affects the soul's incoming astral body, so that certain qualities are emphasized while others are diminished.

It can be likened unto a certain die through which soul stuff must pass through, creating a certain pattern in the substance of the astral body of the child. Another way to perceive of this would be to place an array of magnets of varying sizes and polarities on the underside of a plane, and then drop iron filings upon this. The result will cause a certain pattern, to be observed on this plane, which corresponds to the arrangement of the magnets; it is this pattern which the study of one's astrological chart attempts to discover.

It must also be understood that this does not occur to an incoming soul by chance. All souls which enter the physical plane through the birth experience, do so for specific reasons; and they choose (are attracted to) specific parents based upon their desire to be with them for personal reasons, because of the environment in which they will be raised, and on the basis of the astrological influences under which they will be born.

I'm not certain when the choice is actually made, or if it's the same for all souls. I have heard of souls coming to couples prior to conception, and soon after same; and have also heard (which makes a lot of sense) that the soul influences the development of the fetus (choosing among a large gene pool) so that certain physical results are achieved.

So, though an abortion would not prevent a soul from ever having a life, it would put an abrupt end to its plans for using the chosen vehicle, and disrupt any plans it had made to fulfill its intended purpose at that time. If the soul later comes to the same parents, it may bring with it a subconscious anger for having been denied its earlier plans. I suggest, then, that women who are unhappy to find themselves pregnant, make a sincere and persistent effort at establishing communication with the soul that has chosen them, and explain your feelings; working out some mutually agreeable alternative.

A type of prayer, or letter-writing before bed could result in a dream wherein the soul expressed its feelings as well. If the soul then agrees to remove its claim, it will terminate the pregnancy for you, and the miscarriage will make the abortion unnecessary. Then if it comes at a later time, it will not be so adversely affected.

Astrology, as a psychological tool, is a science that can assist a person to better understand themselves and their own personal weaknesses, as well as their strengths. This knowledge can help a person to better accept themselves as they are, and can be of assistance in better dealing with one's challenges in life; but, as the Bible states, will not "save" a person (any more than physics will).

*ESP or extra sensory perception consists of psychic abilities which are actually very real soul abilities which all people possess. That these seem to be abilities, that only gifted psychics have, is because most people either dis-acknowledge their own psychic impressions, or they haven't learned how to develop them. Many "gifts of the spirit" are manifestations of these natural senses of the soul body. The higher a soul's vibration the better their ability to use these senses of the soul; the denser a person is, then, the less likely ESP will be experienced.

*Communication with Spirits can be a dangerous thing to do when one is not acting with the very highest of intentions. Also, even when one means well, one must be able to discern the quality or reliability of any information received. Familiar spirits are those close to this plane; astral entities, or the souls of loved ones who have died. Their guidance cannot always be trusted; and if a lower consciousness is contacted, the results can be very troublesome. Unless one knows what one is doing, it's still best to avoid this.

That said, I was once given a warning from a "familiar spirit" (a message I received at a Spiritualist Church) that saved me from having a very serious accident that could have killed, or maimed me for life. Also, some spirits in the higher realms of consciousness use mediums to assist in providing welcome guidance to individuals. So, there are benefits that can be obtained from higher souls in spirit form who are trying to offer assistance to us here on the physical plane. Some of these are referred to as "Holy Spirits", and some "gifts of the spirit" are a result of these higher souls' communication with us. The gibberish, for example, which is often referred to as "speaking in tongues" is, in my opinion and affirmed by Cosmic Awareness (C.A.C.), a language of spirits on a higher dimension, who speak through people of a high enough vibration who are able and willing to open themselves up to be mediums for the holy spirits to use.

*Medium-ship is pretty much a description of a way in which familiar spirits may be contacted. For all the reasons mentioned above, one must be careful that lower forms are not contacted. It helps to ask for protection from higher realms (prayer), but if one's own vibration is low, or if the intent is not of the highest (curiosity and ego-based motivations are low), one can experience problems. The use of Ouija boards, and attempts at automatic writing are ways in which people open themselves up as mediums to allow a spirit to use their body for expression. Ouija boards are particularly dangerous because most any spirit can use it. When attempting automatic writing—as with automatic speaking (gift of tongues as an example)—care must be taken to assure that one's vibrations are high, that one is protected, and that motivations are high. And even then, any messages that come must be considered with careful discernment.

*Meditation is a method of attuning oneself with some desired concept or energy field; preferably that of Oneness with God, or something similar. Meditation can also be used as a receptive instrument to allow higher forces such as God, to influence one's life: the attitude of surrendering to Diving will or guidance, or to be used as an instrument of Divine will.

Edgar Cayce stated (though not necessarily in these words); that in prayer, we speak to God, while in meditation God speaks to us. I'd amend that to say; meditation is being receptive to a reply.

There are four areas of concern that need to be considered here; but the rewards of this practice make the practice incredibly beneficial for most people. First, the meditator needs to be in a reasonably healthy mental state; I do not recommend this practice to those suffering from neurosis, or schizophrenia. I also do not recommend the average person to engage in the practice when under severe emotional duress.

Secondly, one must be careful not to put too much energy upon any emotionally based subject; because there is a risk of amplifying that emotion. Meditation should be thought of as "taking in" or eating. The specific energy which one meditates upon is like food for the soul. In this way it is a most beneficial practice. One can become much more loving, trusting, and psychic as a result. But if lower emotional energies are focused upon (taken in) during meditation, one can become over-balanced in that regard.

Thirdly, since meditation is a form of medium-ship, whereby people open themselves up with some specific intent; care must be taken that one is protected from attack or influence, by any forms of lower consciousness. The same advice with regard to medium-ship is recommended: be in a high state of vibration (or consciousness) yourself, and only allow entities of higher consciousness in your presence. One technique is to visualize oneself surrounded by an impenetrable field of light energy or love energy. Another technique is to pray to God or some other high consciousness (whichever one puts the most trust in) to protect or guide them in their practice.

And finally, that the technique used to get into a meditative state does not adversely affect the body by unbalancing the body's energy systems (chakras). This can come about by directing too much energy to a particular chakra or group of chakras.

Trusting in Tradition:

It's not so hard to recognize Satan's (our ego's) influence with regard to lusts for power and praise, or even in the pursuit of earthly passions and pleasures. And when one thinks about it, one can even recognize its influence in leading us to feel better than others and make judgments about them, even to the extent of condemning them or denying them forgiveness. One can even perceive its influence behind fears, especially when they relate to the expressions of others that are different than our own. But there's another area under the rule of ego which is less obvious and even seems to be a good thing to promote; so this area (of Satan's rule) can be the most difficult one to break free of. Failure to do so, however, could be a serious detriment to one's continued spiritual growth and development.

I heard a story once about a woman who made an excellent pot-roast from a recipe she inherited from her mother. In fact the mother had obtained the recipe from her mother before her. When this woman was preparing her dish, she had her young daughter at her side, so that she would learn how it was made, and be able to one day pass the technique down to her children. As the child watched, she noticed that her mother carefully trimmed the hunk of meat until it was in a very uniform rectangular shape. The pieces of meat she cut off were put aside in a different dish to be used for other purposes at a later time.

While the mother was beginning to spice the meat, the girl asked why she trimmed the meat like she did. Mom just smiled in her wise say, patted her girl on her head, and assured her that this was the way it was done. "Don't be concerned. It will come out just wonderful;" the mother assured her. "But why cut off so much of the meat;" the girl asked. Upon this repeated query, the woman stopped to think. She just didn't know; it was the way she was taught to do it, and the results were always good, so she never questioned why. She assured her that there must be a good reason, or else it wouldn't be part of the instructions she received from her mom. And with that she completed the recipe; and sure enough, it was delicious.

The young girl was an inquisitive youngster; so the next time she saw her grandmother, she made a point of asking her. To her surprise though, her grandmother brushed off her question as well. "You don't need to know why, my dear; just do it as I taught your mom, and it will be fine." Now the girl was thinking that there must be a secret they were hiding, so she became increasingly insistent. Finally granny had to admit that she didn't know either; but that it was the way her mother had taught her; and she had watched her make it very often. There was no doubt that this was an important thing to do, because each time she watched her mother prepare the meat, she was careful to trim it just as she later showed her daughter, the girl's mom.

Well, the girl was really curious now, but her great granny had died years ago, so she couldn't ask her. But then she thought of her great Uncle; maybe he'd know. Maybe he knew why great granny trimmed the meat so much. Well, the girl had to wait a long time before the family went to visit him during the holidays. But she was sure going to try to get to the bottom of this mystery. To her, it didn't matter that the result was always as desired; she wanted to know why as well.

Finally the day came when she could ask her grandma's brother; and when she did, explaining the big mystery, and how neither mom nor grandma seemed to know why, he just burst into laughter. In fact, the girl's look of sincere earnestness made him laugh even louder. When he finally settled himself, he told her that, yes, he did know why. "You see, my child, your great granny was very poor and only had one very small roasting pan. If she didn't trim the meat just right, it wouldn't fit into the pan."

Ok, now that was a long story, but I felt that it presented my opinion very well. It seems to me that a lot of religious dogma, laws, and beliefs just aren't questioned. Dogma is passed down from generation to generation, with each being assured that if it was deemed to be best by others, then it had stood up to the test of time, and therefore was beyond question now. The thing is—as I pointed out when discussing the origin of religious laws—times change, and people change. As a society, we are more mature now, than societies were hundreds and thousands of years ago. The same laws and traditions just aren't necessarily appropriate anymore. And at least it's my opinion, that they should be questioned time and again, with each generation, and each change in culture.

Jesus had once identified himself to his followers as being "the way, the truth, and the life", and at one time challenged a disciple of his, when asserting that if he wanted to know truth, then he would have to leave his family behind, and follow after him; stating further that whomever clung to his mother or brother was not worthy of him (truth). I believe that the message which Jesus was trying to put across was that one cannot hold onto tradition and the beliefs that are handed down through generations, and be open enough to be able to accept the wisdom contained in higher or greater truths. It was fortunate for the people living at that time, to have a teacher like Jesus who could provide a more enlightened truth; but how about now?

Though many of us may raise questions, who is there to provide the answers we seek? One's own religious leaders are expected to be following tradition; passing down what they were taught as a representative of their particular religious body. They'd probably be disciplined if they chose to make changes on their own. The obvious answer, then, is to go directly to God.

Every religion should be teaching people how to establish their own connection to the Supreme Source; so follow the guidance you have been taught. And if that doesn't work for you, try your own method. Be persistent, and sincerely earnest like the young girl, and you will be answered. I'm sure of it. If one method doesn't work, try another; God has a lot of different ways to provide us with answers.

And be alert for coincidences! I've received "the next step" through junk mail. I've also received an answer when something someone is telling me just "rings a bell"; and I know in my heart that it's the answer. I also pay attention to my dreams. But the source I most rely upon is the feeling of rightness I somehow sense within. It's hard to describe. But when I consider something, and run through the options, or listen to another's opinion, I sometimes get an inner feeling about something, that it's right, or that it's the answer that I'd been looking for.

Let me give you a simple example. While writing this book I often have to think if this or that is appropriate to say now or later; or if it wouldn't be better to skip that and highlight this, or say this other thing that way rather than this way. If I just confused you, maybe you can get an idea of how frustrating it can be for me at times. Anyway; while writing one day, I got an uneasy feeling about a subject that I wanted to address, so I was unsure about including it. At first I went around the topic, but then I ended up coming back to it, and decided to include it after all. Though I thought it might bother some people too much, I also thought it raised a good point. As I was writing, a friend called, and we chatted for a bit. On her own, she started talking about the same subject, but from a different angle, and I realized that her calling at that time, and raising that topic, was God's way of suggesting that I back off. When I remembered that I had previously felt the same thing, but later changed my mind, I committed myself once again, to pay closer attention to the way I feel inside when I write.

What's the message? Establish your own personal connection with God, be open to Its guidance however it comes, trust your feelings (not emotions!), and be open toward recognizing odd coincidences, or messages that just seem to jump out at you. But regardless of what reply you think you received, question it! And consider the possible ramifications if the advice is followed. God only asks for expressions of kindness and love. Don't be fooled into listening to your ego: the voice of Satan.

OK, I'm getting preachy, and I promised myself I'd try to avoid it, but this is a subject upon which I have a lot of strong feelings. It really pains me that among the few major religions in this small world, there is so much conflict. Even within religions, people become violent and hurtful over differences carried on from one generation to the next. Don't get me wrong, in many ways traditions provide us great benefits. In fact, I've personally appreciated many of the different cultures and traditions I've had the privilege of sharing in my travels around the world and throughout this country. Unfortunately, I've also perceived ways in which improvements could be made for everyone's better good. I've felt that significant misunderstandings were being passed on and on, without any question; merely because it was "the way it's always been done". It's led me to ask; in what do we truly place our faith and trust; in God or in Tradition? I'm reminded of a popular Gospel song: *Give Me that Old Time Religion*; "It was good for . . . it's good enough for me."

A couple of years ago, I had the opportunity to speak with my father's minister about our differences of opinion with regard to Christian teachings. I voiced some of the different interpretations I had with regard to Jesus' teachings, which conflicted with the church's stand. I made it clear that I wasn't trying to convince him to believe as I did (though I'm sure he was trying to change mine—to save me). The major difference between our views on Christianity seemed to center around the subject of Jesus being the son of God. He saw Jesus as a man that was a manifestation of God, and therefore God as man was only present in that singular body of Jesus. I perceived of Jesus as a man who became capable of achieving a higher consciousness, allowing him to express that higher awareness of God. But in my perceiving that same higher consciousness to be available to anybody who raised their consciousness sufficiently to be able to attune to it, I didn't perceive of Jesus the man as being the exclusive son of God. In fact, I felt that the "only begotten son of God" wasn't referring to the physical entity Jesus, but rather to the consciousness that Jesus possessed throughout his ministry. In that respect, I felt that anybody from any religion, who raised their state of vibration to a sufficiently high level, could experience and express that higher state of consciousness called "the son of God".

This difference in opinion proved to be irreconcilable. He didn't seem capable of even considering the possibility that my view-point had merit, much less that it could be accurate. In the end, however, we established the true central aspect to our stale-mate; I trusted in my own feelings as to what was true and right and he trusted in what the church had taught him. To him, the church's position had withstood the test of time, and therefore must be right and beyond reproach, regardless of any seeming inconsistencies, or times when things that Jesus said weren't taken as being true after his resurrection. I couldn't help but think: "the blind leading the blind?" I dared not voice my thoughts though.

When I was about to leave, he asked me; "So you think I'm just wasting my time here, then?" I immediately responded; "Absolutely not! You know that what you are doing has great value to your congregation; you can see that every day. It's just that I perceive a higher truth, a way in which all people—not just Christians—have access to the love and mercy of God."

After I got home I thought about his comment some more, and realized that his concern is a universal one. This minister is sincere in what he teaches and in the service that he provides for those who depend upon him; and they are sincere in their desire to draw closer to God. But I could also recognize that this man had his counter-part in every major religion on this planet; and each of them had followers who were also counter-parts of his congregation.

All these people, though members of widely different religious traditions, were all sincerely seeking to do God's will as best as they knew it to be. God would certainly honor that, and respond to each and every one of them as best as It was able. And It would use every means It could to try to reach those who went astray and try to lead them to a higher truth if they would just be open to receiving it.

Unfortunately, it seems to me that most people are content to just follow their own tradition. After all, they receive validation from their peers every time they meet; and this is something that they might not want to jeopardize in seeking a greater understanding.

As I'm writing, I'm also living with my aged parents; both of whom are suffering from Alzheimer's disease. It's not just their memory loss that is a problem, but they have both lost the ability to recognize when they're thirsty. As a result, I have to keep after them throughout the day to drink fluids, as they won't do it on their own. My father is particularly difficult, because he doesn't like to be "told" what to do (especially by his boy); and will attempt to pacify me by taking a sip or two, and then just putting the glass aside. So, I have to keep going to him, time and again, each time insisting that he needs to drink.

Well, he gets weak and delusional when too dehydrated, so I become more domineering when he begins to show symptoms. During one of those periods, I had him sit in a straight chair and drink a large glass of diluted juice, and not move until it was emptied. I then went to get something for my mother to drink; and heard him comment to mom; "I don't think he likes me." I immediately replied, as emphatically as I could, that I loved him; that I loved him very much; and that this is why I keep after him to drink. I told him that it was <u>because</u> I loved him so much that I kept after him to drink; because if he became too dehydrated he would die; and I wanted him to keep on living."

I've recounted this episode, because this is the same way that I feel about each and every one of you who are reading this book. If I appear to be overly critical when addressing some topic, bossy or over-bearing in any way, please don't take it to mean that I don't like you or that I'm mad at you; I love you all very much! But Jesus offered everybody (not just Christians) what he called water; which—when drank—would cause a person to thirst no more. This "water" is forgiveness of sins; and it grieves me that so many of you refuse to drink it, by refusing to offer it to others ("for if you do not forgive others of their sins, then neither will your heavenly Father forgive you of yours), and as a result retain your feelings of guilt which denies you the life that is so freely being offered to you.

This passionate feeling of concern is also reflected in the way I feel about everybody the world over; regardless of religious belief; or even if the very idea of a God is rejected by some. And because I can feel such love for all people, I can't help but feel that God does the same, and even more. In fact, I know It does; It's shown me <u>that</u> in a most demonstrative way. I just find it difficult to accept that others don't also feel the same; and I want to do everything I know how to do, to bring both you and others to that higher understanding, and feeling of love and oneness.

I view every religion (including the one called Secular Humanism) as like a beautiful cup; layered in gold, decorated with gems, and inscribed with inspiring words; but it seems that too few people actually use the cup to drink from. And every time a devout person withholds their love from another, it's as though they've turned it upside down. There are waters of life flowing from God to fill everyone's cup to overflowing if people could just practice the love that is freely offered to them. Yet even the most fervent believers turn toward judgment of others, condemning others, refusing their forgiveness for often petty offenses, and even using acts of violence against others for the sake of defending their own religious beliefs and traditions. They use their cups to do battle!

I perceive the God of each and every religion to be looking down with compassion and disappointment as Its "children" dressed in garments of white laced with gold throw mud at each other while squabbling over which one of them God will deem to be the prettiest or most handsome.

I've been to charismatic churches and been uplifted by the beautiful music and inspiring fellowship shared among those present. During hymns and moments of prayer I've felt an incredibly high energy that was truly inspiring. But then the sermon would commence and all that high energy would come crashing down as words of judgment and condemnation were levied at those outside their little circle. I wondered if they didn't feel the same let-down. Couldn't they perceive that they were essentially taking their Savior back off the cross; denying what he had accomplished? I suppose not. After all; though Jesus said that he died for the sins of all people, it's too easy for people to allow their ego (Satan) to influence their thinking, in causing them to believe that only they are worthy of receiving the benefit of Jesus' sacrifice.

I've had Jewish friends who've invited me to services and rituals in remembrance of sacred occasions within their tradition, and been moved by the spirit of reverence and kinship that they hold for God and share with each other. From my experience, the Jewish people are among the most helpful and supportive of cultures to those within their religious group. Yet all that love they hold for God, and share among each other, they so often seem to deny to others outside their faith. They seem so caught up in preserving their own traditions, that they feel threatened by others from different traditions. Can they really believe that God favors them alone? I suppose they do, as virtually every other major religion feels the same. Wouldn't it be wonderful if all people could share the same love for God and each other (regardless of religious affiliation), that the Jewish share with their own?

I've sat in meditation with Buddhists both in this country and Tibet; I've taken part in sacred ceremonies and rituals offered the seeker, and taken part in some of their classes; becoming enriched by their philosophies and teachings. I've become acquainted with a Buddhist foundation called Tzu Chi (Compassionate Relief), which has branches around the world; wherein they help those in times of need, regardless of race or religious affiliation.

Yet I've also witnessed the abject poverty under which many live, and seen moneys that could go toward assisting them, go toward buying gold to adorn the statues and temples. I've seen monks who could be working productively to raise needed capital and assist those in need, sitting as beggars themselves, and living off of the handouts of those who barely have enough for themselves. And I couldn't help but wonder that if perhaps a better way to withstand the temptation to form undesirable attachments to the pleasures of the world, might be to take more of a part in the opportunities that the world offers, and demonstrate—through sharing—that one is not ensnared by them. It just seems that if avoidance was a better way, then why come here in the first place? It's like locking the candy away, so the temptation can't be acted upon. Wouldn't it be better to demonstrate one's resistance to temptation by putting the candy in a dish in the middle of the room and just passing it by; or offering it to guests when they visit?

I've taken part in Hindu meditations, and listened to wise Gurus offering words of wisdom, and presenting teachings that were profound both in scope and social value. And I've wished that I could have had the opportunity to receive the blessing of Shaktipat: the bestowing of spiritual energy upon an individual. I wonder how it differs from those I've experienced in Christian charismatic churches, or through Buddhist ceremonies.

Yet when I perceive the way the poor and disadvantaged are ignored out of a false belief that they must be allowed to experience their karma, I shudder. Don't they realize that their indifference will produce like karma for themselves? How can anyone justify the refusal of help to those in need, when it is within their power to help? I realize that nobody can help everybody, and that handouts to beggars aren't always the best way to provide help. But I'm reminded of a short story I once read somewhere.

A man was walking along the shore in a sheltered bay of the ocean. It was at low tide and many sea creatures could be seen stranded or dead along the water's edge. As the man walked, feeling a bit sorry for all the sea life that had to meet its end in this way, he noticed a young boy reaching down and picking things up to throw into the water. Upon getting closer, the man recognized that he was selecting some of the creatures that seemed to still be alive, and it was these that he was attempting to rescue by throwing them back into the water. When the man got close enough to talk to the boy, he asked him why he was doing what he was. Didn't he realize the futility of what he was doing? Certainly he couldn't save all of them. The boy, with starfish in hand, simply replied; "I know that I can't save all of them, mister, but I can help this one." And then he threw that one out into the bay.

I've known Moslem men, and been impressed as they dutifully laid down their prayer rugs at the appointed time, offering their prayers to Allah of 99 names. If only other religions could likewise recognize the same expansive nature of God. While in Egypt, I was awed by the beauty of the Mosques I visited, and the great show of piety expressed by the worshippers. And there was no question about God's presence there. The feeling was incredible; very similar to what I've felt in large Catholic churches.

I especially felt privileged to receive the blessings of Allah from Moslems I met there, even though they knew I didn't share their religion. I felt that they were acknowledging that we worshipped the same God, even though our religions were different. But why wouldn't they? After all; there is no God but Allah. All who pray to God (even though they might give It a different name) are praying to Allah.

That Moslems put so much attention to prayer, I'm led to wonder how much better it could be for them if they followed their prayer time with five or ten minutes of sitting in the silent, receptive state of meditation. Once one has emptied themselves of their concerns during prayer, opening self up to receive the love and blessings of Allah could turn out to be a very valuable and personal experience. It always feels good to be able to pray in the presence of God; but when one sits in meditation and actually feels God's energy or "touch" within one's own being, the experience can be transformational. It seems to bring God so much closer; yet the reality is that we can get closer to God in that way.

Though I find a lot of reasons to appreciate the practices if the Islamic Religion, when I see the women so hidden from sight in their heavy garments, I can't help wondering how burdensome that must be for them. Like the Buddhists who avoid life in order to escape the temptations that the senses provide, Moslems seem to feel that they need to remove the temptation that viewing a woman might elicit. Don't they think that Allah wouldn't be more impressed if a man could stand side-by-side with a woman dressed as she chose, and demonstrate through his conduct that he was able to resist that form of temptation?

I've been privileged to take part in Pagan ceremonies and rituals wherein gods of nature, and even saints and gods of other religions were honored. I've become acquainted with some of the methods of performing creative acts by using ancient methods of manifestation; and observed how they can be used constructively for both personal and social benefit. And I've been impressed by the honesty and openness in which they honor God through all Its expressions; not denying the beauty and value of the natural earthly aspects of life.

But I've also witnessed the consequences of those who used poor judgment in raising base emotional energy to accomplish their intentions; and found it necessary to take measures of my own to remove the lesser spirits which were unintentionally attracted through the expression. I've even been called upon to assist people who have been under attack by lesser spirits, to escape the violation caused by dark forces which were conjured up by others who ignorantly used their knowledge for unenlightened purposes. Don't they realize that they're playing with fire?

The moral code of the Wiccan community is "And it harm none do what you will." Is it so hard to know what causes harm? Acts—even with the best of intentions—when using powers and energies of which one is partly ignorant, can indeed cause great unintended harm. Please; be careful with the powers you use; and don't ever share your knowledge with those who would use it for "dark" purposes. Unrestricted sharing of some types of occult wisdom can and does cause harm. To those who share their knowledge: please be discerning.

The first time I visited Egypt, locals were empowered to guard the temples and pyramids, and this arrangement provided an easier means of gaining closer access to some of the sites than the later police would allow. This afforded me the opportunity to obtain private tours not available to the general public, and to obtain a less official account of this ancient civilization. By traveling with various spiritual groups on all three of my visits there, I was also able to take part in a wide variety of rituals which were deemed to be appropriate to the specific type of purpose for which the various sites along the Nile were supposedly dedicated toward. All-in-all I obtained a deep appreciation for that ancient culture. And through rituals within the Great Pyramid at Giza, I felt a connection to early Masters such as Jesus who reportedly studied and participated in spiritual initiations there.

But even though I was able to climb to the top of two of the pyramids and meditate within the King's chamber inside the Great pyramid, the most memorable experience I had was at Karnak. This was a very large complex of many temples; and very much in ruins. Upon arriving one evening to view a light show, we were directed to find seats on a set of risers which over-looked the whole area. As I climbed, seeing more and more of the area, I began to become emotionally distraught. When I reached the very top and looked around I became lost in my feelings of emotion and sat on the very back ledge of the risers so as to be apart from the crowd. A guard was nearby; but he didn't bother me, though he kept others from likewise sitting on that ledge (it was a long way down to the ground below). I was grateful for his show of tolerance; feeling that he was being sympathetic to my obvious emotional state.

I was feeling as though I had some part in the construction of these great temples, built to honor the gods of the time; and it was disturbing to see them all in ruins. But what brought me to tears was the realization that, though our intentions were good, our efforts were misdirected. I realized that it was not buildings of stone that God desired of us; it was hearts of love. So, what I was seeing before me, seemed to be a demonstration that all the time and effort that was put into creating these monuments to the glory of God, was misdirected and proven—by their ruin—to be nothing more than acts of futility.

I felt that somehow, sometime in the past, I had shared in the misunderstanding, and was now being shown the error of my prior beliefs. It was, to say the least, a humbling experience. Though I appreciated the guard's tolerance, I didn't share with him my feelings. I think he must have understood them, though, because he took me to his room and offered me a cup of tea while he shared some stories with me. It was very comforting to connect with this simple man whose job it was to guard this special place.

Perhaps because I've always had an attraction to the romanticism of the Native American culture, I've quite enjoyed some Native American ceremonies; even taking part in some of their rites and rituals. Anything that involves nature and the great outdoors is appealing to me. I think I'd be content to spend the rest of my days in a hammock or canoe in some undisturbed part of this country. As a result I really feel for the way in which early settlers destroyed the native culture.

Once I took off for three weeks driving through the lower states out to Arizona and back; visiting early settlements and museums dedicated alternately to those of the Europeans who were settling here, and those of the native population which was gradually being displaced by same. In exposing myself to the sentiments and struggles of each culture, it was easy for me to recognize why things worked out so horribly. I keep thinking of what Jack Nicholson said in the movie *Mars Attacks*: "Why can't we all just get along?" My conclusion is that we feel so threatened by differences, that we use them as an excuse to feel superior to others; and therefore justify our acts of aggression against them. And when a motive exists for bettering one's own prosperity or standard of living in the process, then it's even easier to motivate others into feeling fearful of those with differences, and elicit their support for one's own desire to commit violence.

Of course the early Native American community set themselves up for their own demise. By practicing acts of violence and genocide against neighboring tribes, they demonstrated that their level of spirituality—though impressive as it was in relating to nature—was seriously lacking in the area of most importance: love and respect for others. According to Edgar Cayce, their attack by settling Europeans would not have occurred had they not failed in this regard.

Perhaps the most adventure I've had in exploring different religions and cultures was in exploring the ruins of ancient civilizations in the American Southwest, and Central and South America. I particularly enjoyed participating in Shamanic rites and rituals at various sacred sites, and in learning from local Shaman about the religious beliefs and customs of the various cultures I visited. It was very surprising to me, how much the Shamans' descriptions, of the beliefs and practices of the various cultures, differed from those I read about in the tourist and archeological records. Is it possible that a Shaman would pass down his knowledge to a future Shaman, and the archeologists would never be interested enough to ask for their knowledge? Could it be that they were secrets? I think rather that

Historians and Archeologists draw their material from the written records of the missionaries and early explorers who brought these cultures to ruin, so that the records may have been written in a way that could justify their plundering and acts of genocide.

As with other ancient religious cultures, at one time the civilizations that lived in the Americas were very pure in their teachings and practices. In noting the similarity of their structures, and also to those in Egypt, I believe that Edgar Cayce was correct in stating that they were influenced by people from Atlantis who settled there after that continent's demise. But more importantly, I also feel that it was Jesus who—after his resurrection—"walked the Americas" as the book "He walked the Americas" suggests. That these early religions resembled Christianity to a degree, in worshiping a Trinity of God figures: Sun, Moon, and winged serpent (the god-man: of the earth and of the sky), gives credence to that possibility.

From the teachings of the various Shamans I had the pleasure of learning from, I concluded that these early civilizations started out with a large degree of spiritual wisdom, and very positive rites and rituals, but were later corrupted, either from within or from without, by invading cultures, which set them up to be taken down by the invading Spanish. I feel it to be a great shame that the fervent desire of missionaries to spread Jesus' teachings of love and forgiveness of sins could not show more mercy upon these civilizations. I wonder how different this world would be now if the spread of Christianity had been motivated more out of love. I also wonder how different things would be now, if all religions could express more of the feeling of love in their relationships with each other. Maybe one day we'll be able to find out.

THE TREE OF LIFE

"The Road Not Taken":

In the mythic Garden of Eden were two trees; the Tree of Knowledge and the Tree of Life. These trees represented paths that souls could take in their journeys of spiritual growth. In referencing Robert Frost's famous poem; "The Road Not Taken": some souls chose "the one less travelled by". This is the difficult path through the physical plane; and while on that path, souls often have occasion to "sigh"; perhaps out of regret for "the road not taken".

Now, Robert Frost wrote this poem as a comment upon his current life choices, without any thought—I assume—in regards to "Adam and Eve's" choice; but the analogy fits so well I felt compelled to use it. It's the "sigh", actually, that I want to highlight, as it infers that one wished that the other path could have been taken as well. In fact, in the poem, the desire is expressed to come back and take the other path as well, though with a sense of acknowledgment that this will probably not be possible. Well, the good news is that with regard to the Genesis story, one not only can, but will come back to take that other path. "And that [makes] all the difference."

Symbolism of the Tree of Life:

I've heard different interpretations of what the Tree of Life represented in the mythic Garden of Eden, and I believe that there's truth in every one of them. I even like Zecharia Sitchin's more literal interpretation (recommending his books; particularly *The 12ᵗʰ Planet*), though I think that some of his assumptions are slightly off.

In ancient Hebrew mysticism, the tree represents the Qabalah (Kabbalah), which maps out relationships with regard to different aspects of the soul body and their interrelatedness (a valuable course of study for those so motivated). Eastern mysticism focuses upon chakras or energy centers within the soul body, and describes how these correspond to the physical body. According to Edgar Cayce, these are the points of contact between the physical body and the soul; and are what St. John was sometimes referring to in his Book of Revelations. Because of the significance of these centers with regard to meditation and spiritual development, I'll come back to this subject later.

A meaning of the "Tree" that I'd like to offer, though, relates to the drawing I presented in the fourth chapter describing humankind's multi-dimensional nature, as well as comments I made with respect to consciousness; in that—though we <u>are</u> in fact One, since we are not consciousness of being One with the All, then it's equally valid to state that we're individuals. So, the meaning I'd like to suggest is that the Tree of Life represented our state of consciousness that existed before we entered the physical plane and lost the awareness of being a part of the whole; losing awareness of our multi-dimensional soul. In fact, some people have lost that awareness to such a degree, that they can't even be convinced that they even have a soul or a spiritual body. It is this soul body which is immortal, and in losing consciousness of it, it can be said that this tree was cut down.

Multi-dimensionality of Soul:

At the beginning of the third chapter, I offered a crude graph to describe paths that souls may follow in their exercise of free will; and later conceded that since a soul can perceive that it's separate from God, then it can be stated that it is—in consciousness—separate and an individual. Our perception, then, is that we "fell" into lower realms of consciousness by choosing to express ourselves in this dense reality; and it was from this perspective that I offered many of my opinions throughout this book.

I hope that I don't confuse you now, if I assert that we didn't actually "fall"; it is truer to state that we (our souls) "reached" down into lower states of consciousness. It could also be stated that we extended our soul bodies into lower vibratory levels. We did this by creating a denser body and putting that on; much like a scuba diver puts on a wet suit or a fire-fighter puts on a protective suit of clothing.

To understand our true nature, it must be realized that we—in being multi-dimensional souls—exist (in body, mind, and spirit) on a number of vibratory levels; and that each of these levels have their particular qualities in body, mind, and spirit. Now, I know that this is a lot to grasp (and difficult to explain clearly), but in order to learn from our experiences here and find our way back, it's helpful to have an understanding of what's going on.

I previously stated an assertion by Cosmic Awareness that all deities which we can imagine are aspects of our own self. The same can be said with regard to all demons which we can conceive of. Each have their reflection in self, else we would not be able to conceive of them. In considering the higher forms of consciousness such as spirit guides, angels, gods, or God Itself, it's helpful to recognize that these reflect higher states of our own consciousness. When we pray to God, we are also praying to that dimension of our own soul which remains at the frequency or vibratory level of God. This is what I intended to detail in the drawing I presented in the fourth chapter; where we reach up (so to speak) through the various levels of our soul to reach the God consciousness. The "we" I am referring to in this statement relates to our illusionary consciousness which believes itself to be separate, but in reality isn't. This is the consciousness that pretty much everyone is at, all the time.

Trinity of Soul:

Now, to make it a bit more complicated: "we" are also body, mind, and spirit. It's easy to perceive of ourselves as a body because it's what we see in the mirror all the time, and have to scratch from time to time. It's also easy to perceive of ourselves as mind, because when we're on the hammock it's our mind that is active and not our body (unless the mosquitos are out). Our mind is what makes decisions and forms perceptions and creates beliefs. Recognizing ourselves as also being spirit isn't as easy, though, and some people even deny that they have one. The best way to get a handle on this may be to consider with what spirit you are considering this particular subject, or pursuing this activity.

It gets more confusing when we try to put the two concepts together, but it will later be helpful when describing how we rise through the frequencies to get closer to God.

A Trinity of Multi-dimensionality:

The body's multi-dimensionality is pretty much like described in the drawing; whereby gradually denser bodies reside within further denser bodies until all are (one inside the other) inside the physical body. It must be remembered, though, that they only <u>reach</u> into the lower bodies, because they also extend "above" the denser body into ever "lighter" spiritual bodies.

During normal waking hours when the dense physical body is active, these higher vibrational bodies are more attached to, or within, the denser bodies into which they have extended themselves. When the physical body is at rest, though, they are freer to expand outside the denser bodies. The degree to which they are stuck or free is also dependent upon the vibrational frequency of the dense physical body. Unless a physical body is seriously impaired or under drugs, the general health is a factor in determining frequency. Diets of heavy meats, for example, lower the vibration; while seafood and vegetarian diets raise the vibration. Toxic substances stored in body tissues also affect frequency; and this is why many religious groups recommend fasting to allow the body to clear out these toxic elements. If the body is under duress, though, the higher bodies may not be "comfortable" in the body and will separate to some degree. An extreme example would be the introduction of drugs which induce unconsciousness.

The mental body's multi-dimensionality is also reflected in the drawing, but it relates to the types of thoughts and attitudes that one uses to learn with and form beliefs. At the lower frequencies, the mental body perceives of itself as being separate from the whole, and as it rises in frequency, perceives of itself as being more: first a part of a group, then a group of groups, and eventually the whole. The various minds are also the thinking, perceiving mechanism of each type of body; so there is the physical consciousness, the astral consciousness, and etc.

Another way to describe the mind is as Carl Jung proposed: that there is a subconscious mind and a super-conscious mind in addition to the conscious mind which we are always aware of. In this regard, the subconscious mind would relate to the astral mind, while the super-conscious mind would relate to the mind active in the higher frequencies.

The spirit's level of frequency is best measured in the degree of love or self-interest (ego) that it inspires the mind to act upon. A low spirit can perform acts labeled as evil and equated with a devil, while a spirit of high vibration will be more loving, and can be equated with of a god or an angel.

Ascending to Heaven:

It is the goal of every soul to eventually return to Source by retracting its reach into the denser realms. This might be equated with raising the frequency of vibration of the soul at the deepest expression; in this case this physical reality. In order to return to God, then, we need to attend to those influences that challenge ascension in the vibratory rate or frequency of consciousness.

The lower the frequency of the astral body, the more "sticky" it is; it acts like glue, remaining more closely attached to the physical body. The higher the frequency of this emotional body, the more light-hearted, optimistic, or happy the person feels; and this makes it easier for the astral body to lift out of the denser physical body at night. This is why both mood and spiritual development have an effect upon a person's ability to experience some forms of psychic phenomena that depend upon the astral body being able to "go out" in search of information. Sometimes the ego can go with it, and the consciousness will then perceive of itself as going outside the body for some experience—thus an OBE.

I've already discussed the need to deal with issues of guilt, judgment, and refusal to forgive. I've already pointed out the obvious that attachments to pleasures of the flesh, passions, and other sensory stimuli also keep us grounded. All negative feelings or expressions, which weigh a person down, and cause one to become depressed, are antagonistic to spiritual ascension.

Love of self and others, forgiveness which frees self and others, humor, kindness, helpfulness; all these things help to raise consciousness to higher levels. All this stuff you know; so I'm only referencing it here.

What I'm trying to get at is the subject of how to let go of the things that weigh us down, and embrace the influences which enlighten us. Religion is supposed to be providing us with this guidance, yet many of us are faithfully practicing our religion's teachings, and engaging in the rites and rituals which they offer, yet are still unhappy or depressed, and functioning at low frequency levels. Perhaps I can offer some suggestions that will help to remedy this condition.

Turning Within:

The most important thing any person can do, in order to accomplish any task, or to discover any truth, is to turn within for guidance. Unfortunately, most people look outside of themselves, asking others. And those who do "go inside" are not reaching the highest levels of consciousness; instead they listen to the voice of their own ego, and pursue acts of vice and greed, based upon selfish motivations for power and praise. They may also act on the basis of their emotions and make choices based upon anger, jealousy, condemnation, and fear.

It has been suggested that two entities sit upon our shoulders, speaking into our ears, trying to influence our decisions; the one on the left—the devil, and the one on the right—an angel. I think this is partly correct. Instead, however, I think it to be two aspects of our own mind competing for our attention: our ego (which may at times be influenced from negative sources), and our conscience (through which we may receive guidance from higher sources).

I suggest that we learn to distinguish which voice is speaking to us at any given moment, and make the conscious choice to listen only to the latter. In fact, I suggest that we make it a point of trying to establish a sound relationship with higher sources of guidance, and use them to enrich our lives. Some of our greatest inventors, scientists, and artists (of all types) have achieved success through this means. And this avenue is available to all of us, except for those with severe mental handicaps, or strong sociopathic tendencies (who even seem to lack a conscience or connection with higher consciousness).

Prayer is a valuable means for accessing this source, but it is not the only means. Or, perhaps I should say that prayer exists in many forms. Prayer is the concerted effort to communicate with unseen forces either within one's own consciousness, or in some unknown spiritual realm. And it can be expressed either through a type of verbal or mental communication, or through an expressed intent or inner desire.

But the request is only the beginning. It must be followed up with an openness to receive a reply. This can be obtained through some outward manifestation (as I indicated in the introduction with my own experience), through feelings or inner promptings (inspirations), through dreams and visions, or through meditation experiences. And whatever is received, however it comes, must be met with some degree of skepticism in order to discern whether it comes from a reliable source, or from some level of our own ego.

Once determined to have come from a reliable source (based upon the ideals expressed by it), the guidance must be followed up on through some course of action. Too often we do receive helpful guidance, but allow our fearful and doubting minds (or ego) to dissuade us from following it. This happens most often when we are inspired to act contrary to public opinion, or to the opinion of family and friends who might be critical.

I once heard a statistic that 95% of Americans believe in God. Well, that number may be different now, but it doesn't really matter if they don't listen to It. I wonder what percent of Americans pray to God but listen instead to a priest, minister, Rabbi or Guru; or worse yet, to their own selfish ego (Satan).

In "Dawn of Unity", I suggested that we accept personal responsibility for determining our future, and take back some of the power entrusted to government and other structures of authority. In this book, I suggest something similar. For too long, we have gone to religious authorities to tell us what God wants of us, and to tell us what we are to believe. Now I'm suggesting that we act with greater maturity, and establish our own direct relationship with That Which Is—the "All In All" that we call God. I can perceive of no other way for us to grow as spiritual beings and achieve the type of Divine Awareness that God desires for us. I believe that this higher state of consciousness (as expressed through the entity called Jesus) is available to us all and is what Jesus referred to as the Kingdom (consciousness) of Heaven (not a place, but a state of consciousness). How can we ever hope to become one with God, when we allow our own egos, and the opinion or authoritative control of others, to stand between us. If we are ever to become mature in the spiritual sense, I can see no other way than that of personal effort, and I'm sure that God and Its agents will support us in that expression.

Meditation:

There are potentially as many forms of meditation as there are people who practice it, because there are so many techniques that one can use to facilitate the process. Through the practice of meditation (think of mediate or medium) we create a condition within our body and mind which establishes a means of connecting with another consciousness. Because one can essentially meditate on anything that has identity, the practice can be used for a number or purposes; not all of them beneficial. This has led some people to brand meditation in general as being "of the devil" or alternately as being a form of relaxation. Properly used, it is neither.

By far the best application, and the most popular use, is in achieving an attunement with higher consciousness. This higher consciousness can be thought of as a higher dimension of our own soul, or a more universal consciousness such as the Christ Consciousness or God. In terms of vibration: in meditation we attune ourselves to a specific (preferably higher) frequency in order to receive input from that frequency level. It can be thought of as adjusting the dial on a radio to receive music from a particular station. In the following chapter, I'll suggest ways in which it can be used for more mundane or practical uses, but my intent here is to offer a way in which one can become more loving, more virtuous, more psychologically balanced, more divine, and more open to receiving guidance and assistance with one's reaching upwards to return to one's source.

There are many books on the subject of meditation, and I'm sure that many are excellent. For the beginner, though, I highly recommend books from the A.R.E.; particularly because they focus on the spiritual use of it, and relate it to religious dogma. When Jesus asked his disciples to "wait in the upper room" at Pentecost to await the Holy Spirit, he was asking them to sit in meditation. "Waiting" is the attitude that dominates in meditation. One sets the sails, so to speak, and then waits for the winds to come and take them where they want to go. At Pentecost, the wind was actually heard (not uncommon during meditation; I've heard it many times, and so have others I've spoken to. In fact, many different types of sounds can be heard.), and it led them into becoming Apostles; vehicles for the Holy Spirit to use to further Jesus' teachings.

Chakras:

The "upper room" refers to what some call the third eye on the center of the forehead. This is considered to relate to the Pituitary gland—the master gland of the body. Though it's not actually at the top of the head, it is the highest chakra; and the one through which higher consciousness connects with our physical body. The shepherd's staff is the shape in which energy rises; up from the root chakra to the crown chakra at the top of the head, then down to the third eye. The energy raised in this way is different than what some call kundalini. I don't recommending messing with that "snake" unless you really know what you're doing, as its influence can be powerful; even put you in a mental hospital. That's why its feet were symbolically cut off in Eden. Leave it alone; it will rise on its own when appropriate.

Two energies that are best to work with (though with some caution) are the upward flowing energy from the earth, and the downward flowing energy from the Divine chakras above the head (these have different names and numbers which I'm not concerned about here). The "Star of David" is a symbolic representation of these two energy systems flowing in balance. View the six pointed star as two over-lapping equilateral triangles; one pointing up, and the other pointing down. As the symbol suggests, my recommendation (though I doubt you'll hear of it anywhere else) is that you try to keep these energy flows in balance during your preparations for meditation. I don't know of anyone having problems by focusing on either to the detriment of the other; in fact many don't even refer to the downward flow, but my intuition tells me that this is best. It does, after all, symbolize the meditative process; wherein the meditator is reaching up, and higher consciousness is reaching down. Holding the intention that the energies are equal is equivalent to holding the intention that the meditation is a success. A simple way to affirm this intent is to just imagine that one is inside the Star of David when meditating. Don't be concerned if it's considered to be a Jewish symbol; they won't mind you're using it, and it won't make you Jewish unless you want it to. In fact, though it's a Jewish symbol, I doubt that very many Jewish people use it in this way. If you're Jewish, on the other hand, use of this symbol should benefit you even more. Shalom!

Another simple way to balance energies is by reciting either the Lord's Prayer or the 23rd Psalm. Each of these contain references to the respective chakras (the A.R.E. has charts to detail this), so by reciting them verbally or inwardly, the respective chakras are energized and balanced in a subtle way. This won't increase the magnitude of the energy, though. They merely awaken and balance them in a harmonious fashion.

The highest two chakras work best together, and if one begins to feel pressure at the center of the forehead (not between the eyes as some claim), withdraw attention there and focus on the crown. These two work best as one, and when energized together can trigger other desirable results. The third center from the top—the 5th from the bottom—is the throat chakra and is associated with communication, arts (a form of communication), the will, and medium-ship. For this reason, this one must become energized in order to augment the meditative process.

The lower four chakras relate to the more physical person, while the upper three relate to the divine aspects. For this reason, it's best not to focus too much energy on the lower four to the detriment of the upper three; a possible exception being the heart center in the middle. It relates to—well—love as well as identity (self) and healing. When it is energized in the desire to help others, or upon a feeling of compassion for others, sensations may be felt in the hands. These are minor chakras (the body has several but I'm not concerned with them here), relate to healing—a manifestation of love and caring. If you feel energy or warmth in your hands then you can use that for healing purposes if and when appropriate.

The chakra below the heart—at the solar plexus—relates to practical pursuits; success, prosperity, acquisitions, and other things relating to physical desires which aren't sexual. Greed is a negative use of this energy.

The chakra below that is in the area of the navel and relates to sexual energy. This is usually an easy center to energize, so care must be taken not to over-do it. Some people intentionally build this energy and then try to force the energy upwards through the other chakras; but though this can be done, it can also be dangerous because if the energy doesn't subsequently flow up and balance out, an excess can remain there and cause problems.

Also, astral entities can be attracted to the strong energizing of this center; because they can feed off of the energies.

The root chakra is at the base of the spine and relates to self-preservation issues. It also should not be over-energized, as it can relate to anger, fear, and violence: responses that are natural to a person who feels threatened.

Raising energy for Meditation:

There are many methods to raise energy to assist in meditation, and visualization is a factor that has a place in all of them; but the intention should always be to keep the energy centers balanced. One way to accomplish this is by focusing on each center in turn for the same amount of time, or with the same intensity. Another is to maintain a back and forth flow of energy that washes back and forth through the body. One can also envision something like a fountain above and below spewing energy up or down. Another is to just imagine swirling energy around the whole body. I've had success with visualizing different colored lights shining on me; first red, then orange, yellow, green, blue, indigo, and violet. With each color I imagine I'm absorbing only what I need, and I don't focus any much longer than others.

The "Middle Pillar" meditation is also a nice technique. It uses the symbolism of the Qabbala—the middle pillar of same—to raise the corresponding energy centers in the body. There is not a one-to-one correspondence, though, so the middle pillar centers may include two or more chakras.

Perhaps the best method to use at the beginning is to use the breath, and imagine energy flowing into and through the body and then out again; focusing on no particular chakra at all. This just treats the whole body as one energy center. But do feel or imagine that the energy is flowing equally throughout; don't just bring it in and out of the lungs.

One can also imagine liquid light flowing down through the top of the head and flowing all the way through and out the feet, flushing all negativity out of the body. Once one feels clean or cleared, then one could imagine becoming filled with the liquid light until overflowing.

Another technique is to simply imagine energy flowing back and forth, up and down through the body. No colors, symbols, analogies, or breath (do breathe though); simply use the focused intention of the mind to move energy. Visualize or imagine the energy moving sequentially throughout the body, up and down, as though clearing out the system.

Chanting is also a technique used by a lot of people the world over; and with good results. Not only does it increase the energy, it helps to raise it to a higher frequency. Chanting for a few minutes can greatly facilitate the meditation process that follows. It could be done before or after working with energy balance. It needn't be done out loud, but the sound can be mentally repeated. The words used are often referred to as one's mantra; which means mind tool. Besides helping a person keep to keep the mind focused so it doesn't wander, the word used has a meaning that is focused upon. The technique then serves two purposes; it also serves as an affirmation.

Perhaps the most popular sound is AUM, where each letter's sound is given equal attention. It's also helpful to feel the vibration of the A at the heart, and as one moves to the U sound, visualize or feel the energy moving up to the throat—vibrating that area. Finally the M vibrates the top and front of the head. This sound is equated with the sound of the universe—of the highest vibration; so it's like feeling a union with God.

Another popular sound is HU which is considered by the Eckankar religion to be an ancient name for God. Eckankar is a religion that recognizes the multi-dimensionality of soul, and incorporates the laws of karma and reincarnation into its teachings and practices. They chant the sound of HU as a spiritual exercise to express their love to God. This helps to raise the practitioners' energy to a higher frequency; particularly when they are equating it with a feeling of love.

You may use suggestions from various religions, a variety of books, or from other people; try several until you find what works best for you. You may even change techniques from time to time. Check out your book store or the internet. I already recommended the A.R.E.; but another source I recommend is Astara (www.astara.org); they provide an inexpensive course in booklet form that goes into very great detail about the chakras and meditation. Their material may be too detailed, though, for someone who doesn't want to venture too far in this direction; but you can make up your own mind.

Benefits of working with Energy:

Some meditation techniques focus merely on relaxing, with little emphasis on the energy that can aid the experience. If you realize that we need energy for anything we do, however, it's easy to recognize the value of increasing the amount of energy available. It's like putting the foot down a bit harder on the accelerator in a car so one can more easily climb the steep hill.

Bringing energy up from the earth and through the body upwards also has a grounding effect which helps to stabilize the respective bodies; while bringing energy down from "on high" aids in establishing a connection to God and the realms of higher consciousness or high self.

Also, the very act of focusing on a process of balancing and energizing, gives the mind something to do so that it is less apt to wander; thinking of problems or jobs to be done.

Benefits of using Breath:

When using one's breath all of the above benefits are received plus two additional ones. By focusing on breathing, more oxygen enters the body; and with the body at rest, there is more excess physical energy (oxygen + glucose = energy) available to supplement the energy drawn up from the earth.

Additionally, breathing is predominantly a subconscious function. So, when the mind takes over control of this function the subconscious mind becomes more active. First it asks what's going on, and pays attention to the intention of the meditation, facilitating the process. And if the same techniques—including time and location of meditation—will learn quickly what's going on and help to facilitate the process. Also, being freed from having to operate the breathing process, it can devote more attention to what one wants to accomplish. Symbolically, using breath during meditation is like Aladdin rubbing the lamp, so that the Genie will appear and do his bidding.

Inner Cleansing:

Upward flowing energy from the earth through the lower centers can be likened to clean water flowing up through the stream-bed of the lower four chakras and above, flushing out debris that has accumulated there. This debris is the blockages and areas of density that are held within our astral bodies. These may be areas of hurt, anger, fear, etc. that have been stored there on an emotional level. By flowing energy through the astral body, these can be cleared out or brought to the surface to be dealt with. This is another reason why energy flow is best kept in balance; too much force in one area can bring up past emotional issues for you to deal with.

Rebirthing for Cleansing:

There is a process related to meditation, though, where the intention is to raise energy high enough to free up these blocks. It's called "rebirthing". This is done with a qualified practitioner to guide the process. One breathes much more than normal and for much longer periods of time to raise oxygen levels and energy much higher than normal. It's like flushing out the emotional body with energy in the same way a plumber might flush out your sewer system with water. And you can believe that the results are sometimes similar. During rebirthing, the person may experience any of a number of strong emotions or physical sensations—including movements and tightening of muscles. It can also produce visions and recall of past traumas; which, when brought to the surface for recognition, can be resolved and released. After the experience a person can actually feel lighter; and will often feel freer, more happy and loving.

If you want to sample just a bit of this yourself, like sampling a dish before buying, lie comfortably in bed, and start taking comfortable slow deep breaths in and out without pausing, so you maintain a continuous cycle of flow. Once the continuous cyclical rhythm is established, start to breath deeper and faster; but do so gradually to remain just a bit above the comfort level. Try too much too fast and it will become too uncomfortable to continue. What you will start to feel at one point are physical sensations like tingling of the skin; these are easy to work through. Later you will likely start to feel an impulse to move your body; you can feel free to do this if you don't let it stop your breathing in the process. Eventually you will begin to feel emotions such as fear or remorse; and this is where it's good to have a facilitator. The facilitator will motivate you to keep breathing when your subconscious mind is telling you to slow down or stop. In fact it will help you to keep your mind on what you're doing because you might tend to doze off or get so "spacey" that you will forget what you're doing and settle back down. It's sort of like falling asleep at the wheel, except you come to a comfortable stop rather than an abrupt crash. A facilitator will also allow you to feel safe, so you won't quit out of fear. And it will comfort you when the emotions arise to be accepted and released. Some facilitators offer prayers and/or add spiritual energy to help heal and bless you during the process and aid in other ways as well. And if you start to experience severe physical movements, the facilitator can deal with them in the best way.

Benefits of Downward flow of Energy:

The benefits of bringing energy down from above are very much the same as with upward flowing energies, except the energy has a different quality and function. Rather than likening it to water flushing debris from a stream, it is more like air flowing through an air duct, blowing out cobwebs. It could also be likened to light scaring bats out of the belfry.

Where upward flowing energy deals mostly with emotional issues, downward flowing energy deals with attitudes and memories, which interfere with one's connection to divinity. Past life issues and memories can surface as a result of this flow of energy. As with the upward flowing energy, this energy is raised in the rebirthing process and is part of the reason for its success at helping to free people from mental and spiritual blockages.

In meditation, though, the energies are not raised to the extremes that they are in a rebirthing session; actually the opposite. In meditation, one wants to relax so much that one ceases to even become aware of the body.

Purposes or Intentions:

This is the most important element of meditation to consider, for in meditation one takes into the trinity of their multi-dimension souls the type of effect that they intend or set as a purpose for meditating. If you have a problem, for example, and wish to use meditation to help resolve it, you could inadvertently augment the difficulty. This can occur if you start thinking of the problem itself—especially on an emotional level—while meditating. It can be helpful, though, if you are able to keep your focus on the desired solution. As an example, consider that you want to become more patient with your children. You decide that you want to focus on patience, becoming more patient. If during your meditation your attention shifts to the reason why you want to become more patient, you could start to feel frustration or anger at the cause of your impatience, and end up feeding your soul with that energy. The best thing to do, then, is to avoid meditating for that purpose just after some occurrence that has stimulated the need. Wait instead until you are relatively calm and the subject isn't a present emotional issue.

If you recall what I said about ILP, you may remember that I said that this Infinite reservoir of Living Potentiality is everywhere present to be awakened or formed into any use that can be conceived of. The mind uses this Potentiality to create thought-forms which manifest as plans or energies. Healers use it for healing; Qigong and martial arts for Chi energy; and you can use it for any intention which you desire to fill yourself with during meditation. You can imagine drawing it into yourself with the breath (because it's in the air), through your body with either flow of energy (because it's present in the higher frequencies of spirit, as well as the lower earth energies), or you can affirm that it's within your own body and just focus on it building the intention where it's desired. As examples, meditate on being more loving by focusing on your heart being filled with love; on being smarter or sharper by focusing on your brain being fed with that quality; or on healing by focusing on an ailing part of your body being transformed by the ILP in the corresponding organ being awakened into a healing energy.

Perhaps, though, the best use of meditation is with regard to changing mental attitudes that relate to spiritual growth and connection with Divinity. Use of affirmations is an excellent way to do this; and this method is the one recommended by Edgar Cayce via the A.R.E. Suggested affirmations include being a channel of blessings to others, being kinder and wiser in every way, surrendering to the will of God, etc. My favorite is just a simple feeling of attuning myself with higher consciousness; it's like surrendering, and includes all the other good ideas. I sort of feel that my own energy patterns are harmonizing with higher patterns, as though I'm letting go of the blocks and attitudes that conflict with those held in the higher realms.

There are lots of books and material on the use of meditation, methods of meditation, and preparation for meditation. If you're like me, you'll try different ideas and change them from time to time. Regardless which techniques or affirmations you choose, do try to be regular and persistent. The first few attempts might be difficult as your mind is probably used to wandering when you sit back (or lie down) and relax. Be patient and persistent; it may not take very long before you begin to gain success.

Preparation for Meditation:

There are many ways to prepare for meditation; but when you consider that the success will depend upon cooperation from your subconscious mind, the best methods are those which involve the subconscious mind in the process. These methods utilize some type of ritual, no matter how simple; but to begin, more involvement works best. Later, when you've established a routine you can start to make modifications to suit your comfort.

Washing your hands or face, preparing a setting, putting on light music, lighting a candle, or producing some fragrance are ways to get the subconscious mind involved. So also is writing down an intention or a prayer.

I already mentioned how prayer helps to establish a connection with Divinity, and this I recommend in all cases. Prayer also acts as a means of protection; not as though you'll need it, but so that you will feel safe. It also serves a way to set the intention and start to slow down the body into relaxation. But the most beneficial aspect of beginning with prayer is that it allows you to focus your mind on what you're doing, and clear out all the emotions, thoughts, and feelings that might otherwise come up to interrupt the process.

Through prayer, you can empty yourself of all the negative feelings and emotions that are on your mind. Properly done—and pray until you feel you are done—your mind and emotions will be empty and clear; because you've already expressed all those things that are troubling you, and placed them in God's hands. Some people imagine a large box and put all their concerns there before meditation; closing the lid afterwards.

After you've set aside your concerns and established your intent, then you can start to work with energy. If you want, you can also chant for a minute or more to establish a higher frequency of energy (you'll feel it change) before you begin to work with the energies; balancing and harmonizing them. You may even start to experience energy shifts or meditation phenomena during this process. Of course you may also fall asleep or start thinking of things.

If (perhaps I should say when) your mind starts to become active, just put it back to either mentally chanting or working with the energies. When you feel deeply relaxed, and feeling good, then you can begin the most important step of focusing upon your intent or ideal; whatever you feel to be best at the time. This is when the mind is most apt to start wandering because it easily becomes bored with this step. While working with the energy it was busy; now it's not. So, if it wanders, just gently bring it back home, and start again.

Self-hypnosis techniques suggest counting backwards from some number; going deeper, deeper, deeper with each number. This works for meditation as well. It can be done in the relaxing phase, but if the mind becomes active, it can be done again in this step. Count from 12 to 1 maybe going deeper, more relaxed, etc. They when you again feel good, focus on the intent again.

If phenomena occur such as flashes of light, colors, or sounds, just try to go with these higher energies; let them take you wherever they want to go. These sensations can be startling and even frightening, but try to just go with them or let them be. At least that's the advice I've been given. The flashes of light don't disturb me much; I actually feel more connected when I see them. But I haven't yet learned how to "go with" the sounds. They keep pulling me out of my relaxed state; maybe one day. (Sigh)

Another phenomenon you will eventually begin to experience is a flow or vibration of energy. They are almost never from spirits trying to possess you; but that might be your first impression, especially if they are strong. Ask yourself how they feel. But if you put some attention toward asking for protection, they're not likely to be negative spirits; or spirits of any sort. Most likely you're feeling your astral body separating a bit from the physical and your consciousness went with it, so you're now feeling the vibrational energy of a lighter more vibrant body. I feel this all the time almost and I love the feeling.

I've felt negative energies before as well, and they either cause me to feel as though something's wrong or they are perceived as a pressure on the chest. If it's the latter, focus on a tiny spec of brilliant white light in the center of your chest, and feel it getting gradually bigger until it fills your chest; then expanding more to fill your body and beyond. If it was an astral entity it will leave of its own accord.

At some point you might tire of focusing on the affirmation or intent, or feel that you've sufficiently established it. At this point just focus on the center or top of your forehead and put your attention on seeing. Yes; keep your eyes closed. Also put your attention on listening. In these two ways you are entering a receptive open phase which allows you to receive guidance or a response. Ideally it's an act of surrender, as you've already done your part. Now you're just watching, listening, and waiting. Do this for as long as comfortable and then slowly start to return your awareness back to your body; and when you feel fully awake, you can get up. If you're meditating before going to sleep as I do, then just move into your sleeping position.

Phenomena:

There are three types of phenomena that I and other meditators occasionally experience: sights, energies, and sounds. Different opinions about with regard to these, but most suggest that they not let you distract you from your practice. I will give you my <u>current</u> opinion.

Early on I described the two-fold movement of energy; one directed up toward higher consciousness, and the other coming down from higher consciousness. It is my opinion that sights are a perception of these downward energies. They feel as though I'm either seeing energy itself, or I'm seeing higher spirit bodies that are composed of energy. In either case I accept them with a feeling of gratitude, but try not to let them interfere. After all; if one comes, more may be following.

In discussing the sensations of energy or vibrational changes, I wish to refer to what I said about us being multi-dimensional; having bodies of different frequencies, one inside the other. During meditation these can begin to separate (also in sleep to a degree), and the feeling of energy changes is perceived when the consciousness moves with these energies. To back up this belief, I'll recount an incident:

Many times when I'm meditating and feeling a higher vibration, I'll also begin to see as though through my closed eye lids. Now often what I see are visions; generally symbolic in nature, but other times it's difficult to know if one is actually seeing something, or if one isn't rather picking up an image from some memory. In many cases, I've concluded that visions are often images stored in memory from prior events.

This makes it difficult to know what's really happening when one "sees" something during meditation. Regardless, it is the "experience" or "perception" of some event that seems to be what's significant. One doesn't always need to know what is really happening. Occasional perceptions of outdoor scenes which seem natural, as though I'm in the yard or looking out the window of a moving car, are good examples of this type of experience. But sometimes I'm seeing something in the room or building that really feels as if I'm looking at some true object.

On one occasion I was seeing the wall near my bed from a perspective as though I was a few feet from where I was laying. It was strange because I was fully aware of lying in bed feeling the comfortable sensation of vibration. What occurred to me though, was that the details I was seeing were also vibrating at about the same frequency. In another similar experience I had; also when seeing the wall, the wall seemed to be tilted at an angle. I thought this strange, so I intended to move my energetic body: the one that felt to be vibrating. I succeeded in moving my energy body (or at least it felt like I did) and the slope of the wall shifted accordingly. I was convinced that somehow the "me" that was seeing was also the "me" that was vibrating and slightly separate from the physical body (which was unmoving in bed with its eyes closed).

When I hear sounds I associate many of them with movement of my conscious self (the one perceiving the sound) into higher bodies of my multi-dimensional self. It's as though by leaving one body to enter a lighter body, my physical brain (which interprets sound) experiences an energy shift that it translates into sound. I'm not sure how it works, but I'm sure that it is a phenomena associated with my consciousness entering higher bodies.

That I hear a variety of different sounds makes it even more interesting; and once again I must state that the subconscious mind will bring up sounds stored in memory, and play these back for some intended effect. Before I changed to a cell phone, I'd often be awakened from sleep by the sound of my landline phone ringing just once; as though my subconscious mind wanted me to wake up; using it as an alarm clock. What's supportive of this notion is that now that my only phone is a cell phone, I will occasionally wake up upon hearing its particular tune being played. I will also occasionally "hear" my father calling me by name. The message is that the subconscious mind can produce any type of sound it wants, and for any of a number of reasons.

Sometimes I hear clicking noises, crinkling noises, popping noises, snapping noises, sounds like wind rushing by, sound like a gun being fired, and these I relate to movements of energy through the head that affect the nerves associated with hearing. Perhaps these all relate to the degree of the energy shift; and the brain interprets the differential as different familiar sounds. Regardless; when I hear these type of sounds, I take it as evidence that my consciousness is actually moving into higher dimensions; which was the goal of the meditation in the first place: to become more at one with higher spirit or God. I just wish they weren't so distracting! The advice I've heard from others is to just go with the sounds; easier said than done.

Guidance through Dreams:

I highly recommend meditating before going to sleep in the bed upon which one sleeps. It may cause you to fall asleep during the meditation, so a second period of meditation in the morning is also recommended to make up for the period lost in sleep. I also find meditating at the end of the afternoon or just after dinner to be beneficial as the physical body (at least mine) enjoys a nap around that time, and relaxation is automatic. Anyway; the benefit of meditating in bed before going to sleep is that the subconscious begins to confuse sleeping with meditating, and one wakes up in a type of meditation. And even if one doesn't wake up at all, the meditation can occur during sleep and some interesting dreams result.

I guess you're already guessing my next recommendation. Dreams are an excellent means of obtaining insight into problems and guidance in general <u>if the dreams can be remembered and written down before being forgotten.</u> My next suggestion is that you start a dream journal in which you write down as much of a dream as can be recalled; even if it's just an impression of the mood or theme. Writing down even the tiniest bits lets the subconscious mind know that you're paying attention and are open to receiving messages. It's like checking the mailbox regularly. Once it becomes established that you're paying attention and receptive to input, you will begin to obtain dreams which can help with problems; providing insight. And the more you write, the more you will be able to recall; because—like a muscle—with repeated action, you will remember more and more. You will then be able to receive answers to, or guidance with respect to, problems you expressed in your prayers.

Another interesting and quite enjoyable result, of doing this faithfully, is that it brings the ego consciousness more into contact with the dreaming consciousness. An inevitable result is that on occasion the two will meet in the dream, and you will experience a lucid dream wherein you are conscious (to some varying degree) that you're in the dream, yet also sleeping and having the dream. In the most vivid degree of lucidity it's very difficult to know if you're really dreaming, because it seems so real. Many times I've had the experience when I considered if I was in a dream and concluded that it was real; only to realize later that it was a dream.

The most challenging part of keeping a dream journal is waking self up enough after a dream to write it down. Very often one just doesn't want to move. But if one falls back asleep, most—or all—of the dream is lost. By forcing one's self to move and write the dream, however, seems to have an effect of strengthening the conscious ego mind's ability to move out of the physical body's sleeping state and into the dream state. I don't completely understand why; but it seems to aid in experiencing not only more lucid dreams, but in also in stimulating the occurrence of out-of-body experiences

Out of body, in my opinion, is a state where the conscious mind has moved into a lighter body, and that lighter body separates from the physical (though still connected by a thread of energy). In these experiences one can travel incredible distances in a flash, or fly along like Superman. It's often hard to tell, though, if one is truly having an OBE or if one is merely having a lucid dream. It's not of importance here; I'll let you have your own experiences and tell me.

Uses of the OBE:

Once in an OBE, there are several things that one can do for constructive purposes. In fact, the lucid dream state is so close to an OBE, that similar uses can be applied. I also have a theory that in a lucid dream the light-body is "out", but the consciousness is asleep. On a very few occasions I've been able to "wake" from a lucid dream and find myself in an out of body state. I was sort of like sleeping while driving I guess.

Anyway, contact with entities in the astral plane can be made from this state; and though this might be frightening to some of you, just realize that even if they appear hostile they can't hurt you. I've been grabbed and all I did was express love to them and they let me go. You could also project God's light to them, or bless them. I wouldn't suggest trying to fight them or express any negative energy if they appear negative to you. Don't let me frighten you, though, I've had several OBEs and only one or two were hostile; and even these mostly threatening.

The reason I recommend this use of the OBE is that there are a lot of stuck souls in the astral plane who don't know where to go, and there's too few people able to help them. If an entity from a higher realm comes to them, they can't see them any more easily than we can usually see ghosts. At best they can feel energy. And that's often the way I first perceive an astral being when I'm in a lucid dream state. It's happened several times that I'd be in such a dream and feel energy surround or touch me. By now I know what the feeling is, so I try to talk to it. Eventually it materializes or becomes visible and all I have to do is offer whatever counsel they need so they will want to move on, and then give them direction. Sometimes I lead them to a higher plane, and other times I tell them to go to the brightest, whitest light; and there's always something appearing to which they can go. It's as if higher consciousness led me to them, or they to me because the higher entities weren't being recognized by the disincarnate beings, so they couldn't communicate. I guess the job that I performed is like that of a go-between. Anyway, it's something you can do once you establish a healthy and strong connection with higher consciousness, and have a sincere desire to help "lost" souls.

Spirit Guides:

Sometimes during meditation I mentioned seeing lights and associating them with entities from higher planes. When I'd see energy patterns I'd interpret these as energies sent to me from the higher planes to somehow help me, or better attune me. But the entities that sometimes come can have an intention in making the visit, so if the light sustains itself long enough for me to think of it, I try to go toward it. At this point it will sometimes take off with me following—in spirit. That's another type of OBE whereby someone came to get me.

But more often higher entities appear in dreams to give guidance, and these instances shouldn't be ignored, but respected. Try to be nice to them; one suggested I do something that I had been chastising myself for procrastinating on, so I wasn't ready to hear it again in my "dream". I hope he was forgiving after I finished cursing at him. (Funny thing, I haven't seen him since). Look, we're all human; we make mistakes and I've made my share—more than I'd care to admit. But we keep trying; right?

T AKING 9 ACTION

Fulfilling God's Will:

While I was in my youth a couple of things bothered me that I wish to share with you now. One was that we'd go to church and sort of get a pep-talk, and then come home and it was the same thing: challenges with friends or neighbors, personal problems, and feelings of guilt because of personal weaknesses. Somehow, though, we accepted them because we were forgiven of our sins and were going to heaven when we died; and though God or Jesus was always asking us to do things differently, and offering advice on how we could ideally get along better with others, we didn't feel we really needed to. We were forgiven after all; so our failing to follow God's recommendations only made it more difficult here and now. Later we'd get our reward. We may not have been really happy, but we were comfortable; we were experiencing what everyone else was anyway.

The other thing was a part of this. Occasionally, I'd be reading the Bible (one of those less frequently read New Testament books beyond the often-read Gospels) and read what was expected of us, now that we were Saved and had Jesus in our hearts; only I wasn't doing what it said I should be doing! And I'd read another verse inferring that if I wasn't (and that was true), then I really hadn't "believed" as I was expected to. The "good book" also made claims to being able to ask for healing, and answers to prayer if I had faith, and the prayers or requests for healing didn't happen; I'd even ask "in Jesus' name" and it didn't help. When I'd go to the minister and ask him, he'd just remind me that I was forgiven anyway and would get my reward then. What he told me—what the church taught—just didn't seem to agree with what was stated by Jesus or his apostles.

What now?

Well, now I'm older and I believe that I've finally come to terms with the questions of my youth. Regrettably, what I've come to decide is true, while making sense of what Jesus said, contradicts what the church teaches. And though I've been able to deal with the challenges that this discrepancy has created for me; it leaves you readers with the problem of what to do about it. You can just disregard what I've suggested—and that would be the easiest approach in the short run—but if I'm right, it will cause you more problems in the end. Now, I've had a lot of years to readjust my thinking, and work my way through things, but you may not have much time if you do feel that there's merit in what I claim to be true. So, to assist you in that regard, I've suggested some ways in which you can catch up, so to speak. Please take them as tips or suggestions, not as mandates. I'm not trying to be your daddy; just trying to make up for any challenges I've presented you with.

Try to Forgive Self & Others:

If you do choose to truly seek forgiveness of all of your sins, and truly be released from the consequences that un-forgiven sins bring into your life; not desiring to return again to this physical realm and deal with them through more challenging circumstances, then let me outline a protocol that you could use. You can make modifications if you want.

1. Make a list all the things about yourself that you wish you could change. These should be things for which you feel guilt or shame; things that bring feelings of remorse or regret. They may be habits or attitudes, or they may be things you did and now regret. These are the things for which you presently don't <u>feel</u> forgiven for.
   Now this may cause a problem for you, for if you now list them, you are afraid that you will be denying your faith, and on <u>that</u> basis God may take back the forgiveness the church claims that you already have. To get around that, accept that you will go to

heaven regardless (just as the church states), we're only disagreeing as to when. Also, you can accept that you are already forgiven (as the church states), but that you just don't feel forgiven because you still feel guilt, so you're attempting to bring yourself to be able to forgive yourself. Does that make it easier?

2. Make a second list of things that angers you about what others are doing or have done to you. These are things which—when considered—cause you to feel negative emotions. These could include world affairs and events, but only list them if they particularly rile you or bother you to the point where you get an emotional response (push your buttons). This list should certainly include individual deeds wherein somebody hurt you or your feelings, and for which you feel resentment or anger. These are the things and people whom you want to be able to forgive.

3. Made a third list, drawing from the second, of specific personal conflicts that you have with specific people which remain unresolved. Often-times these are single events or a cluster of events centered on one specific topic. Preferably these are with family, friends, or co-workers. These are top priority.

4. Relative to the previous list, reference each entry with your best guess as to your own fault or failing that contributes or contributed to the situation. If you truly feel no fault, then list a weakness that allowed the situation to occur.

5. Now compare the list of your own faults against the list of others' faults. Note any similarities. These faults can be worked on together; for as you forgive others, you forgive yourself; and when you truly forgive yourself, forgiving others will come so naturally, it won't even feel like you're doing it: like it just isn't necessary anymore because there's no anger, resentment, or judgment.

6. Hopefully your lists won't be too long; because they need to be addressed one at a time. I suggested that list 4 be given top priority only because they affect you more intimately, and will bring the most observable results when resolved. You may choose other priorities. To start, you can try with ones which you feel might be the easiest. Anyway, try to arrange these target areas in order of priority.

7. From the first list, make note of the weaknesses about yourself that don't seem to have resulted in conflicts involving others, <u>and</u>

which seem to be a part of your personality. These could include compulsions or personality traits, which may be difficult to change. These will be worked on last, or at the same time but in a different way; it's up to you.

8. Don't share these lists with anyone! You'll likely be adding to your lists if you do!

9. Starting with the easiest and/or most personal: select from the following techniques and try them. Refer back to the section in this book where I also made suggestions; I don't intend to repeat them here. Consider that I have provided two groups of suggestions. And good luck.

1. You're not going to be able to make big changes in your own personality, and you're not going to make significant changes in others. But in truly desiring to change, and in making the best attempt, and by praying for help, you will have appeased your feeling of guilt for not trying. And for most of the entries, that's all that's required to allow yourself to forgive yourself: you're satisfied yourself that you're desirous of change, and willing to change, so what's to feel guilty about?

2. Get a copy of AA's 12 step program; either the book or the simple list. Try to apply them to the personality traits—the difficult ones—as you work more diligently with the others.

3. When beginning to address each item, pray and re-pray the "Serenity Prayer" until you can really feel that you've meant it, and the prayer has been understood. It follows:

Serenity Prayer

Grant me the serenity to accept the things I cannot change,
the courage to change the things I can,
and the wisdom to know the difference.

4. With person—to person issues, especially those which involve another's personality, pray the prayer of "Loving Indifference" over and over until you really feel its impact. Follow it up with a prayer for God to provide you with an opportunity for resolution.

Loving Indifference

Dear God, this child is yours just as I am yours;
let there be harmony between us.

5. Crucify your ego! Many conflicts occur because you can't admit to error, or (even when you're sure you were in the right and the other wrong) don't want to let the other be able to make the claim and get away with it. Essentially, you're holding onto the conflict so you won't look bad. Let go of it. Let your ego burn. Think of the ego as Satan. Crucify it. Call or email the other person and tell them you regret the conflict; and want to know what you can do to be friends again.

6. Ignore the entire issue and conflict if it is a long standing one. Think of some nicety you can do for them, and pretend that the conflict never existed. Act toward them as though they were your best friend and always have been. You'd be providing them with an out as well, so they're not likely to even bring up the subject. If they do, you could pretend that you don't remember it (like you've forgotten about it). If they remind you, or insist, you could just say you regret that it happened; you value their friendship and are sorry for your part in it. Only if they choose to make a big deal of it (if they are after your ego) do you need to go to step 5.

7. Don't focus on people's faults, rather on their virtues. Recognize that they have shortcomings just as you do. Do you know what winter camouflage looks like? It's mostly white, but contains areas of black and shades of grey. People are like that, you included. Try to focus on the white, and ignore the black and grey. Take some advice from Polly Anna.

8. If you haven't already done so, refer back to the suggestions I gave earlier, together with the insights about karma. How can you not forgive something for which you are also guilty, and how can you not forgive someone who hurt you back for something you did in a prior life? You're just getting what you deserve. You don't have to know the details, or even if there _is_ merit to the supposition. You're allowing that it might be true, so accept it as a likely probability and let the seeming injustice go. You've paid the price; now the slate is clean. Move on.

9. Check out organizations that offer self-help or transformational programs. Years ago there was EST, and I heard good things from someone I met who went through the program. Well, I understand that Landmark Education has bought all the rights to the material that went into that program, and they offer several programs. I have no familiarity with them, but they might be worth checking out. Scientology also offers transformational programs, but I've heard less than good things about the organization. I don't know personally, so I won't say to stay away, but do use caution with respect to any organization, especially those which require a personal commitment which equates to power over you. The best programs to try are those which are offered without further obligation. Beware of structures of power; power corrupts!

10. To prevent further problems, and to help accept these, accept that you don't have a right to <u>expect</u> others to change for you. In fact, you don't usually have a right to expect anything from others. It's in having expectations not met that we get angry; so don't expect anything. If you don't feel you need anything from others, you won't be disappointed in getting nothing, and you won't create new feelings of resentment.

Forgive your Religion:

You might feel that your religion let you down for telling you essentially that you didn't need to forgive others or cease to judge them. Accept that the leaders of the religion are in the same position that you are; and even worse. If they change their beliefs, then they're out of a job. Besides, you chose to believe them even though you've read the bible and read where Jesus taught otherwise. So accept that though they may have presented you with a misconception, you chose to accept it. It was your own ego, and desire to be accepted by the group that led you to be overly trusting. Accept your own error, and don't blame your minister, priest, or whatever.

And forgive yourself as well, because you probably weren't ready for the truth anyway. The error was possibly intended to teach you the lesson <u>now</u>. So be happy that the Holy Spirit has now inspired you to make a better choice. And let it all go. There's a saying: "When the student is ready, the teacher appears." Accept that <u>now</u> the teacher is here for you because you're ready; and be glad for that. And say a prayer for those who aren't receptive now because they still aren't ready. You could follow up the prayer by suggesting to your friends that they look at this book and tell you what they think. Or easier yet, direct them to my website: <u>www.dawn-of-truth.com</u> and ask them what they think of it.

10 PROPHESIES

Chicken Little:

It seems that throughout my whole life there have been prophesies with regard to the end of the world. I recall while attending classes at a parochial grade school I was taught to expect the end of the world to come and Jesus to return to declare his kingdom on earth. I don't dare count how many times some individual or group has even predicted a certain date for such an event. Yet, here we are; and all those who made the predictions were seen as "Chicken Little"; declaring that, "the sky is falling". It's easy to conclude, then, that nothing will happen on the fateful day of Dec. 21, 2012; right? Well, maybe.

Most of the predictions in the past have centered on references in the Bible which also included a prediction that Jesus would return at that time to save his own and set up his own kingdom. That other religions also look for a Messiah, or return of an enlightened teacher, seem to infer that there may be some credence given this consideration.

The Book of Revelations is famous for offering prophesies of future events; very similar to those of Nostradamus in that they are so difficult to interpret, they're practically useless. Or, for that matter, can be used to validate most any desired prediction; because of their vagueness.

Revelations also predicted an Antichrist being, and a couple of "beasts", and a child to lead us all to a peaceable kingdom; but we haven't seen any of these characters either. Except that the number 666 does seem to be a part of the product code assigned to things we buy and sell.

There have also been prophesies of cataclysmic events such as a comet called Wormwood due to bring us our doom, and a third world war that would destroy the world "with fire" causing people to suffer from radiation. But people were supposed to suffer from solar radiation anyway because of the hole in the ozone layer.

Edgar Cayce predicted volcanic eruptions, Atlantis rising, and water levels rising—possibly due to a tidal wave in the Atlantic. I forget what was supposed to occur to cause that; maybe a comet, volcanic eruption or the rising of Atlantis. His predictions of coastal water levels rising could be a result of melting ice caps in the Antarctic; but who knows?

Cayce also predicted devastation in Japan and Northern Europe, and none of that has occurred either; at least with the magnitude predicted. Perhaps this was a prediction of the effects of WW II; rather than that of a natural disaster. Could it be that predictions just don't usually occur in the same way that we expect them to?

It seems that California has been predicted to suffer the "big one" and fall into the Pacific, for years now; is "she" still awaiting her doom?

One prediction I was looking forward to was the mass appearance of Aliens. I recall that some predicted that they would come to rescue "their chosen". That sounded a lot like something to avoid; though if one were Jewish; it did sound like Jehovah could be returning.

A prediction that I was not looking forward to, was the New World Order, and all the class riots and gang violence which were supposed to accompany that. Hopefully "Big Brother" has given up; but one never knows. I do keep an eye out for attempts by the government to make this more of a totalitarian state than a democracy; and I have to admit, that we do seem to be moving along in that dire direction.

Well, if you check what's hot today; I guess that the Mayan prophecy has displaced the one from the Great Pyramid, and that's the new one to consider. All the old biblical prophesies, Nostradamus and Cayce predictions seem to have been ignored for some time now.

Maybe this time it will be it. But the question arises; what is the Mayan prediction? Is it for total devastation or for a significant change of some sort; to change consciousness perhaps?

It's real easy to hear all these people "crying wolf" to get the feeling that there are no wolves and never will be. After all, if an event fails to come enough times, chances are that it will never occur; right? Of course, I'm not a successful gambler either. So, I'm not betting that the Mayan prophesy won't occur in some way. It may in fact come in a way we aren't expecting. Actually; all the prior prophesies may be about to become realized, but in a way that we aren't expecting.

A Change in Consciousness:

Well, I consider it to be a given that this world needs to experience a change in the way that people interact with each other on the basis of religious beliefs. And in my opinion, this is all necessitated by erroneous assumptions or teachings about God and other religious assertions. Clearing up these misconceptions or misunderstandings is pretty much what this book is about.

So, I guess that by going to the trouble of writing and publishing this book, I've pretty much expressed my hope that there is a change of consciousness coming. Also I hope it's soon; and I would be very gratified if I could think that my efforts had at least a small part to play in it.

In making my prediction, I'm not so much considering what other people have predicted to occur (though I've certainly considered their views), as I am considering what I believe must occur in order for things to meet my own expectations of what's best, and what God would desire.

What I think is best for people, is that most people in this world make a clear assessment of how things have been progressing, where we seem to be heading as a society, and just how they want the future to unfold for themselves and their children.

As for God's desire; I think It really does want Its Kingdom to become manifest on Earth. That's to say that we on Earth start acting from a different state of consciousness; one reflective of God's consciousness. The question being, though: how does God intend that Its desire become accomplished; through what type of events?

Personally, I'd like to experience a change wherein people stopped killing each other, stopped invoking fear in others with dire prophesies, and stopped deciding who God likes best and who God is sure to punish. And I'd also like any changes that did occur, to occur in a manner wherein nobody could come along later and say; "See, I was right and you're wrong!" I'd hate to have to be sharing a world (or what's left of the world) with a bunch of braggers.

I'd also like to meet some friendly and intelligent Aliens, but only if they came to help in ways that we can't, and didn't try to take charge in any way. Maybe it's my ego, but I just don't think it right that someone comes to our world from somewhere else, and starts to tell us what to do. I've been an American all my life, and I kind of respect the ideals which give mankind the unalienable (pardon the pun) right of self-determination through a Democratic Republic. No matter how highly evolved they might be, I don't think an Alien Oligarchy is the better way. Helpers under our choosing and control, OK; but let's just remember who's world this is.

I will say one thing in favor of their sudden appearance in a demonstrative way; they sure would shake things up a bit! They might even cause a sudden change in consciousness to occur! Of course, I'd prefer that people the world over just decided that they'd had enough of violence and greed, and realized that cooperation and something like love for others was a good thing. I get really tired of seeing "Peace on Earth, Good will towards Man" every year for a couple of weeks, and then back to the same old Orwellian philosophies like "war is peace", and "giving money to the rich is good for the poor".

Yes; I think this world is due for a shift in consciousness; in fact I see it happening already, and all over the world. People are clamoring for an end to the disparity of wealth and power that exists everywhere. I believe that all people have a natural, God-given right and obligation of self-determination, and I'm hoping that when enough people agree to that premise, that beneficial changes will indeed come that will result in a beneficial shift in consciousness.

A Look at History:

While there have been predictions of the end of the world since Biblical times that have not occurred, there have been changes in consciousness. There was the time when people realized that the earth wasn't the center of the universe, and another time when people realized that the world was round rather than flat. I think we're due for another change like that. Hopefully we'll come to realize that war doesn't solve problems, but rather makes problems worse. Now that is a shift that I'd like to see; and I think that we're finally coming towards that realization.

A Pole Shift:

Edgar Cayce once prophesied that there would be a major pole shift sometime around the end of the century, and many years later author John White apparently felt the same for he wrote his famous book *Pole Shift* to make the same prediction. But here we are years after this shift was to happen and the poles are still there. Magnetically they've been experiencing a gradual movement, but nothing like that which was predicted. So what happened; another sigh of relief that those who make wild predictions are just somehow delusional?

As with end-of-world prophesies, I think people are picking up on a subtle subconscious impression that something that needs to happen is going to happen; they just interpret the impressions in the best way that they know how. One has to admire them for their willingness to risk being laughed at, and appreciate their feeling of concern which led them to express their idea. And who knows; maybe they are right and just misconstrued the timing of the event(s).

I have no impressions one way or the other about the likelihood of the earth's physical poles actually shifting in a significant way. If it does happen, though, I will meet the results in the same way I've met other events in my life; one day at a time, doing what I can in the moment. I suppose that's what everyone will do if it ever happens. I doubt that one could actually plan in advance for such an event; the ramifications for any one individual are just too difficult to predict.

I have, however, read one prediction with regard to a pole shift that does feel accurate. And though it may not come about as rapidly or destructively as the other pole shift predictions, it could actually result in a much more profound shift. This prediction is for a shift in the way people view the world; or respond to world events. It might be more accurate to call it a paradigm shift. Gerald O'Donnell—founder of the Academy of Remote Viewing and Influencing Reality through Time and Space—has made a prediction that the pole shift will come about as a change in the way people relate to their world: people will shift from acting out of fear, to expressing love. And that's a polarity shift I look forward to experiencing! But what could cause such a shift to occur in human expressions?

Do we like to Fear, or dare to Love?

I'm reminded of the time when the twin world trade center towers were struck by planes. Some people ran for their lives; for them it was natural to be fearful; and they let that determine their actions. Others, however, were moved out of a feeling of concern for others, and accepted risk in trying to rescue those in harm's way. It's regrettable that those who chose to act out of love ended up leaving this world, while those who acted out of fear have remained; maybe in the times ahead things will have different results.

End of a World View:

What if all the people—Mayans in particular—who perceived an end to the world, were actually picking up on subconscious impressions that there was going to be an end to the way people responded to life? More specifically; what if a shift in consciousness is in the process of unfolding wherein people will end their habit of responding out of fear, and begin to start acting out of a feeling of love for others? That would certainly constitute a major change in consciousness that would bring an end to the world that we read about in the papers and hear about on the news. It would also constitute a polar shift and end-of-world event that I would truly like to experience. But one would have to wonder: just what could cause such a change?

A New World View:

Can you imagine such a polar shift or change in consciousness really occurring? No more "Chicken Little" running around yelling that "the sky is falling"; instead we'd have a lot of kind and compassionate people daring to do what they can for the well-being of others. We'd be running in to assist those imperiled by any threatening event, and begin to share more of what we have enough of, with those who are suffering lack. And more importantly, we'd stop fearing those whose religious beliefs differ from our own, and be willing to respect and love them instead. I wonder what changes will occur in the economies around the world when people stopped hoarding money and resources out of fear for their own financial security, and instead started sharing their wealth out of a feeling of compassion for those suffering in states of lack?

A Utopian Dream?

Well, it seems I've gone from contemplating the possibility of a catastrophic event, to considering the possibility of experiencing a most blessed occurrence. Am I a visionary or a dreamer? To tell you the truth; I consider myself to be both. And not only that; but I think that this world we live in is pretty much a dream in itself, and as such can be re-dreamt. So why don't we all try to hold the same vision of a world full of loving people, setting their own worries aside to embrace those in greater need or risk of peril, with their love. If we can commit ourselves to doing that, then maybe we will be able—as a loving society—to be able to deal with any cataclysm that might occur in this world. We might even be able to prevent some from occurring. Just deciding that we will no longer support our government in acts of aggression against other nations, will do a lot to begin the movement toward the world of peace we've only dared dream about, or wish for, as we mailed out our Christmas cards every year.

Separating the Sheep from the Goats:

The Biblical New Testament spoke of a day of judgment when "sheep" would be separated from "goats"; the inference being that the good sheep would go to heaven and the bad goats would burn in hell. This always bothered me; not just because I didn't like to hear of people suffering so badly, but because there was no middle ground: no mercy for those stuck somewhere in the middle. I was assured, though, that God was a just and fair judge, and it would be clear just where to draw the line. And since the lines were drawn around people's religious beliefs, then there wouldn't be much question anyway.

As I got older and thought more about "Judgment Day", I agreed with assertions that this referred to a person's moment of passing over; when their life would flash before them, and they'd judge themselves for the things they did. This judgment would then determine what type of life they would need to be born into for their next incarnation.

Now, however, I'm rethinking this Biblical Prophecy. I'm thinking that both of these view-points can be validated at the same time, though not exactly in the same manner. Consider this: for thousands of years, some of us have been reincarnating over and over again to grow in the spiritual sense and gain the wisdom that we came here to acquire. This has increasingly led us to desire peace over violence, to forgive rather than seek retribution, and to be loving rather than selfish. But while we've been learning—moving up in class so to speak—new students have been entering the school and are still requiring lessons on violence, anger, and greed. It's because our school has a large population of both old students and new, that it's becoming increasingly uncomfortable for everyone.

As a result of this consideration, I believe that a splitting of reality is due to occur; and that this is the judgment day whereby the sheep are to be divided from the goats. I don't perceive it as a punishment, though; but rather as a better opportunity for all to be provided with the most appropriate education. In fact, I believe that the students (souls) will choose which school they will be more comfortable in. People who like to play violent games and fight over what they can get are just not going to want to live in a world where everybody gets along and shares what they've got.

In terms of the pole shift, or shift in world view: I think that there will be a lot of souls who will want to live in a fear-based reality, and who won't want to change their view from fear to love; they might even thrive on instilling fear in others for the sense of power and control that it gives to them. And I'm sure that there are lots of people who thrive on the emotional stimulation that fear elicits. These people might prefer an even more fearful world with lots of dire circumstances to stimulate their emotions, and validate their beliefs that violence and greed are necessary in order to survive.

My conclusion, then, is that God or Higher Consciousness should be able to create a way whereby some of us can experience a reality of greater peace and love, while others can experience a reality of increasing turmoil; within which they can exercise more fear, violence, and greed. Actually, I believe that this is the intention; and that I've got a pretty good idea as to how it can come about.

Changes that do not Serve the Ego:

Whenever I've heard about people's beliefs with regard to prophecies of coming events, I've always had a wish that they wouldn't be proven to be accurate. This is because I cringe at the thought of someone going around boasting about how right they were, and how wrong everybody else was who doubted them. In fact, the prediction about the return of Jesus to prove to the world that the faithful Christians were right in their beliefs while everyone else was wrong, also bothered me; and I consider myself to <u>be</u> a Christian. I would truly love to meet the guy (my big brother); just not under those circumstances. Somewhere inside of me is a belief that the human ego, with its desire to believe that it's better than others, is something that's just not to be encouraged. So I don't believe that God would do anything to validate some self-righteous individuals' reason for boasting; thereby feeding their egos.

The same goes for any prophecy that is to bring this world into greater peace and prosperity. If it occurs in a demonstrative manner wherein everybody will be forced to acknowledge that some specific group of people was right, and everybody else wrong, then in a metaphorical way, Satan would be served in the process. The new paradise on earth would contain a bunch of boasters, claiming how superior their own belief was.

And by considering the opposite perspective, all those who were wrong would be forced to live in a reality that proved them wrong; they'd live in anger at their God which lied to them; or at the very least misled them in not letting them in on the secret.

So, in rejecting the notion that <u>anybody</u> will be able to boast about the accuracy of their own prediction of a sudden and catastrophic event, and feel themselves wiser that those who didn't believe, I put some thought into just how a shift in reality could manifest in such a way that would appear to be a normal course of events; wherein everybody's beliefs were validated.

A Dimensional Split:

I know that it might sound unreasonable to expect that a separation of humanity could occur in a way that was not obvious to the people so divided, but somehow that's just the way that I feel it will work out. I strongly feel that a separation is necessary too. I perceive the world to be like two groups of people each trying to pull in opposite directions. If this world is, in fact, a place for learning; and not an unlikely cosmic accident, then there must be a way for a shift, or splitting of reality to occur gracefully so that both sides will perceive the world as changing in their favor (or rather, perceive no split at all).

If one considers that all reality, which we perceive of as being solid matter, is rather a vibrating field of energy being perceived as density because we are in sync with it, then all one would have to do to make a shift, is to move out of sync with one reality and move into synchronization with the alternate reality. Then each reality could move on its own course without anyone being the wiser. From each group's perspective everything would appear to progress along the path that they hoped it would.

To demonstrate this concept of synchronization, imagine that a large coupling is attached to the end of a variable speed motor. An electrical technician who wanted to measure motor rpm (revolutions per minute) would put a chalk mark on the coupling; and while the motor was running, shine a beam of light from a strobe at the coupling. He would then adjust the frequency of the flashing light from his strobe until he could clearly see the chalk mark on the rapidly spinning coupling, making it appear as though the motor wasn't even running. The illusion results from the fact that he can only see the mark when his flashing light is illuminating the mark at the same time that the mark returns to the same position. By reading the frequency on his strobe, then, he now knows the speed of the motor, because the two are in sync. He doesn't dare touch the coupling, though, because he knows that though it appears to be stationary, it is actually spinning very rapidly. This is why we perceive matter to be solid, when we know from grade school science classes that in reality it's mostly empty space.

Now consider what would occur if the motor represented our present reality and the strobe our own state of vibration. A lower rpm or strobe frequency could represent a more dangerous and fearful reality, while a higher rpm would then represent a more peaceful and loving world.

Let's imagine, then, that we add a second motor spinning at the same speed; and position it so that its coupling is next to the original one. Now let's change the chalk marks so that one motor shows a dangerous and fearful image, while the other one shows a harmonious and loving image. Now if we changed the speed of the motors slightly, the technician would have a choice. Since he would only be able to perceive a clear image of the (reality) in which his own strobe (own personal state of vibration) was in sync with, he would need to adjust his strobe frequency (state of vibration) in order to continue to be able to clearly perceive the image of reality that he <u>wanted</u> to see. He couldn't see both. If the motor speeds continued to deviate, he would continue to readjust his frequency to accommodate his chosen "view-point". Also, because of his continued focus upon the one image, he wouldn't notice that there was a second motor holding a different image. He would only perceive of the necessity of his readjusting to adapt to a changing reality. And isn't this what we do all the time, as we adapt to events that occur in our world? Some of us become more fearful, and others become more helpful to those in need.

Consider what would happen if there was only one radio station in a certain area, and all residents were left with no alternative but to listen to the type of music that the station played. Now those who liked heavier sounds would write to complain about the lighter music, and those who liked the lighter sounds would write to complain about the heavier music. To resolve the problem, and to satisfy all their listening audience, the station installed a second transmitter. At first both transmitters operated at the exact same frequency playing the same music. Gradually they then began to change the frequencies of each; playing more heavy music at one frequency and more light music at a slightly different one. Over time, the listening audience would need to keep adjusting the tuning of their radios to better pick up the music that they liked and were more focused on. After a period of time the transmitters were at significantly different frequencies and all the viewers were tuned into the station of their own choosing. From the perspective of each group of listeners, the music became more and more to their liking, not realizing that there were now two stations playing different songs for each group.

This is similar to how I perceive a shift to occur. I don't know how rapid the adjustment will be made, but I believe that the frequency of this dimension will shift into two bands resulting in two distinct dimensions of reality. And I think that people's own focus upon what draws their interest and attention will be the factor in determining which reality they will end up following. All people will move in the direction of their choice and not even realize that they were moving away from a reality that they had the opportunity of choosing instead.

Now, I know this will raise questions about animals, plants, and minerals. But as I expressed in the fourth chapter, we are all multi-dimensional; everything that exists in this dimension of reality also exists in different frequencies. The difference is only how dense the reach is. It's hard to conceive of each of us having a being-ness already in existence on a higher dimension, but that's only because we aren't usually aware of it. What I perceive happening, then, is that each reality will contain all the same "creatures"; they will just adapt differently on each. Some may even become extinct on one reality, while they flourish on the others. It will, essentially be their own spirit's choice where to manifest, and on what dimension of reality.

To better clarify this concept of multi-dimensionality, consider a group of islands in some ocean. Our perception is that these are individual and exist only as land masses on the top of the water. Yet we know that in reality they also extend far down to the ocean floor where they are recognized as being mountains: mere projections of the one planet earth. This pretty much describes my view of reality and who each of us really are. We can't perceive of the other dimensions of ourselves that exist in different ocean layers, but they are there. And like with mountains in the ocean, the ecosystem is different at different depths. Similarly, we as a multi-dimensional soul do express ourselves at different dimensions of reality, though the consciousness expressing in the physical plane is generally not aware of its projection at different frequencies of reality.

Now, consider that these mountains had the capacity to project up or down in order to satisfy the desires of the various ecosystems. Initially, they're happy where they are. But were the water level to gradually begin to drop while the waves began to get increasingly higher and more turbulent, different mountains may decide to adjust their height to their own desires. Islands that desired a more pacific experience would rise higher to escape the rising waves, while other islands would drop in order to stay just at the water's shoreline; the one moving to escape the turbulence, the other to get more.

I know that it is difficult to really get a grip on what we truly may be as multi-dimensional souls when our consciousness is almost always locked inside a physical vehicle which we see in the mirror every morning. Yet some people have been able to move their conscious awareness into other dimensions of its soul and had glimpses of a more expansive self; and also of a more interesting reality. Take some time to read books that describe experiences that have been described as out-of-body experiences and you'll get a peek at a far greater truth that is very difficult to grasp; even for those—like me—who have had such glimpses.

Anybody who has astral projected has found their awareness to enter into an astral dimension almost identical to this one. Many experiments in Parapsychology have documented this, and been confused that there were slight differences. They had assumed that when a person astral projected they would still be in this dimension. They aren't; when astral projecting in an astral body, a person is in an astral dimension; and that is the reality that they later report in detail. What's even more interesting is that when astral projectors talk to friends in the astral realm, they think that they are speaking to the individual on the physical dimension; they can't perceive of a difference. But when they return to the physical dimension and speak with their friend, the person doesn't know what they are talking about. They have no recollection of the incident. In fact, often the friend is at the same location reported to have been observed when the projector was in the astral dimension, but was actually doing something quite different than that reported.

Now, I'm not trying to base my supposition upon the credibility of these reports. I've experienced for myself how different my home looks when I perceive that I leave my dense body in bed and travel around in a lighter body that can float and fly and move through objects. Most things are the same, but different things are arranged on tables, a window is where it shouldn't be, and pictures that should be on the left are now on the right. Once in a while, an entire room is different, as though someone interchanged one of the rooms of my house.

Of course I can't prove to you what is real and not real; I'm not trying. What I am trying to do is to offer a plausible way, in which the shift I believe to be in the process of occurring can indeed occur; and in a way that is not discernible to most people.

Though I earlier described a radio station playing two types of music, I think that what we will observe is what Gerald O'Donnell predicted; though he probably isn't predicting it to occur in the way that I describe. I haven't read his material enough, though, to express any opinions about it.

Prophesies are for Warnings:

I have read a lot of predictions from others, though, and there are a lot of groups telling people not to be afraid, no matter how things seem; that things will eventually turn out to be wonderful. I believe that these groups are intending to help people; by guiding them away from focusing on fearful emotions, and are leading them into envisioning a world-wide movement toward the "love pole" of the shift. To an extent, I agree with their intent; but I also point out a caution: Prophesies are usually given for a reason; and that reason is to motivate people into making changes in their expressions. If a change is necessary for some people to make, then by assuring everyone that things will be OK, some people may suffer the consequences or miss the opportunities that a change could have averted.

Somehow people must be able to come to a recognition of what prophesies are actually forecasting for them in their own lives; particularly with respect to what changes their soul is being desiring of them. People must be able to go within their own consciousness, in order to get a feeling with regard to what they will need to do, themselves, in order to achieve the reality that they desire; and to avoid any unwanted future situations. If personal choices or changes are required, then this is something that people must determine for themselves, by listening to their own Higher Consciousness; the responsibility is not best delegated to others, in expecting others to determine what's best for them.

Prophesies are not to invoke Fear.

Besides hearing predictions that everything will be fine, I've also read a lot of references to various people and groups predicting dire catastrophes and promoting fear among people; telling them to prepare for one horrible event after another. These are those whom I believe are leading the gullible into a reality that could become self-manifested by people's own focus on the negativity. One must wonder just what motives the doomsayers have, in making their predictions.

To those who find themselves becoming victimized by such dire predictions, and succumbing to fear: I say; go within. Reconsider your beliefs and expectations; they can only lead you into experiencing more of that which you focus upon. In other words; "Be careful what you [expect], you just might get it!" So, listen to your heart and not your emotional gut.

A Shifting into Planet A and B?

In the newsletters I receive from C.A.C. (also available at <u>www. cosmicawareness.org</u>), Cosmic Awareness often describes a splitting of realities in a similar manner as I describe. We do have our differences in opinion (I think), but I only feel comfortable in describing what I feel; regardless of what others suggest. But if you are interested in this source's description, I highly recommend that you take a look.

Cosmic Awareness describes our world dividing dimensionally (not physically) into two realms which It identifies as planet A and planet B. It also describes planet A as being on a higher plane of existence while planet B will drop to a more primitive state. Cosmic Awareness also emphasizes the necessity of all to focus on the positive and resist those impulses to focus on fear; and I strongly concur with this. I admit, though, that I'm not clear just how Cosmic Awareness describes the process as occurring, but I'm not really sure just how I envision it to occur either; I can only offer my best guess based upon what I feel to be valid.

Keep Smiling; have Faith.

Regardless how the future will unfold; the one thing that those, who are touting a coming new world (where life will be more harmonious) agree upon, is the need to remain positive and not fall into states of fear. They suggest very strongly that the focus upon fear will tend to draw one into experiencing the fearful realities. This fits very well with what Cosmic Awareness suggested to be Planet B, and Gerald O'Donnell suggested as being one dimension of the pole shift, and what I described as a splitting of a school into two distinct school systems.

The message, then, is to be careful that you don't fall into the trap of succumbing to fear; and instead be positive in both your outlook on life, and in your expressions with others. Pray and meditate upon what is best for you to do; trusting in your own ability to receive personal guidance from within. Pay attention to your dreams, the opportunities that become presented to you, and your own inner feelings. In this way you let your own soul be your guide.

And let your light shine to assist others; be caring, and helpful, especially when encountering those in states of panic or need. Do all those good things that you know to do from a heart that is full of compassion for others; and trust that Divine Providence will lead one out of any difficulty, if or when it comes.

Choosing Your Future Reality:

In describing what I feel to be a future occurrence soon to become a reality in this world, I can't help but be concerned about people—good people—who are desirous of living in a more loving and harmonious world, but at the same time are full of dark emotions; angry at some, jealous of others, feeling guilt for personal shortcomings, and judging others for their faults.

In my view, these are they (and you may be among them) who have—at present—an uncertain future. Now I don't intend to put you into a state of fear; for if you're reading this, then you've probably already decided that you want to move into a more harmonious reality. And I support you in this quest. But I think that you may need to give ample consideration to what you do truly believe in, and not lean on the claim that is a part of your religion's creed.

I suggest that it's not just fear but one's attitudes toward others that will play a role in separating the "sheep" from the "goats". I suggest that one give considerable attention to attitudes of judgment, anger, and resentment toward others. And since I believe that this coincides with the degree of guilt a person is holding onto, I suggest that this issue be given a high priority; release from feelings of guilt will result in a lessening in dark emotions such as anger, fear, and resentment. These together are those attitudes that lead one into performing acts of aggression against others; which perpetuates expressions of fear and violence. Taken all together, this describes what I perceive to be the greater reality which will become the type of world that planet B will become.

If you feel that this might describe yourself too much, then you might also give consideration to the future that you would really and truly prefer to live in; and try to imagine what you would be doing while in that reality. Would you be envisioning yourself working in cooperation with others in co-creating a better society; sharing your resources with those who lack, and teaching others how to add to their own prosperity? Or would you be competing with others in society; trying to get as much as you could from as many as you could, while giving to others as little as possible? If the latter is more accurate, then it just might be that Planet B would be more to your liking.

On the other hand, if you really do want to live in loving harmony with others; sharing what you have, and helping others to become more prosperous, then I suggest that you follow the suggestions I've offered with regard to overcoming your feelings of guilt; and give serious consideration to forgiving others. Trust in God's love for you; and forgive others as you would have God and others forgive you. This is my version of the Golden Rule.

THE MESSIAH COMETH

The Promise of a Messiah:

S ince mankind's first entrance into this physical plane, God promised a Messiah who would come to free mankind from the consequences of their errors. As a child I wondered why it took so long for God to finally follow through on Its promise; considering how many people suffered and died while awaiting this savior.

As a Christian, I was taught that Jesus was this Savior, and that his death on the cross freed "believers" from the debt of sin, allowing them to "go to heaven" when they died. I often wondered about this, because it was clearly obvious that people still suffered and died (at least in the physical sense) because of their transgressions. I couldn't understand why people had to wait for a time after death for this redemption to take effect.

As I grew into adulthood, I realized that virtually every religion had the very same expectation; that some Messiah would come to free them from the trials of the world, promising a life without suffering. This caused me to wonder if perhaps there was something missing or misunderstood about Jesus' role as a Messiah.

I've since concluded that there have not only been Messiahs, but that Messiahs that have come and left, promising to return again to fulfill the purposes which they originally came for. My conclusion is that it doesn't matter how many Messiahs come to save, if we don't follow their teachings. Saviors don't impose "saving grace" upon us; it's up to us to follow the teachings that they provide, in order to avail ourselves of the grace freely offered.

The Three Paths to Salvation:

We've touched on this subject before; but because so many religious teachings downplay its importance, or relevance to the quality of our lives, that I feel a need to emphasize it once again.

The "default' path to salvation—or redemption from sin—is through meeting the consequences of our actions; known as karma. This is the slow path through suffering, whereby we "reap what we sow", and learn the hard way that selfishness and injury to others leads away from God and Its promises of heaven. Through this path, we grow in wisdom by experiencing for ourselves the error of causing others to suffer. Through this path, we learn obedience to law, by being able to walk in the shoes (so to speak) of those whom we judge or cause to suffer. The Golden Rule is the rule which we are encouraged to follow, in order to escape the consequences of this path.

Those who find themselves on "Planet B" will be following this path toward salvation. It is a path designed for souls who have not yet learned how to love others; who, out of fear for their own survival and well-being, consider it acceptable or justified to cause others harm.

The second path to salvation is that which has been identified as ascension to "Planet A". On this path, people will find the going much easier, as they have learned to apply the Golden Rule, and treat others as they would like to be treated themselves. Those who travel this path are on their way to absolving their karmic debts through service to others. Acts of kindness and mercy help to pay off karmic debt; and come as a result of the wisdom gained through prior experiences of one's own suffering. Those on this path have pretty much learned that to harm others is to bring the same harm to their selves; so out of empathy, they seek to help others to bear their burdens.

The third path to receiving salvation, or forgiveness of sins, is through Alchemy, or the receiving of Grace. This is the path that has been taught by Messiahs over the ages, and ignored or down-played by religions. It is the path that truly brings about a change in consciousness, because one's karmic load is instantly wiped clean; resulting in an ecstatic feeling of freedom and self-approval which turns to self-love. This results in the "cup that overflows [with love]", so that one can't help but love all others unconditionally.

Jesus, as well as other earlier Messiahs have taught the way to receive this state of grace, but because people were too burdened with guilt, or too caught up in their own ego's cravings, to be able to partake of this free gift.

Upon receiving this gift, one cannot go back and condemn another, or judge others. For to do so, denies them the grace which they had been offered. Jesus, through his teachings and parables, made this very clear. Unfortunately, the church misunderstood the necessity of forgiving others, and Jesus' teachings in this regard were invalidated.

One can't blame the church, though, because it's always been people's option to follow Jesus' teachings, and take advantage of this gift without the church's direction. In fact, many faithful people within the church did apply Jesus' teachings in their lives, and did receive the grace which was offered. That the majority of people failed in this respect, is due to their own inability to apply the teachings in their own lives.

Now, as we look once again for an ascension or rapture, whereby mankind will be given a chance to advance spiritually with less of a hindrance from those who remain in ignorance of God's truth, it would be well that people once again consider the teachings of Jesus—and other earlier Masters—and seek grace.

The Necessity of Forgiveness:

In order for people to receive grace, they need to follow the pattern that was presented by Jesus through the Gospel Story. Before "the Messiah" could come—or be recognized—John the Baptist called people to repent of their sins, and through the ritual of bathing in water, washed themselves clean of their sins. This is a crucial first step: repentance.

Following this step, one is then called upon to forgive others. A review of Jesus' teachings will reveal just how often he was teaching on this subject; providing techniques to be used which would allow a person to be able to forgive others. Since I already discussed these, I won't elaborate here.

After repentance, and after forgiving others, people are encouraged not to judge others, nor to condemn in any way. Jesus exemplified in his life, the Way in which this can be done. It requires that the ego be sacrificed. Only by denying the temptation of one's own ego—which would consider itself to be better or greater than others—can a person come to be able to truly forgive and cease judgment of others.

Finally, after the ego is sacrificed, one then awaits the resurrection of the ego in a Christened state. It's the ego which undergoes the "crucifixion" and therefore the transformation; whereby it ceases to perceive of itself as alone and separate, but realizes that it is one with the All. It is this resurrected ego which is the true Son of God; the Consciousness which knows itself to be one with God and all mankind.

What is the Messiah?

Referring back to the Genesis story; Satan (the ego) tempted mankind into following its path through the physical realm. This physical reality is under the rule of ego; because people perceive themselves to be separate from the Whole, and therefore in competition with all others for the pleasures of the physical plane. This is what causes all sin, and therefore, all suffering.

The Messiah was promised to be a deliverer. This was in fact the educated or resurrected ego, the Christ Consciousness which finally came to "be like God" in recognizing its oneness with all others. This is what the promise was; that through repeated lifetimes, mankind would eventually learn that they were all a part of the oneness we call God.

The <u>outer form</u> of the Messiah appeared throughout history to teach people how to live, and how to absolve their guilt, so that they could eventually come to forgive. Since people were largely not ready for the lessons, different Messiahs came at different times to different cultures. Jesus was just one of several; I refer to him because he is the one I am familiar with in the religion I was brought up in.

The Messiah is Within:

The purpose of these Messiahs is to point people toward their own inner Messiah; which is a part of their own consciousness, unrecognized while under the control of ego and the feelings of guilt which ego produce. This was symbolized in the birth of Jesus (the Messiah) in a lowly stable in Bethlehem. This stable represented the subconscious mind (among the animalistic passions). Here, only the wise [men], and those who diligently watched "their flocks" (subjugated their subconscious impulses), would recognize this Higher Consciousness when it came.

The message here is that one needn't look outside of one's self for a deliverer. One needs only to go within, and seek inner guidance from the Divinity which is a part of one's own multi-dimensional soul. It is from <u>within</u> that one receives grace!

Any person—regardless of religion—who truly repents of one's sins, makes a concerted effort to change one's behavior, and forgives others without condition, can seek mercy from the inner Messiah: the Higher Consciousness of one's own soul.

The Messiah will Come or Return Soon:

But don't expect to receive grace or the resulting change in consciousness <u>when</u> you desire it. It comes when Spirit arranges for it to occur. Apparently a catalyst or trigger is required in order to affect the alchemical reaction. If you refer back to my own experience, you will note that it took a phone call for me to experience my state of grace. Your experience will come at a time and in a way and manner that is most appropriate for you. And it will come, as the Bible says, "as a thief in the night", because you will not be able to know in advance when it comes; so be ready.

I might also add; that like me, you may not long be able to sustain this state of consciousness when it first arrives. Eventually the cares of the world may cause you to return in consciousness to attend once again to the demands of karma and life lessons. Think of it as peeling the onion, layer by layer, until you are finally able to learn all lessons which this physical realm demands of us. In patience, you will have another opportunity; and another still, with each experience of Higher Consciousness lasting longer than the prior, until you are finally able to move on, into the higher realms

The Bridegroom Cometh:

If you're a Christian, remember what Jesus said about keeping your lamp full of oil, so that you will be ready when the bridegroom comes.

That advice applies here; for the "bridegroom" in this context is the Messiah Consciousness, or—perhaps more appropriately—the catalyst or opportunity to receive transformation.

Consider the lamp to be your subconscious mind, and the oil to be your capacity for self-forgiveness, or your ability to love others unconditionally. Consider also, that judgments, desires for retribution, refusal to forgive others, guilty feelings, and any types of fear, are things which punch holes in your lamp or cause it to spill.

Jesus was "the Way" in that he set an example for you, giving you a protocol to assist you in forgiving yourself and others; and if you make an honest attempt (one that satisfies your inner Messiah) the final results won't be a big concern, because it's the honest desire to improve, that's more important than actual success.

As the Serenity Prayer expresses, one must be able to discern what changes can be made, and what one must be able to accept and live with as a result of one's own personal weaknesses.

It's a loving heart—one desirous of self-improvement—rather than one's ability to achieve actual success, which helps to expand one's capacity to love. In short, if you can bring yourself to the point wherein you can love yourself totally and without condition, in spite of your failings, then loving others will be easy; for you will grant others that same consideration; recognizing that imperfection is part of the state in which we all live. You won't need others to be perfect, because you will have come to accept that it isn't possible for anyone to actually become perfect in this short life. If this wasn't so, then forgiveness and tolerance wouldn't be necessary; and neither would be the granting or receiving of Grace.

Opportunities for Saving Grace are Coming:

As one does what one can to become the best person that one can be, and leaves the rest to God; trusting that in time and with patience, one will eventually achieve success—whether in this life or the next—one fulfills the requirements to satisfy one's own soul that one is worthy of receiving the transformative power of grace. It is then but a matter of holding fast to that state of self-acceptance, which allows one to be open to receiving grace from Higher Mind—the Messiah within.

The goal, then, is to but wait for an opportunity to experience whatever catalytic event one's Soul requires, in order to feel one's self freed from the bondage of karmic debt. In patience, and hope, one merely awaits the granting of Grace. It is my prayer, then, that for all who are prepared, and so hope, that this Saving Grace comes soon.

Toward this hope, I wish God's blessings upon you all.